MATHEMATICS
THROUGH ART & DESIGN
6–13

Anne Woodman & Eric Albany

CollinsEducational
An imprint of HarperCollins*Publishers*

ACKNOWLEDGEMENTS

The authors wish to express their gratitude to the teachers in these schools for the enthusiastic way in which they took part in the trials of the activities in this book and to their pupils, some of whose work is shown in the photographs of examples:

Alder Coppice Middle School	Dudley
Blanford Mere Primary School	Dudley
Brewood-Wheaton Aston Middle School	Staffordshire
Brierley Hill Primary School	Dudley
Calshot Primary School	Great Barr, Birmingham
Castlecroft Primary School	Wolverhampton
Charminster First School	Dorchester
Graiseley Primary School	Wolverhampton
Highgate Primary School	Dudley
Holt Farm Primary School	Dudley
St Luke's C of E Primary School	Wolverhampton
St Mary's RC School	Wolverhampton
Stowlawn Primary School	Wolverhampton
St Thomas C of E Primary School	Wolverhampton
Uplands Junior School	Wolverhampton
Whiteheath Junior School	Oldbury

First published 1988 by Unwin Hyman Ltd, London

Reprinted 1990

The edition 1992 by
CollinsEducational
77–85 Fulham Palace Road
Hammersmith London W6 8JB

© Anne Woodman & Eric Albany 1988

The purchase of this copyright material confers the right on the purchasing institution to photocopy pages 117–120 only. No other part of this publication may be reproduced, stored in a retrieval system, or transmitted in any form or by any means, electronic, mechanical, photocopying, recording or otherwise, without prior permission of Unwin Hyman Ltd.

Design and Cover: Hine & Limbrick
Illustrations: Matthew Limbrick
Photography: David Wellings

ISBN 0 00 312572 6

Typeset by Nene Phototypesetters Ltd, Northampton
Printed by Scotprint Ltd, Musselburgh

CONTENTS

Introduction		iv
Chapter format		v
Topic/Age Range Matrix		vi
Skills level: 6 to 8 years	Bubbles and Circles	1
	Area 1	4
	Carbon Copycats 1	6
	Line Doodles	9
	Roundabouts 1	12
	Clowns	14
	Cylinders	17
	Starweaving 1	20
	Rainbowshapes	22
	Tessellation 1	25
	Shadowshapes 1	28
Skills level: 7 to 9 years	Carbon Copycats 2	31
	Rotashapes	33
	Fabric Shapes	35
	Area 2	37
	String Prints	40
	Tetraland	42
	Exploded Squares	46
	Starweaving 2	48
	Tessellation 2	50
Skills level: 8 to 11 years	Roundabouts 2	52
	Horizontal and Vertical	55
	Name Games	58
	Cross-stitch Patterns	61
	Tangram 1	64
	Area 3	67
	Shadowshapes 2	70
	Slinky Curves	73
	Tessellation 3	76
	Jack-in-the-Box	81
Skills level: 10 to 13 years	Border Patterns	84
	Shadowshapes 3	87
	Tangram 2	90
	Roundabouts 3	93
	Starweaving 3	97
	Circlewebs	100
	Swoparounds	102
	Folding Star Containers	104
	Islamic Patterns	107
	Tessellation 4	110
Techniques and Materials	Marbled Paper	114
	Paper Spring	115
	Five-pointed Star	116
	Chinese Tangram	117
	Nets for Cubes	118
	1 cm Isometric Grid	120
	'A' Series Paper Sizes	121
	Suppliers' Addresses	122

The examples in the photographs are presented in approximate age order.

INTRODUCTION

This book is intended for teachers and parents of children aged from 6 to 13 years. The general aim of the book is to increase the enjoyment, understanding and involvement of teachers, children and parents in mathematics, art and design.

W W Sawyer defined mathematics as:
> *The classification and study of all possible patterns and relationships. Pattern is anything the mind can recognise as a regularity.*

Very often, depicting mathematical patterns or relationships in a colourful and artistic way adds to a child's understanding and appreciation of them. Children may come to realise that, inherent in many artistic forms, there exists a mathematical precision too often taken for granted. Also it is hoped that children will come to appreciate that natural forms and structures can be interpreted only by using mathematical language and techniques. Symmetry is a dominant characteristic of both the natural and manmade world.

The report of the Cockcroft Committee *Mathematics Counts* (HMSO, 1982) comments that although there are some books linking mathematics to other subjects such as art and science, more are needed. Paragraph 292 of the Report states:
> *Almost all children find pleasure in working with shapes, and work of this kind can encourage the development of positive attitudes towards mathematics in those who are finding difficulty with number work.*

Children will be led to look upon mathematics as a more attractive subject if we draw their attention to the balance between its functional and its aesthetic aspects. Also, by linking it not only with art and design, but also with language and science, mathematics can be used by children more *creatively*; it is freed from the strait-jacket of the textbook.

Whilst undertaking the practical activities suggested, there will be many opportunities to introduce mathematical vocabulary *in context* — to talk about mathematics in a nonstressful situation.

Over twenty years ago, in a lecture to the Mathematical Association of America, Professor Polya said:
> *If a teacher has no experience of creative work of some sort, how will he be able to inspire, to lead, to help or even to recognise the creative ability of his students? A teacher who acquired whatever he knows in mathematics purely receptively can hardly promote the active learning of his students.*
>
> *A teacher who never had a bright idea in his life will probably reprimand a student who has one instead of encouraging him.*

It is important that *Mathematics through Art and Design* is not regarded by teachers and parents solely as a source of ideas to try out on children. Its appeal and format should be such that the adults will want to have a go at the activities themselves.

Anne Woodman & Eric Albany

CHAPTER FORMAT

The topics covered come under these main headings: *rotation, reflection, translation, area* and *tessellation, three-dimensional work* and a *miscellany* section which includes *measuring skills* and early work on *shape*. However, there is bound to be considerable interrelationship and cross-referencing between the topics. The *techniques* and *materials* section contains a list of suppliers mentioned in the book, information on 'A' series international paper sizes and instructions for making marbled paper, paper springs and a five-pointed star. Master sheets of cube nets, tangrams and isometric grids may be photocopied without prior permission.

The items under each heading are divided into four overlapping age bands (6–8, 7–9, 8–11, 10–13) so that, as far as possible, activities can be selected to match the abilities and interests of the children. (See the table on page vi.)

Each chapter includes a brief outline of what is being attempted and is presented in a standard format under the following subheadings.

Materials
A list of such things as card, squared paper, isometric grids, ruler, colouring pencils, pens or crayons, glue, scissors, etc that will need to be prepared in readiness for the activity.

Vocabulary
A list of mathematical words and phrases that will be used in the course of the activity. Some of these may well be new to the children but it will be possible to introduce them gradually and in context while the activity is being undertaken and in the ensuing discussions with the teacher.

Method
Usually a 'safe' method of achieving a satisfactory end result is presented in easy stages making the maximum use of clear diagrams, but teachers who prefer to follow a more adventurous, open-ended approach may wish to modify the activities accordingly. In the case of the older children, instructions could be copied on to workcards for them to use on their own. Alternatively, they may be able to use the book for direct reference.

Teaching Points
These consist of advice to the teacher on how the best use can be made of the materials, hints about organising the activity, what sort of questions to ask and how to make the most of the mathematical ideas that occur during the activity.

Extensions and Variations
Once children have gained confidence with a basic technique, it is often possible to extend their skills in many interesting ways. They may be encouraged to investigate problems linked with the basic activity or to apply previously acquired knowledge and skills in more challenging ways, many of which stimulate divergent thinking and a willingness to pursue open-ended tasks.

References & Resources
A list of books and commercially produced materials which are appropriate for the activity.

TOPIC/AGE RANGE MATRIX

The cross-references to *Mathematics in the National Curriculum* (December, 1991) are given below each chapter heading, and refer to the attainment targets and levels to which the chapter makes a significant contribution, eg 4(1) represents AT4, Level 1. Statements of attainment for each level have not been specified, but these are covered wholly or partially within, or lead towards, the level indicated for each attainment target.

Attainment Target 1 applies throughout the book, which focuses on using and applying mathematics in a wide range of situations.

AGE RANGE	6–8 YEARS	7–9 YEARS	8–11 YEARS	10–13 YEARS
MISCELLANY	Bubbles & Circles 4(1,2) 5(1) Clowns 4(1,2) 5(1,2) Line Doodles 4(1,2,3) 5(1,2)	Fabric Shapes 4(2,3)	Horizontal & Vertical 4(2,3) 5(2)	Circlewebs 4(4)
ROTATION	Starweaving 1 3(1) 4(1,2) 5(1,2) Shadowshapes 1 4(1,2) 5(1) Roundabouts 1 4(1,2,3) 5(1)	Rotashapes 4(2,4) Starweaving 2 4(2,3,4)	Roundabouts 2 4(2,3,4,6) 5(2) Shadowshapes 2 4(2,4,6)	Starweaving 3 4(4) Swoparounds 4(4,5,6) Shadowshapes 3 4(4,5,6)
TRANSLATION		String Prints 4(1,2,3,4)		Border Patterns 4(3,4)
REFLECTION	Carbon Copycats 1 4(2)	Exploded Squares 4(2,3) Carbon Copycats 2 4(2,3)	Cross-stitch Patterns 4(2,3,4) Name Games 4(2,3,4)	Islamic Patterns 4(3,4,6)
AREA & TESSELLATION	Rainbowshapes 4(1,2) Area 1 4(2) Tessellation 1 4(1,2)	Area 2 4(2) Tessellation 4(2)	Tangram 1 4(2,3,4) 5(2) Tessellation 3 4(4) Slinky Curves 4(4) 5(2) Area 3 4(3,4)	Tangram 2 4(4,5,6) Tessellation 4 4(4,5,6)
3-DIMENSIONAL	Cylinders 4(1,2,3)	Tetraland 4(2,3,4)	Jack-in-the-Box 4(4)	Roundabouts 3 4(4,6) Folding Star Containers 4(4,6)

BUBBLES AND CIRCLES †

This chapter suggests activities in which children can explore different ways of working with circles, overlaps and pattern making.

MATERIALS
Plastic drinking straws, powder colours, jars with lids, plastic pots, sheets of paper, liquid detergent, printing pad (see page 3).

METHOD
Teacher preparation: Using a jar with a lid, mix a 'cocktail' of powder colour and equal parts of water and top quality washing up liquid. Make up several colours of this mixture, which keeps quite well. Pour the coloured mixtures into plastic pots of different sizes (the children could collect these in advance) to a depth of two or three centimetres.

1. With a drinking straw, blow into the mixture until bubbles start to collect above the rim of the container (fig. 1).

VOCABULARY
Circle, circular, semicircle, cone, cylinder, rectangular.

2. Place a sheet of paper over the bubbles and push it down gently until it touches the rim of the container.
3. Lift the paper off and you should have a circular print with lots of bubble patterns (fig. 2).

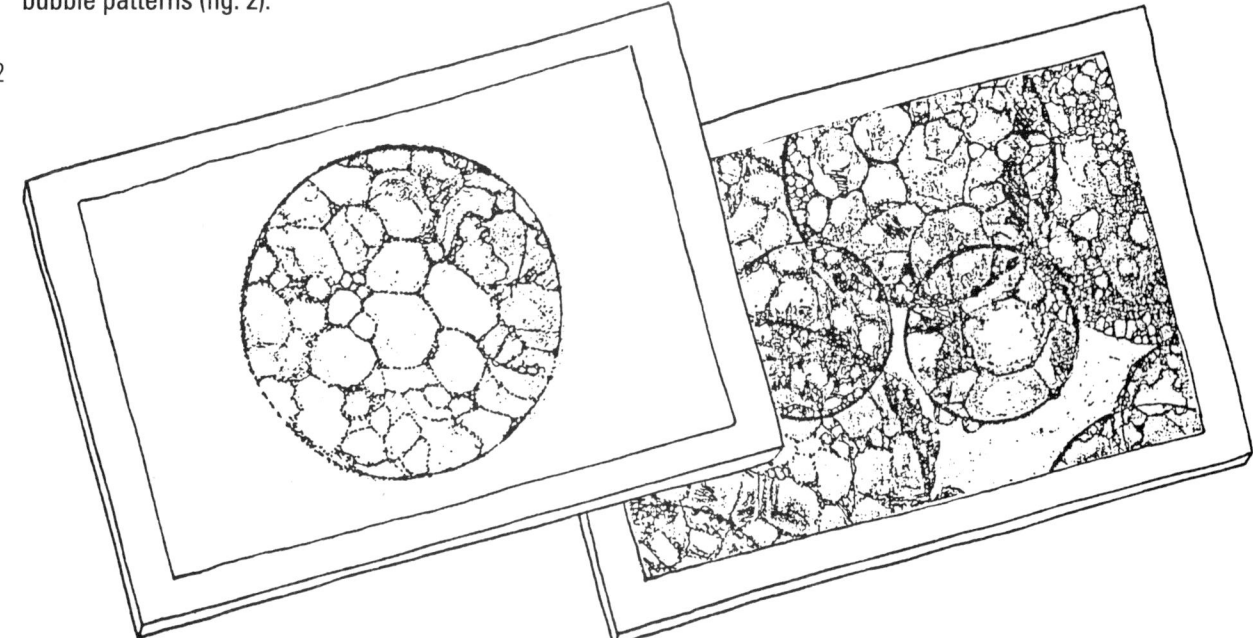

4. Do this several times, using the different colours and different sizes of pots, until the surface of the paper is covered with circles and bubble patterns.
5. Leave the paper to dry.

† *Illustrated on page 2 of the first photograph section*

TEACHING POINTS

1. Some of the remaining bubble mixture can be used as 'ink' for a printing pad, and further circles can be added to the design using cotton reels, corks, or circular ends of open or closed cylinders as stamps. (See page 3 for instructions on how to make a simple printing pad.) Small gummed circular shapes, file paper reinforcers, sequins, etc can also add variety (fig. 3).

2. Bubble print paper could be used in place of marbled paper when making the Jack-in-the-box. (See page 81.)

3. Tissue paper circles look attractive when bubble printed and glued to the design.

4. The designs look effective when printed on circular backing sheets which can be wall mounted or hung as mobiles. Alternatively, rectangular backing sheets can be coiled to form open cylinders (fig. 4).

5. Several circular prints can be assembled on a piece of card to make a 'bubble' caterpillar or dragon (fig. 5).

6. Discussion points might include:
"What shapes do the bubbles make on the paper?"
"How can you blow smaller bubbles or larger ones?"
"How many different sizes of pots did you use?"
"What is the smallest/largest pot we can find in the classroom?"
"What happens to the colours when they overlap?"

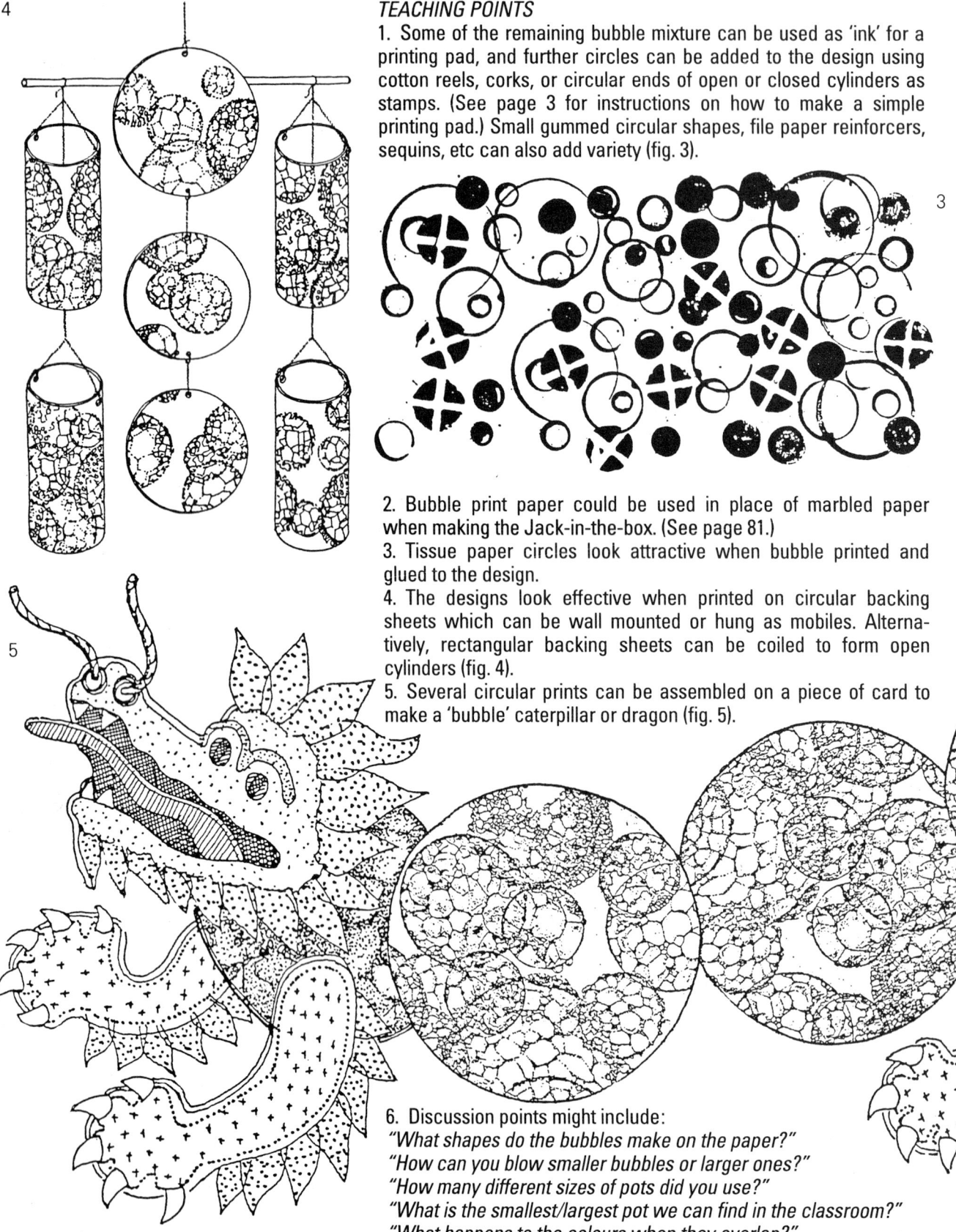

2   BUBBLES AND CIRCLES

EXTENSIONS AND VARIATIONS
1. Get the children to collect as many objects as possible with circular edges that they can draw round — saucers, tins, cups, cylinders, etc. Using a crayon or a candle, firmly mark out circles all over a backing sheet. Paint over these with a thin paint or coloured ink. The wax will resist the liquid wash. Some children may also enjoy trying to draw freehand circles. A more experimental approach could be to draw circles using a variety of media, apply a liquid wash and investigate which of the materials are water resistant and which are not.
2. The techniques described in *SHADOW SHAPES 1* (page 28) can be used with circular stencils and templates.
3. Demonstrate how to draw circles using either the *Triman Safety Compasses* or the Taskmaster *Junior Compasses*, which have no sharp points, and allow the children to experiment with them.
4. Make a collection of circular tops or stoppers — bottle tops, aerosol tops, corks, etc — and classify them in as many different ways as possible. Glue them down in a random or predetermined assemblage.
"Why are most tops circular?"
"Is it the best shape for a lid?"
5. Collect and display examples of circular motifs and patterns that are either manmade or natural forms.
6. "What can be done with a circle to change it into a cone?"
"Can you make a cone from a semicircle?"
7. Computer design programs such as *Picture Builder* allow experimental work with a variety of shapes including circles, with colour, size and orientation as variables.

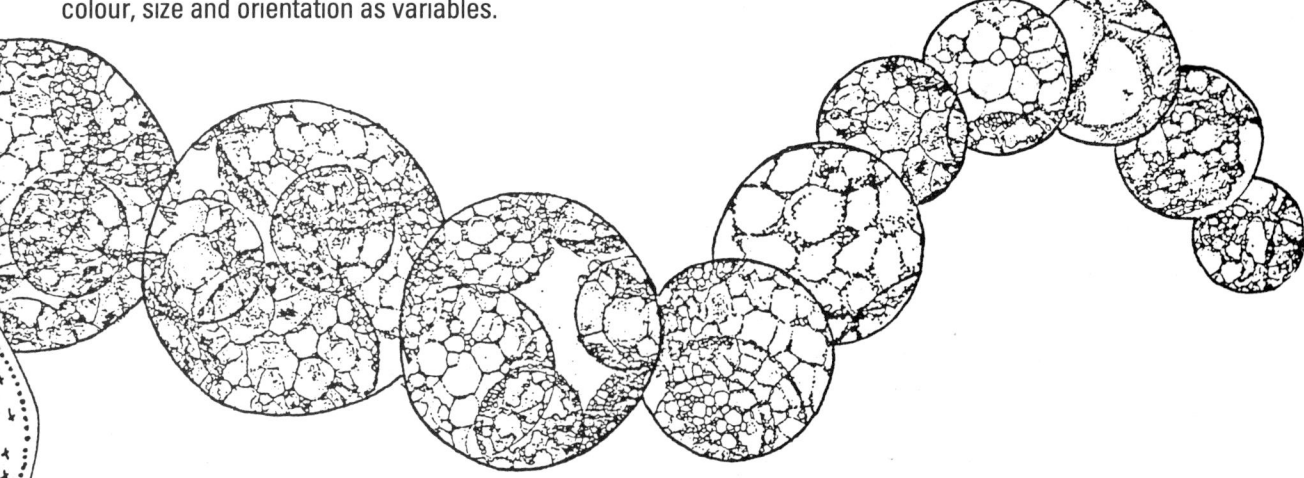

Instructions for making a simple printing pad
Materials: Shallow lid, thin foam rubber or sponge, printing ink or homemade mixture of PVA glue and poster paint (ordinary poster paint will do at a pinch).
Put a thin layer of ink in the base of the lid and cover it with a layer of foam cut to fit. Prod the foam gently until the ink starts to seep through. Add more ink very gradually if necessary, but do not swamp the pad so that it is overloaded. Try some practice prints to test the pad. Commercial office-type pads and ink in different colours are in all leading educational catalogues and work quite well.

REFERENCES & RESOURCES
Junior Compasses Taskmaster Ltd
Triman Safety Compasses E J Arnold
Picture Builder Computer program (RML, BBC, Commodore), Hill McGibbon Software.

AREA 1 †

> **MATERIALS**
> Large backing sheet, crayons and/or poster paints, brushes.

> **VOCABULARY**
> Region, surface, cover, overlap, outline, jigsaw, gap, completely.

The concept of area is often misunderstood, even by older children, and needs to be introduced and developed carefully. The activities in this chapter focus on foundation language and concepts in an informal way, by dealing with covering surfaces partially and completely, fitting together, overlapping, etc — ideas that are common to both area and tessellation.

METHOD
1. Using a black crayon, divide the backing sheet into about ten regions. Make different shapes and sizes.
2. Working from the top to the bottom, paint or crayon each region in a different colour, going right to the edge of every region each time so that the surface is completely covered (fig. 1).

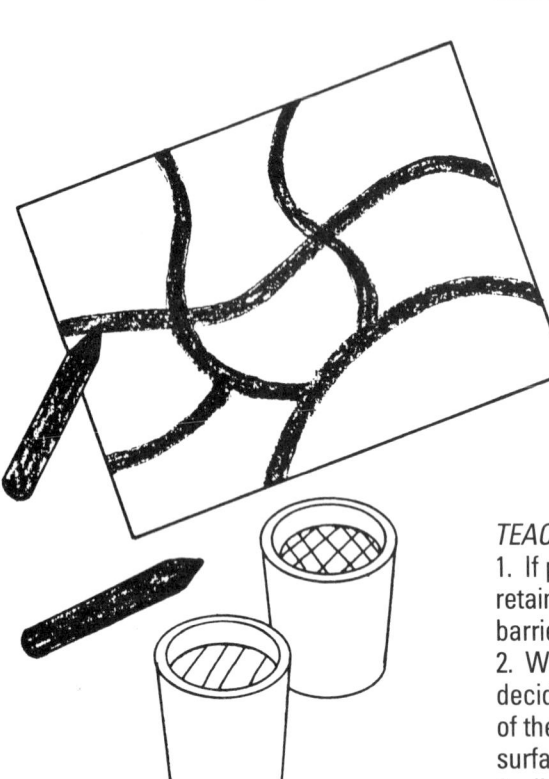

TEACHING POINTS
1. If paint is used, the wax crayon outline heavily applied will help to retain the paint in the correct region by acting as a paint resistant barrier.
2. When demonstrating this activity, ask the children if they can decide which region covers the most or the least amount of surface of the paper. Is there a region that covers about the same amount of surface as the child's handprint?
3. Jigsaws offer opportunities to talk about shapes that fit together without leaving gaps and cover a surface. Some children may enjoy making their own jigsaws but cutting along the lines of their pattern and then fitting the pieces together again without leaving gaps. You could also ask the children if they can put the pieces in order according to area. This may reveal some interesting misunderstandings!

EXTENSIONS AND VARIATIONS
1. As a related activity, provide some paper shapes and think of a 'rule' for the children to follow. For example, glue the shapes down so that
(a) they fit together as closely as possible without overlapping,
(b) they overlap and do not leave any gaps. (Tissue paper is useful here because its transparent quality allows the children to see the overlaps.)

† *Illustrated on page 1 of the first photograph section*

2. Provide a selection of plastic or gummed shapes (fig. 2).
Invite each child to choose a set of shapes that are all the same shape and size (congruent shapes) and to try to fit them together so that there are no gaps or overlaps. Ask questions such as:
"Which shapes are the best for covering a surface?"
"How many of these shapes do you think it will take to cover this book?"

3. Get each child to use either paint or collage materials to decorate a small box so that the entire surface, that is, all the faces, is covered. Area as a measure of the amount of surface is not applicable to 2-dimensional shapes only! Colour restrictions could be imposed; for example, the box is to be decorated in shades of one colour, or in as many different colours as possible.

4. Children can make simple tangram-type patterns of their own using congruent gummed shapes. These can be cut or torn into three or four parts and then glued down so that there are no overlaps and each part connects with at least one of the other parts (fig. 3).

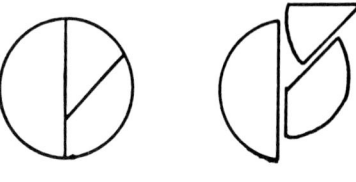
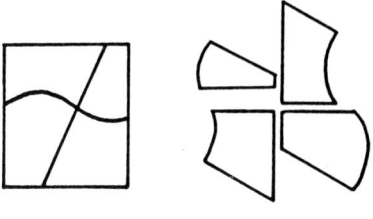
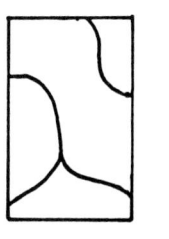
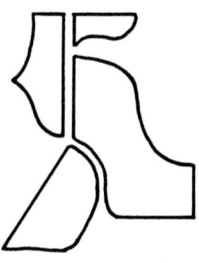

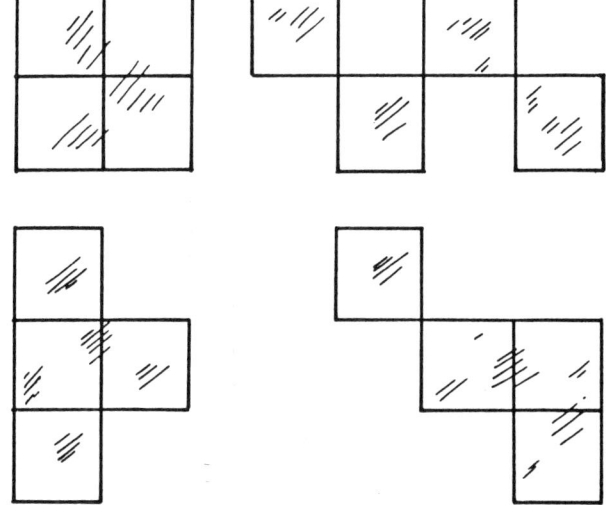

5. A slightly more formal investigation might be to get the children to fold and cut gummed squares into four smaller squares and then find as many patterns as they can with the squares, using the same rules as in 4 (fig. 4).

Suggestions in 4 and 5 above offer opportunities to talk about covering surfaces, no overlapping and the conservation of area.

REFERENCES & RESOURCES
First Squares Philip and Tacey
Fill-a-square Test Board Philip and Tacey
Tactile Tessellations E J Arnold

CARBON COPYCATS 1 †

MATERIALS
Rectangles of tracing paper (maximum size A4), A4 carbon paper, safety mirrors, ball-point pen, felt pens or colouring pencils, scissors.

VOCABULARY
Fold, half, crease, line (axis) of symmetry, symmetrical.

Carbon paper and paper folding are used to create patterns with bilateral symmetry.

METHOD
1. Fold the tracing paper so that one half fits exactly on the other half, i.e. along the axis of symmetry. Crease it firmly.
2. Flatten out the tracing paper and refold it with a sheet of carbon paper folded inside, shiny side facing the tracing paper and the folds touching.
3. Gradually, draw a pattern on the top half of the tracing paper. Keep turning to the back half as you work, and watch your pattern grow (fig. 1).
You can also open up the tracing paper and remove the carbon paper to check on how the pattern is growing.
4. When you like your pattern, remove the carbon paper, flatten out the tracing paper and colour the pattern symmetrically, i.e. so that the colours match on both sides of the axis. Use a mirror for checking. (Fig. 2).

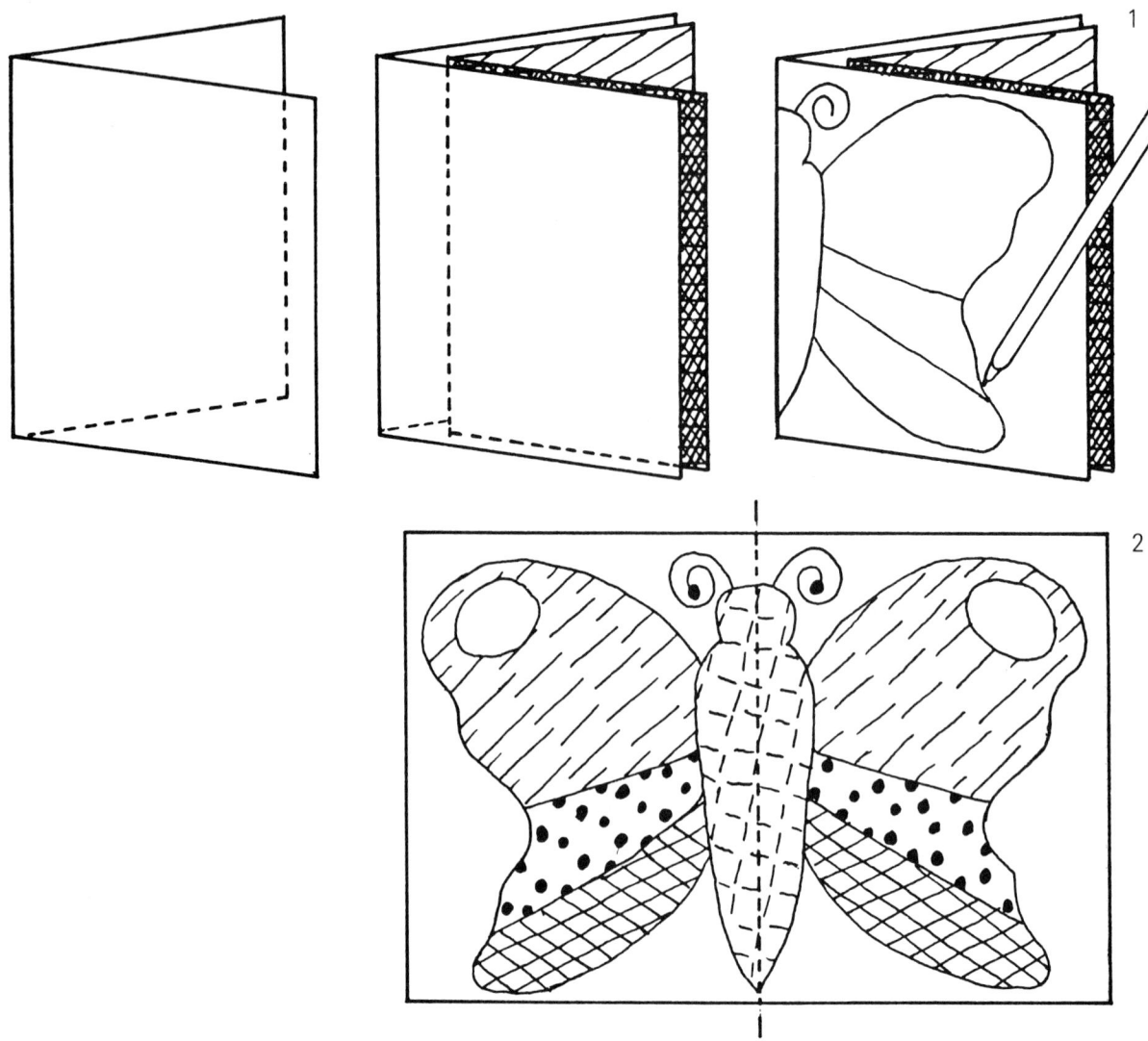

† *Illustrated on page 3 of the first photograph section*

TEACHING POINTS

1. No doubt the children will enjoy making further carbon copycats, and it is a good idea to vary the shape of the tracing paper to include others with at least one axis of symmetry. Encourage children to design a pattern that complements the shape (fig. 3).

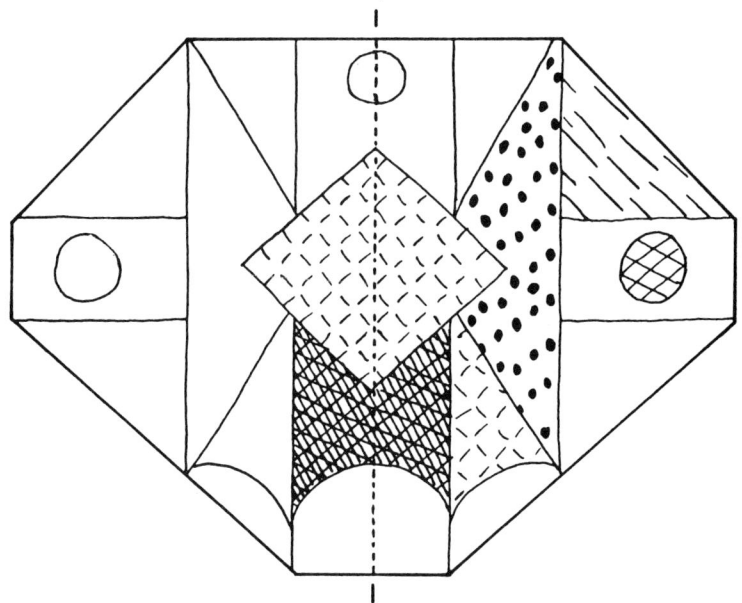

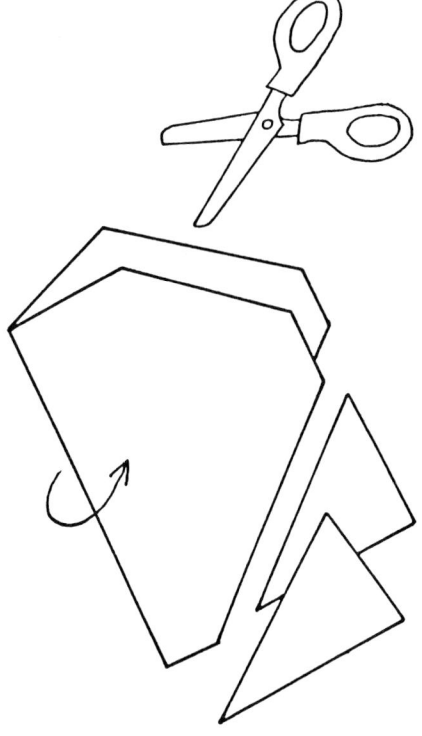

2. Some children may prefer to create a more individualised shape by trimming the edges of the tracing paper before they start on the pattern (fig. 4).

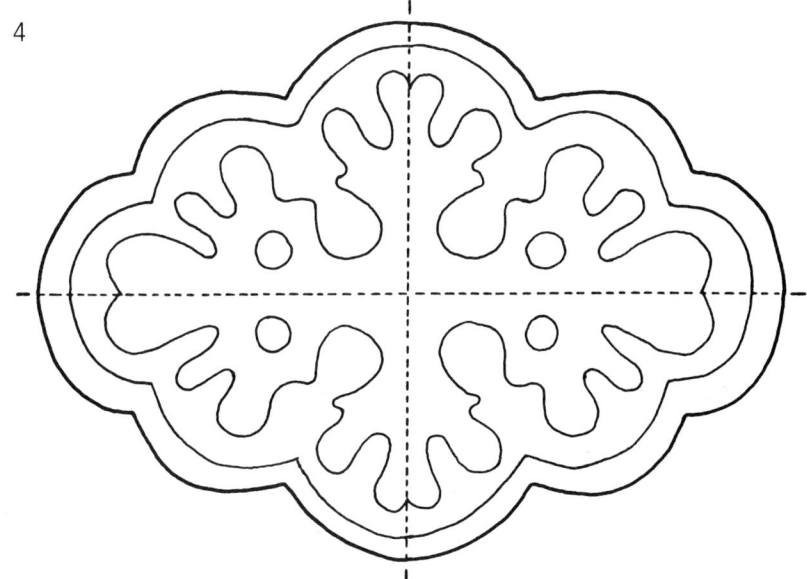

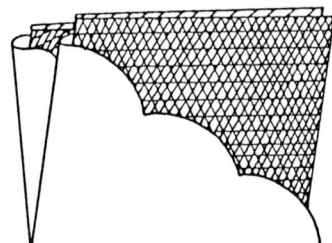

3. If the carbon paper extends beyond the edges of the tracing paper, encourage the children to mask the extruding area, as some brands can be rather smudgy. You may have more than one colour of carbon paper available, which would enable children to produce multicoloured effects.

4. Being able to see through tracing paper gives it an advantage over ordinary paper, as the child can hold the folded pattern up to the light to discover that all the corresponding parts fit on to each other. This, in conjunction with mirrors, which should always be available, helps in the understanding of some of the properties of reflective symmetry.

Other transparent and semitransparent materials could be collected and experimented with to see which work well — greaseproof paper, polythene bags trimmed to form a double page, tissue, cellophane, etc.

5. A simulation of carbon paper can be made by wax-crayoning heavily over a sheet of paper and using it in the same way as carbon paper. It will be necessary to press very firmly with a ball-point pen.

EXTENSIONS AND VARIATIONS

1. As with all mathematical ideas, it is important to present the same concept in different ways. Other equally successful ideas include the following.

(a) Blobs of *Cromar Paint*, or poster paint to which some liquid detergent has been added, can be guided by the fingers from the top of the folded page into a suitable shape. (Ordinary poster paint falls off tracing paper when dry.) Polythene also works well with this type of paint.

(b) String pulls with paint mentioned in (a).

(c) Ink blobs.

(d) Wax crayon shavings placed in a random or predetermined pattern between the folds of the tracing paper and ironed on with a quick dab of a dry iron (wool setting) — but this requires personal supervision.

(e) Paper 'fold and cut' or 'fold and tear' patterns are also popular.

There is no reason why two or more of these techniques should not be combined in one piece of work.

2. Start with a square sheet of paper and experiment with folds along different axes of symmetry — horizontal, vertical and diagonal.

3. Extend children after the free experimental stage by giving them specific patterns to design using the folded paper; for example, a butterfly, a tree, two trees, three trees, two people walking away from or towards each other, a clown standing on another clown's head. Some children may enjoy challenging a partner to make a copy of a given design.

4. *The Magic Mirror Books* by Marion Walter, which require an active investigatory response from the child, are a valuable resource to complement any work on reflective symmetry.

5. Provide examples of patterns with more than one axis of symmetry and see if the child can work out how to fold the paper to obtain a similar pattern. (This idea is developed in *CARBON COPYCATS 2*, page 31.)

REFERENCES & RESOURCES
The Magic Mirror Books Marion Walter; Tarquin Publications
Nuffield Maths 5–11 Teachers' Handbook 2 Longman; pages 94–96
Cromar Paint Berol Ltd
Mirror Resource Pack (Safety) E J Arnold.

LINE DOODLES †

Before starting to use a ruler for measuring and construction work, each child should learn to hold and use a ruler in a controlled way. This is a skill that needs to be taught and practised in the same way as holding a pencil.

MATERIALS
30 cm ruler, pencil, paper approximately 20 cm square, colouring materials, 5 mm self-adhesive circles (optional).

VOCABULARY
Ruler, rule, straight, place, point, position, region, different, collection, cross over (intersect), enough, edge to edge.

METHOD
1. Draw a collection of straight lines using a ruler. The lines can be of different lengths and can cross over each other until there are enough of them to make an interesting pattern (fig. 1).
2. Colour some of the regions (fig. 2).

1
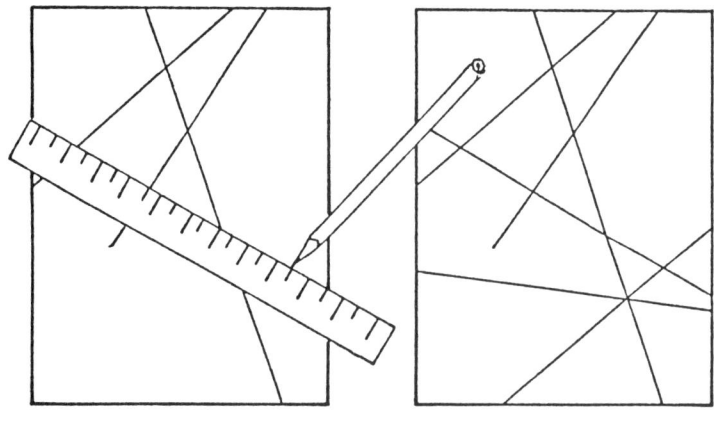

2
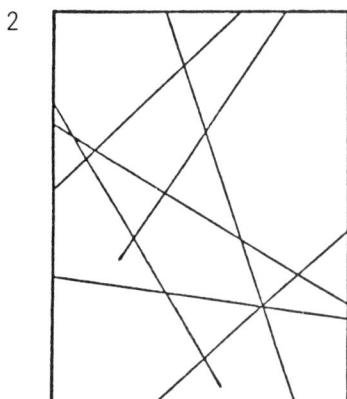
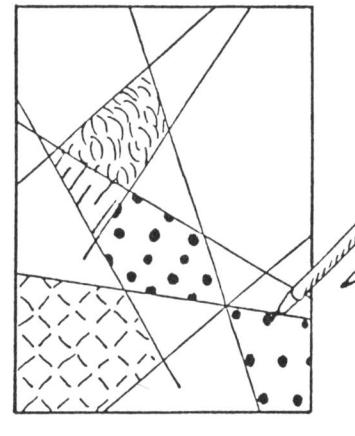
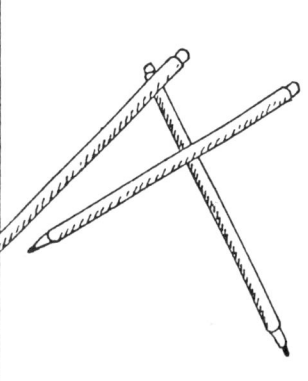

TEACHING POINTS
1. This activity requires direct instruction to show the children how to hold a ruler correctly and merely gives practice in ruling straight lines to create a random pattern. During the activity, the children should be observed and faults corrected.
2. As an alternative to colouring the different regions, ask the children to draw or stick a small coloured circle at each point where two or more lines intersect.

† Illustrated on page 3 of the first photograph section

3

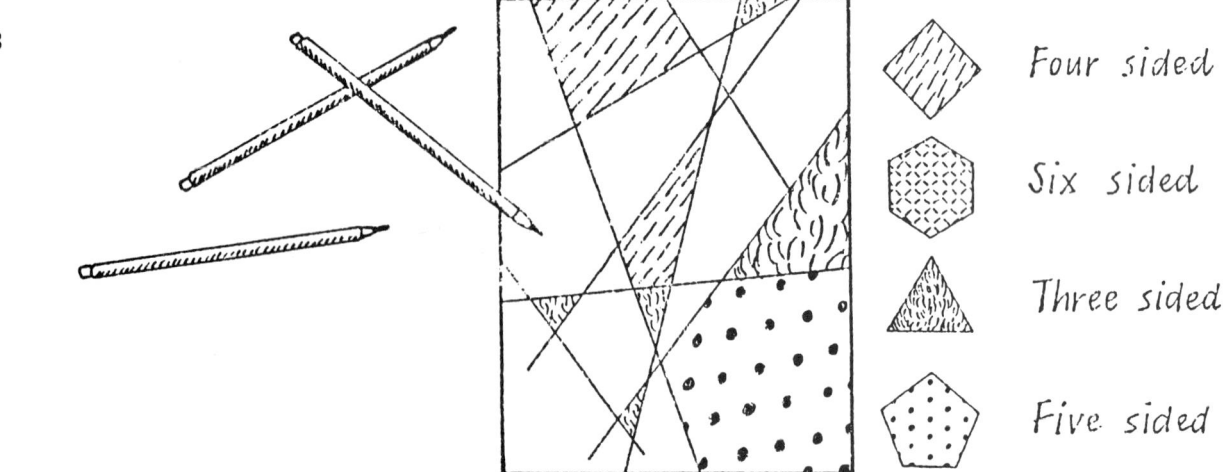

EXTENSIONS AND VARIATIONS

1. Different polygons are created by the lines and intersections, and it may be useful, after step 1, to investigate how many triangles can be found. Ask each child to write a small 3 to identify a region that is triangular or to colour each triangle.

2. Some children may enjoy classifying and colouring each region according to its number of sides, and finding out the family names — triangles, quadrilaterals, pentagons, hexagons, etc. A simple key could be included to explain the colouring system (fig. 3).

4

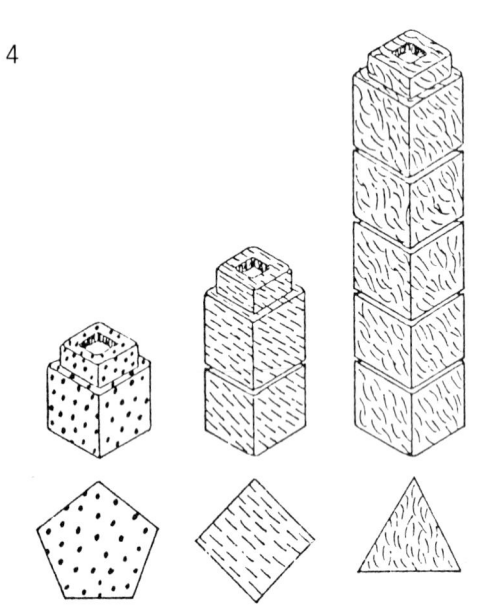

A block graph could be made from *Multilink* or *Unifix* cubes in related colours (fig. 4). Questions could then be asked along the lines of:

"How many triangles are there?"
"Which shape is there most of?"
"How many more triangles than pentagons are there?"

3. In order to give the beginner practice in another ruler skill, that of drawing a line to connect points, position three or four 5 mm circles on a 15–20 cm square of paper. The child is then asked to draw several lines right across the paper from edge to edge, passing through at least one of the oversized points or 'blobs'. For each line the ruler has to be rotated slightly, but the large 'blob' gives a large 'target area' which can be reduced in size as the skill increases. (Fig. 5.)

5

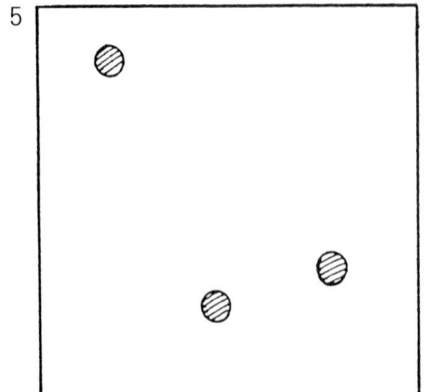 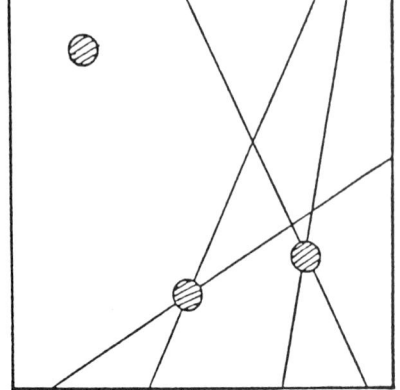 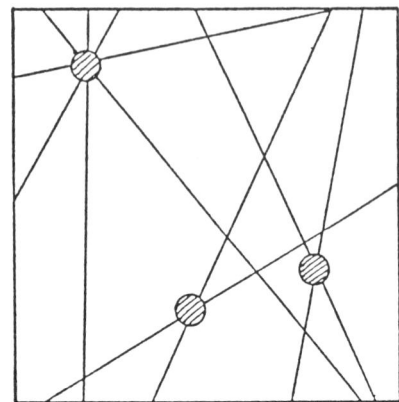

10   LINE DOODLES

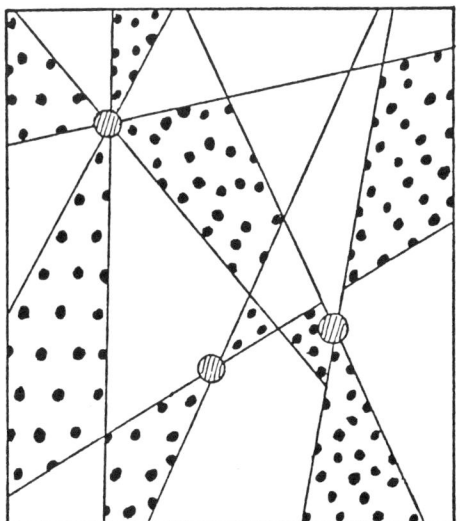
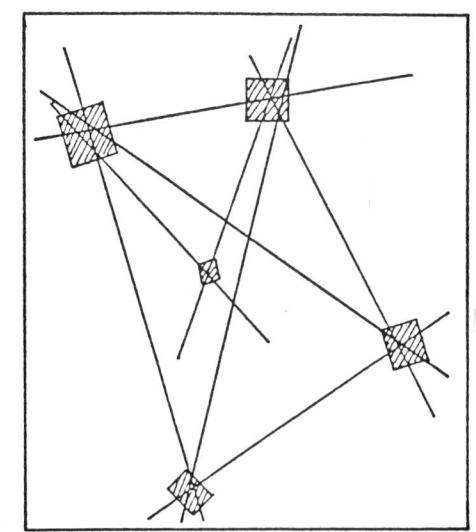

4. In the example in figure 6, some of the polygons converging around the blobs have been shaded.
5. The example in figure 7 uses square blobs of two different sizes and ruled lines joining pairs of blobs.
6. Several straight lines are drawn on the reverse side of a small gummed square, so that strips can be cut out along these guidelines. The strips are then arranged and glued on to a backing sheet. Further ruled lines, in different colours, can be added to the design. (Fig. 8.)
7. Logo and the mouse-driven program Brush complement this activity.

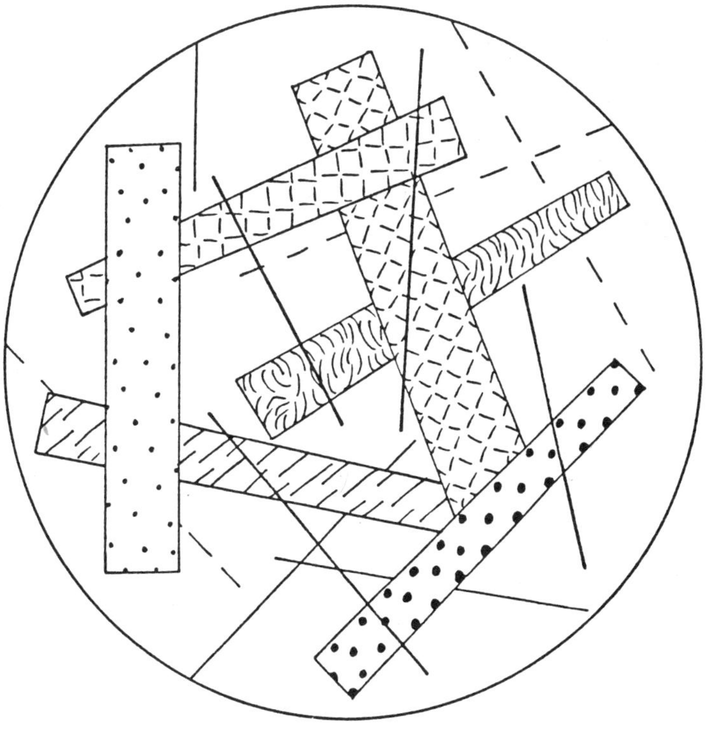

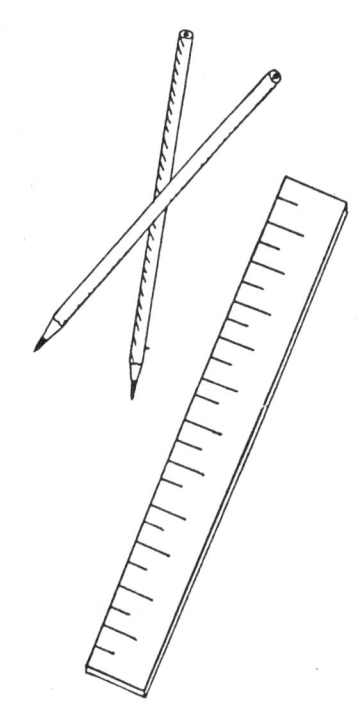

REFERENCES & RESOURCES
Brush Computer program from AUCBE.

LINE DOODLES 11

ROUNDABOUTS 1†

MATERIALS
Template or stencil of a square with sides at least 10 cm, card scraps, backing sheets, pencil, ruler, scissors, colouring pens or pencils.

VOCABULARY
Turn (rotate), square, shape, polygon, same, outline, edge, position, on top of, upright, vertical, one quarter of a turn, clockwise.

This activity provides a simple method involving matching and rotating shapes to create patterns with rotational symmetry.

METHOD
1. Use a template or stencil to trace out a square on firm card and cut it out carefully.
2. Draw the same outline on the backing sheet.
3. Cut out a *simple* shape from one edge of the card. Some examples are given in figure 1.

4. Position the card outline on top of the one drawn on the backing sheet.
5. Trace around the cutout section, holding the pencil upright (vertically) (fig. 2).
6. Rotate the card template one quarter of a turn clockwise so that the cutout section lines up with the next edge of the square.
7. Repeat steps 5 and 6 until the cutout section has been traced on to each edge in turn (fig. 3).
8. Colour the pattern.

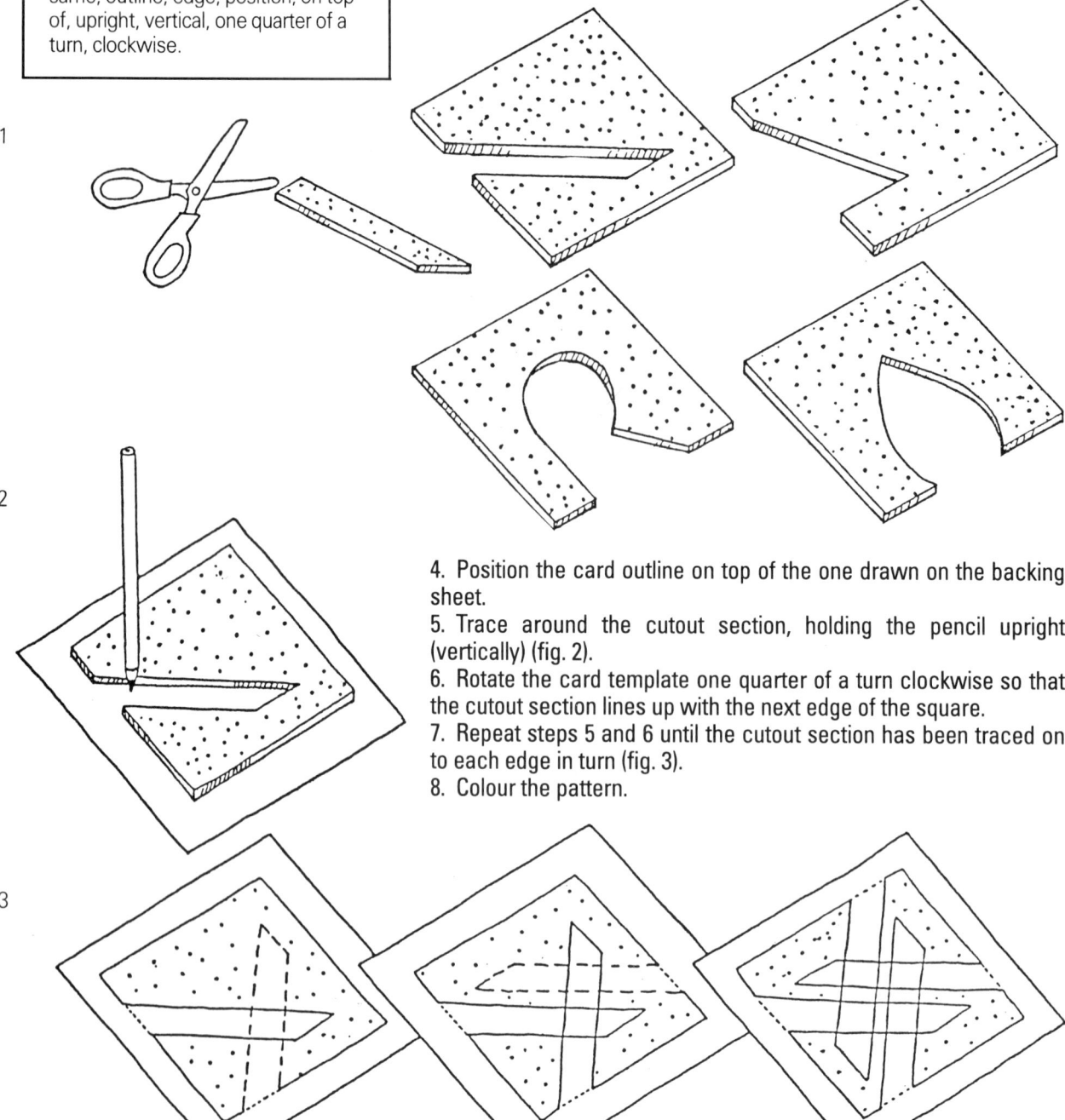

† *Illustrated on page 4 of the first photograph section*

TEACHING POINTS

1. The simple easy-to-trace-around cutouts can create quite spectacular patterns using the *turn and match* technique. The patterns created look the same after each quarter turn — that is they have *rotational symmetry of order 4*.
2. In order to avoid colouring mistakes, it is a good idea to encourage the children to plan their colouring arrangement first, by marking each zone faintly in pencil with the initial letter of the colour to be used (fig. 4).
3. Large scale diagrams can be constructed in the same way by using heavier card and larger templates, marking out the design in heavy black crayon and then painting the pattern.
4. Display several contrasting designs in one group and their templates in a separate group. See if the children can match each pattern to its template (fig. 5).

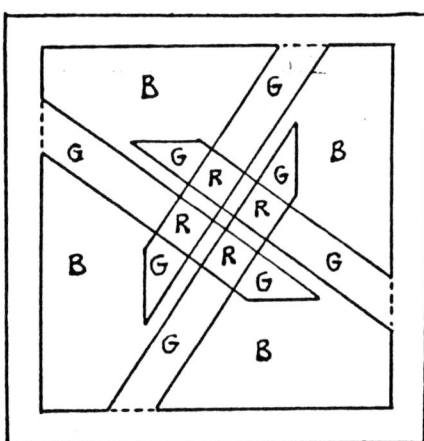

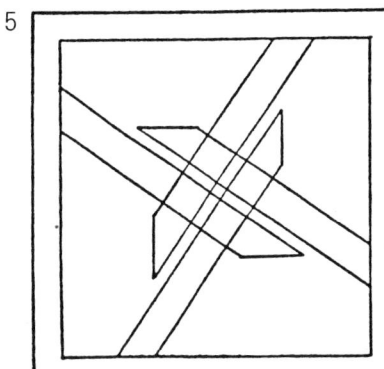
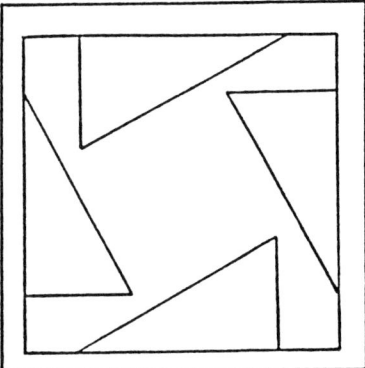
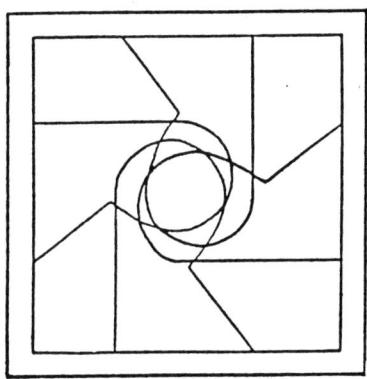
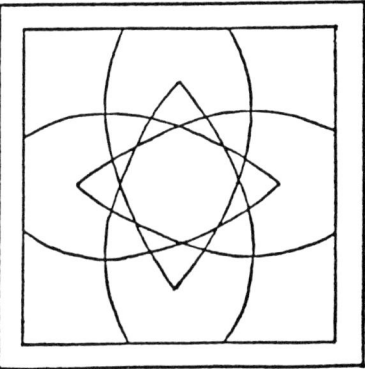

EXTENSIONS AND VARIATIONS

1. Encourage pairs of children to use the same outline and cutout. Ask one to rotate the template in a clockwise direction; the other to rotate it in an anticlockwise direction. What conclusions can they make?
2. Design a cutout so that when the pattern is complete, the cutout sections
(a) will not overlap each other,
(b) will overlap each other,
(c) will meet at the centre without overlapping.
3. Try removing a cutout section from one of the corners instead of an edge, or even try removing a section from both a corner and an edge.

CLOWNS †

MATERIALS
Card shapes for head and body, small assorted gummed shapes (stars, etc), paper strips, glue, scissors, offcuts of card, paper, gummed paper, buttons, sequins.

VOCABULARY
Circle, square, oblong, oval, hexagon, triangle, ends of, on top of, overlap, size, longer, wider.

The children are encouraged to use and assemble a combination of simple shapes and 'springs' to create a clown.

METHOD
1. Choose card shapes for the head and body of the clown and glue them together at the neck so that they overlap slightly (fig. 1).
2. Make four paper springs for the arms and legs. (See *TECHNIQUES AND MATERIALS* section, page 115 for instructions.)
3. Glue arms and legs into position on the body section (fig. 2).
4. Design hands and feet and glue them on to the ends of the limbs.

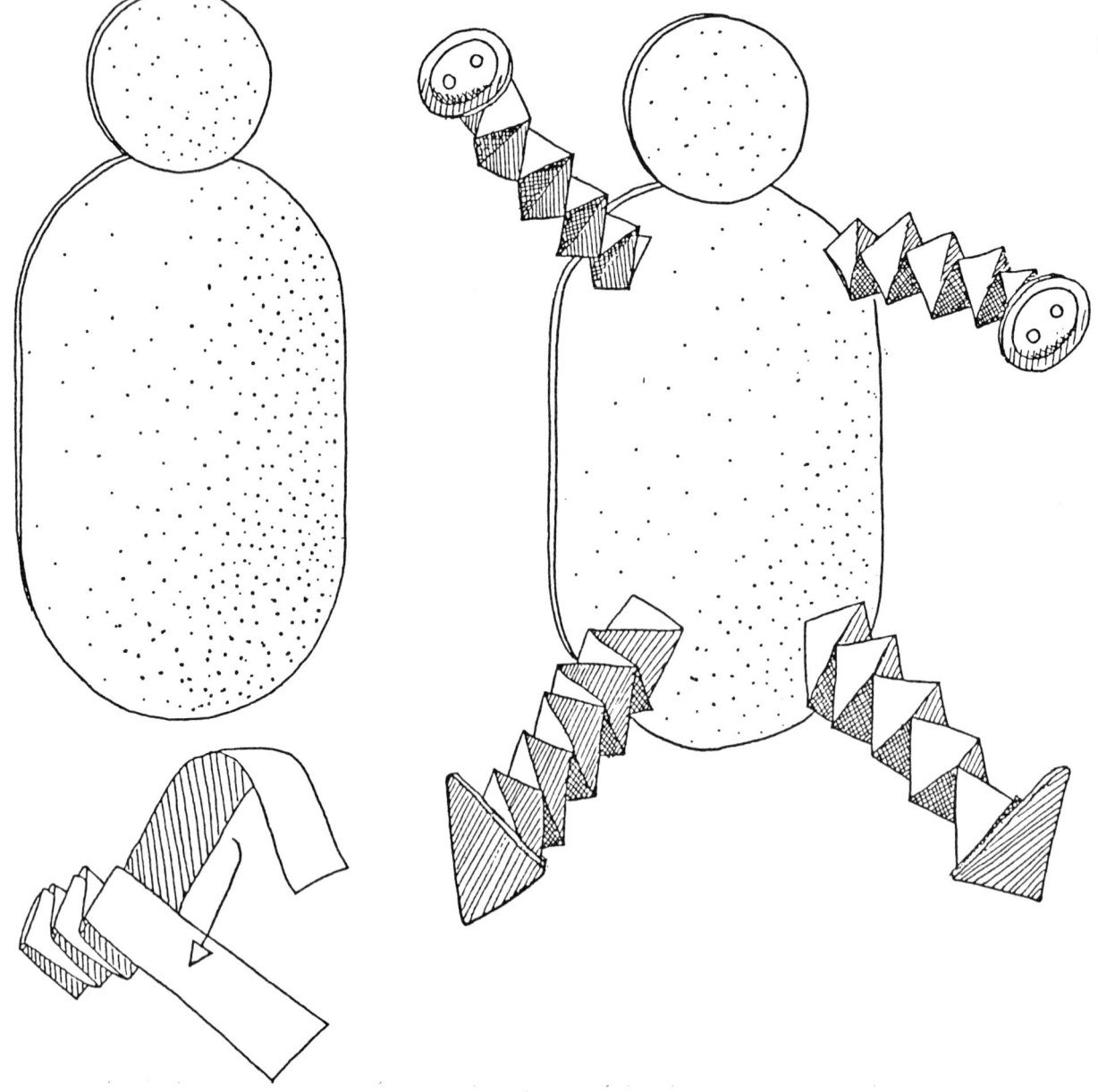

14   CLOWNS   † *Illustrated on page 3 of the first photograph section*

5. Design a hat out of card or paper and glue it to the top of the head. Think of a good shape to make a clown's hat. Some examples are given in figure 4, can you think of others?

6. Add paper shapes, sequins, buttons, etc to create features for the face and decoration for the hat and body (fig. 4).

3

4

TEACHING POINTS

1. Display pictures, posters and artefacts of real clowns and encourage children to observe their dress and make-up.

2. The paper springs offer opportunities for experimental work. Before constructing the clowns, allow children to experiment with different types of paper to find out which make the best springs. Help children to devise a 'fair test' for doing this so that some conclusion can be reached. Results could be put in order from the best to the worst.

CLOWNS 15

"Can you think of a way to make a multicoloured spring?"
"What would happen if unequal lengths or widths were used to make the springs?"

3. The use of descriptive mathematical language can be encouraged during this activity, particularly if a range of shapes, colours, sizes, textures, and lengths and widths of springs are being used.

4. Encourage the children to classify the clowns in as many different ways as they can. If the clowns are displayed so that they can be moved around easily, they can provide a pictorial representation of different ways of sorting into sets, for example: are smiling/are not smiling; have red noses/do not have red noses. Take a turn at classifying them in this way yourself and see if the children can say what criteria you have used. Children should also be encouraged to describe in spoken, written or diagrammatic forms all they can about their clowns, looking for differences and similarities.

"Can anyone describe a clown, without pointing to it, so that it can be identified?"

5. If you focus on curved shapes, for instance, you could restrict the children to using only shapes of this type.

6. With a small calendar or message attached to the body, a clown makes an attractive gift to take home.

EXTENSIONS AND VARIATIONS

1. This activity can be extended to include 3-dimensional shapes. Get the children to collect a variety of different size cuboids. Cover the boxes with suitable paper. *"What is the best way to cover a cuboid with wrapping paper?"* Otherwise paint them with PVA or poster paint to which some detergent has been added. When dry, these can act as bodies for the clowns. Further solids can be added if desired — matchbox feet, for example.

2. The concept of proportion can be introduced in a very informal way:

"What is the best width and length of spring for your clown's body size?"

"Could you make springs small enough for a clown with a matchbox body?"

3. This 'solid body' type of clown can be displayed effectively as a stabile by wedging it into a block of polystyrene packing material with a length of soft wire.

CYLINDERS †

This activity emphasises the vocabulary relating to cylinders by combining prints of end faces and actual cylinders in a collage.

MATERIALS
Backing sheet; card tubes such as toilet/kitchen roll centres or *Smartie* tubes; PVA glue; poster paint in three colours; shallow circular containers and cylindrical printing tools such as aerosol tops, tin lids, corks, etc; inking pad.

METHOD
Instructions for the teacher
1. Get each child to paint-print the end faces of the cylindrical printing tools on to the backing sheet so that it is covered in circles of different sizes and colours. (See page 3 for instructions on how to make a simple printing pad.)
2. Each child should paint at least one cylinder in one of the colours chosen for the circles on the backing sheet.
3. When the cylinders are completely dry, the children glue them lengthwise on to the backing sheet (fig. 1).
4. Display the results horizontally, vertically and at different angles so that the children can see and discuss the cylinders from varying perspectives.

VOCABULARY
Cylinder, circle, horizontal, vertical, lengthwise, end, face, covered, different, sizes

1
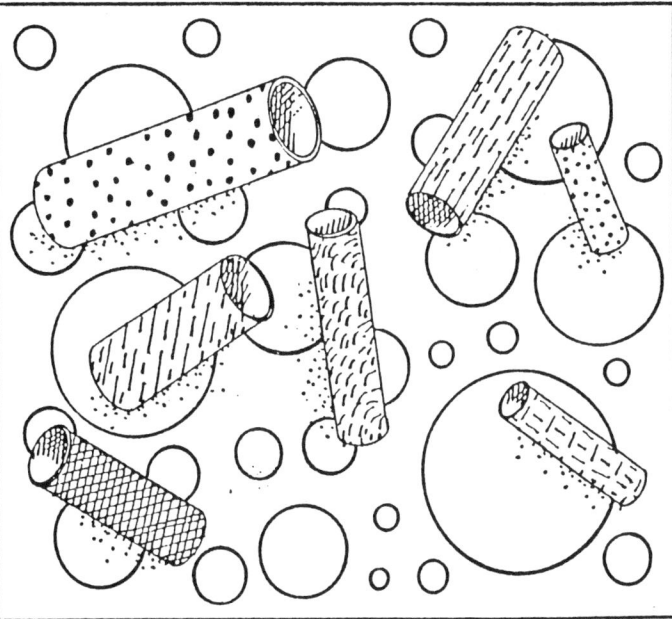

TEACHING POINTS
1. This activity could be organized on a group or class basis and will be much more valuable if every opportunity is taken to discuss the collection of cylinders, which should be as varied as possible, ranging from, for example, a drinking straw to a cheese box. The cylinders should be compared, classified and ordered in as many ways as possible with differences and similarities being closely examined.
2. The circle prints on the backing sheet will allow the end faces of cylinders to be discussed more naturally.
3. As an alternative method, instead of painting the cylinders and waiting for them to dry, get each child to cover at least one cylinder with small gummed-paper pieces, torn or cut and overlapping slightly so that the entire curved surface of the cylinder is covered (fig. 2). Trim off or glue down any untidy edges at the top and bottom, then glue the cylinders lengthwise on to the backing sheet using neat PVA glue.

2
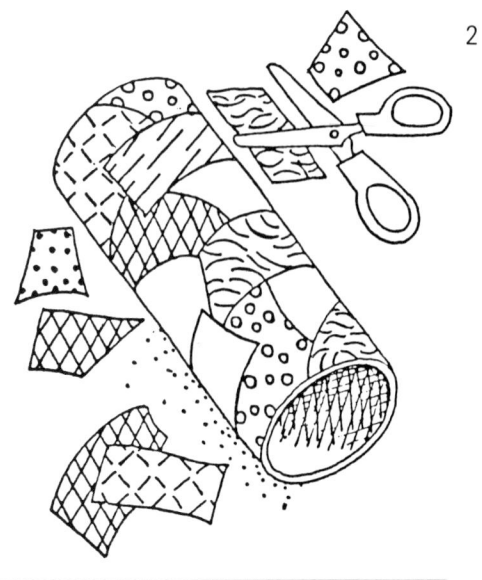

† *Illustrated on page 2 of the first photograph section*

4. When making the arrangement of cylinders, different rules could be imposed, for example:
(a) cylinders must be placed so that they are parallel to the sides of the backing sheet (horizontally or vertically);
(b) each cylinder must touch at least one other cylinder;
(c) all the cylinders must slope the same way (fig. 3).

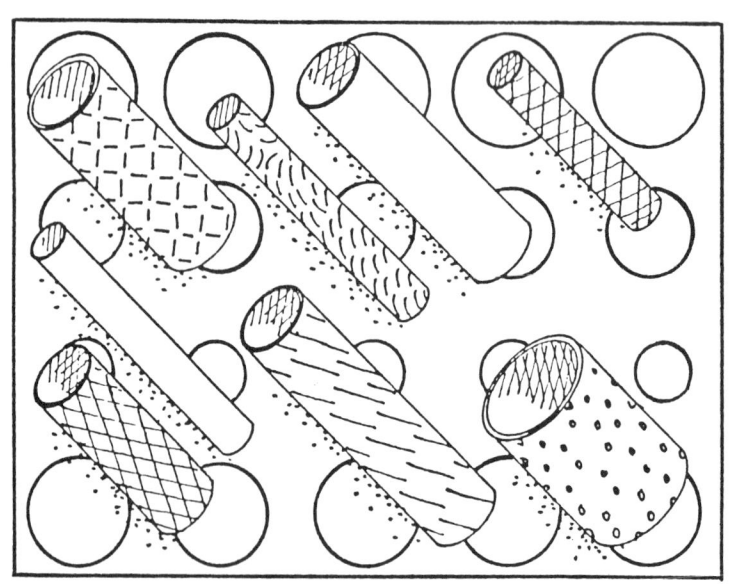

3

4

EXTENSIONS AND VARIATIONS

1. Attach unpainted cylinders to the backing sheet and then spray with aerosol paint.
2. Hang the decorated cylinders as a mobile, threading them in such a way that they can be viewed from different angles — horizontally, vertically, obliquely. The separators themselves are cylindrical — straws, pasta, beads, etc (fig. 4).
3. If the cylinders are glued along one of the end faces, they can be arranged rather like chimney stacks (fig. 5).

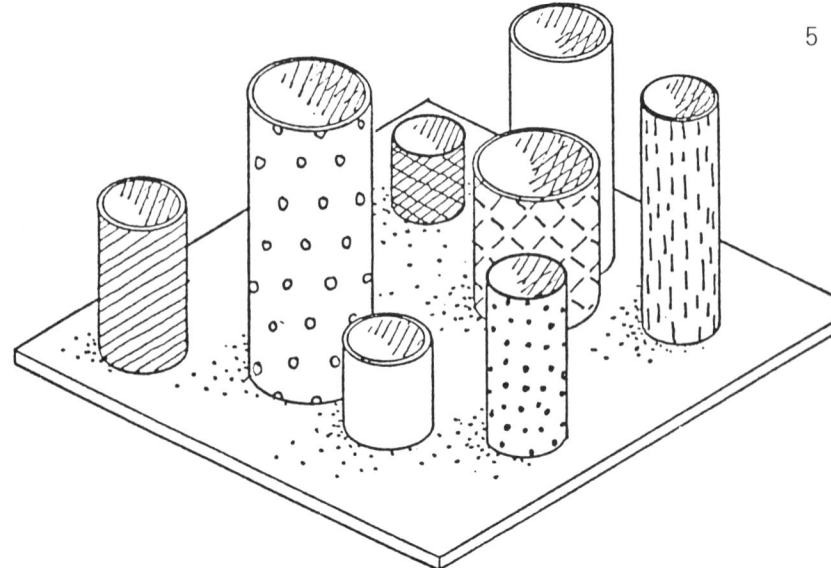

5

Alternatively, they can be grouped to form a 'desk tidy' for, pens, pencils, paperclips, etc (fig. 6).

4. Individual or paired tasks:

(a) Design an object made entirely from cylinders of different sizes. [Popular choices may well include robots, rockets, masks, etc (fig. 7).]

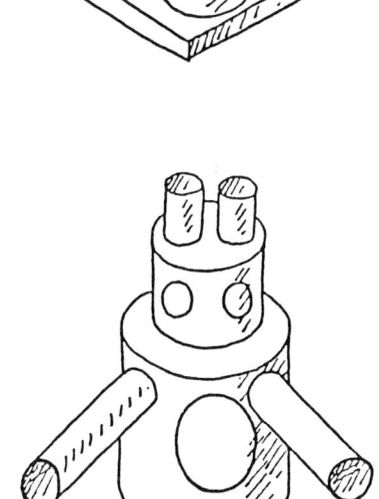

6

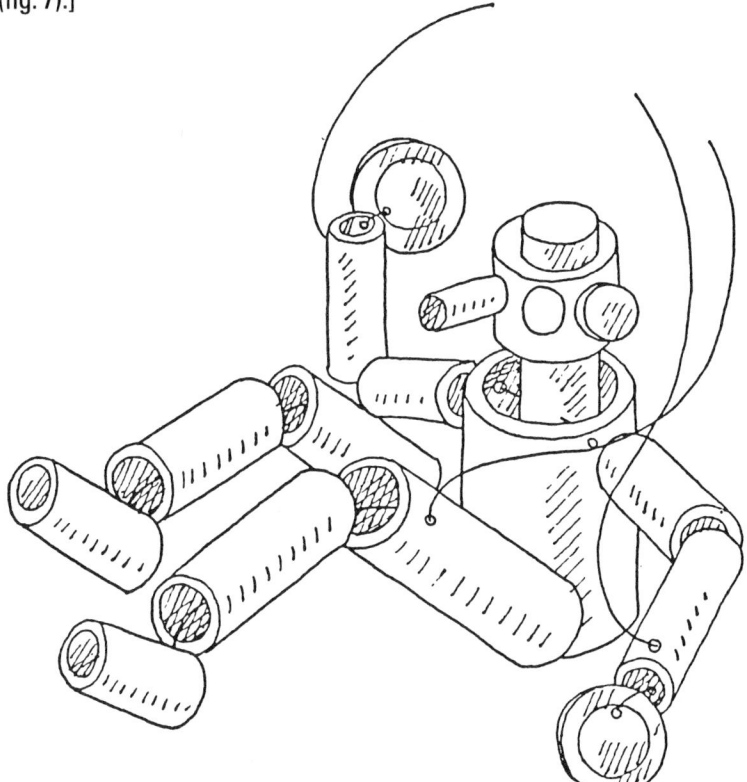

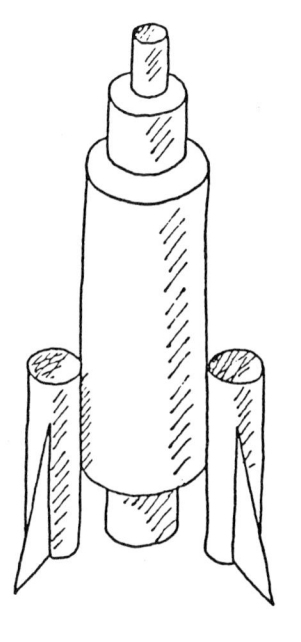

7

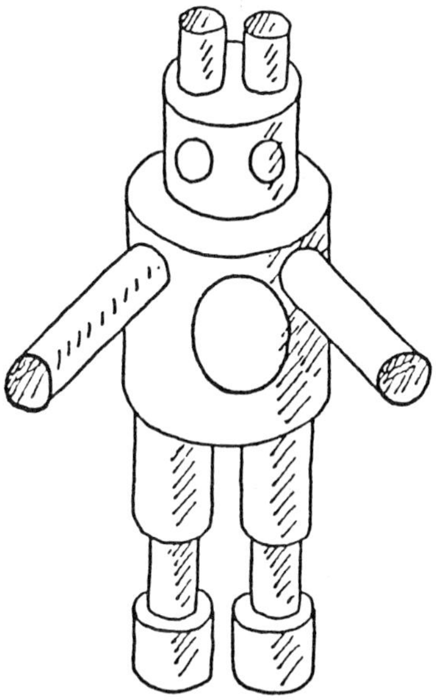

(b) Design and decorate a cylindrical hat from card. Make sure it is the correct size for your head and does not fall off.

(c) Design a label of the correct size for a tin of fruit or a tin of peas, etc. (Provide an empty cylindrical tin.)

5. Develop similar art activities for other families of solids such as cuboids, cones or pyramids (fig. 8).

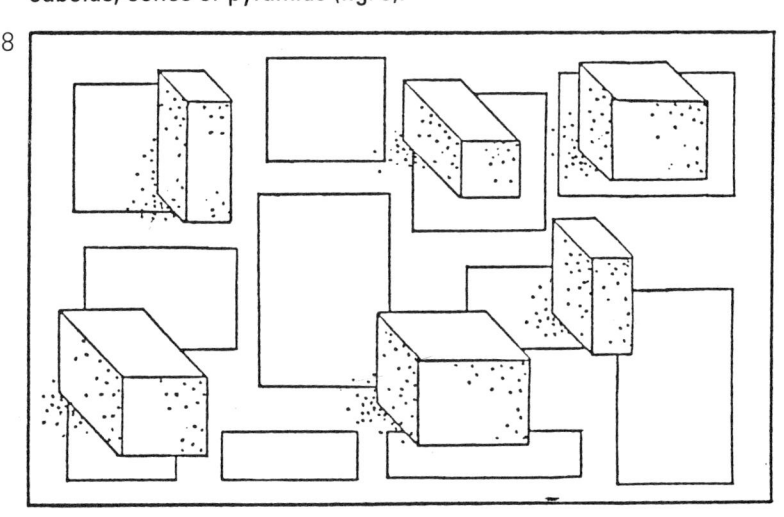

8

STARWEAVING 1†

MATERIALS
Two craft or lollipop sticks; assorted wools; scissors; PVA glue; buttons, counters and sequins.

VOCABULARY
Over, under, right angle, quarter of a turn, taut, square, rectangle (oblong), weaving.

This weaving technique, rich in positional vocabulary, needs to be demonstrated, preferably with a small group of children.

METHOD

In advance use the glue 'neat' to fix the two sticks together to form a right-angled cross with the four arms of equal length. Leave to set firmly. (Fig. 1.)

1. Tie the end of a ball of wool on one arm as close to the glued joint as possible, and trim the loose end.
2. Wind the wool *under* the next arm, round *over* the top of it and then *under* it again. Keep the wool taut. (Fig. 2.)

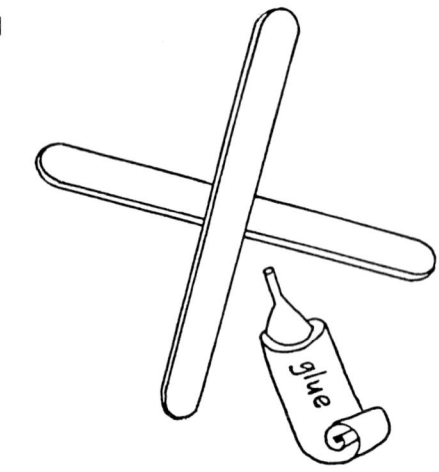

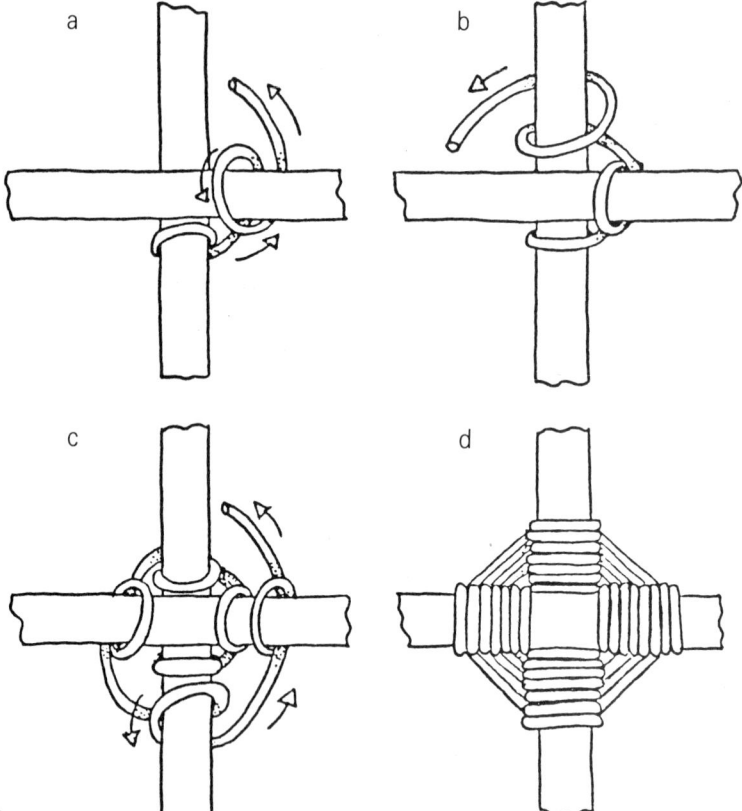

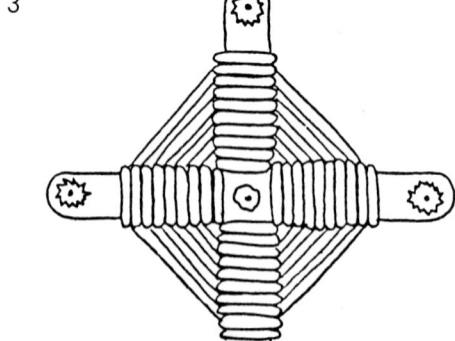

3. Turn the sticks a quarter of a turn then wind the wool *under* the next arm, round *over* the top and then *under* it again.
4. Keep turning the cross in the same direction and do the same for arm 4.
5. Continue in this way, keeping the wool taut at all times and being careful not to leave gaps on the sticks or to overlap the different 'rounds'. After several rounds, the weave should look like figure 2d.
6. Change the colour, texture or thickness of the wool by cutting it and knotting on the new wool.
7. When about 1 cm of the stick ends are left uncovered, finish off the weaving by applying a small blob of glue to the last arm, fix the wool and trim off the end. The shape woven should be a square.
8. Decorate the ends of the arms and the wooden centre by glueing on buttons, counters, sequins, etc (fig. 3).

† Illustrated on page 4 of the first photograph section

TEACHING POINTS

1. Apart from the words listed, there is a great deal of new vocabulary and new ideas that can be raised by discussion. For example:

(a) When displaying the square weavings, it is better if they are mounted at different angles. This will provide an opportunity to talk about whether the square shape is changed or stays the same when it is tilted. We are looking at the idea of *conservation of shape*.

(b) The weaving is rich in symmetry; not only rotational (because it looks the same after each quarter turn) but also reflective symmetry of both shape and colour. This can be checked by using mirrors.

2. Provided every child starts with the same size sticks, the resulting woven squares will tessellate; so in a display it is possible to assemble the units to form an overall pattern.

3. Natural twigs can be used instead of lollipop sticks but they will need to be bound firmly with wool in advance.

EXTENSIONS AND VARIATIONS

1. Before starting the activity, wools could be examined, discussed and classified in different ways — colour, texture, thickness, etc.

2. Starweaving has a very interesting historical background. In parts of South America the 'stars' are known as *God's Eyes* and are woven at the time of a child's birthday. In Tibet they are known as *Ghost Traps*. Two books giving details of the history are listed at the end of this section. The weaving technique is also to be found in basketry and in the construction of certain corn dollies.

4

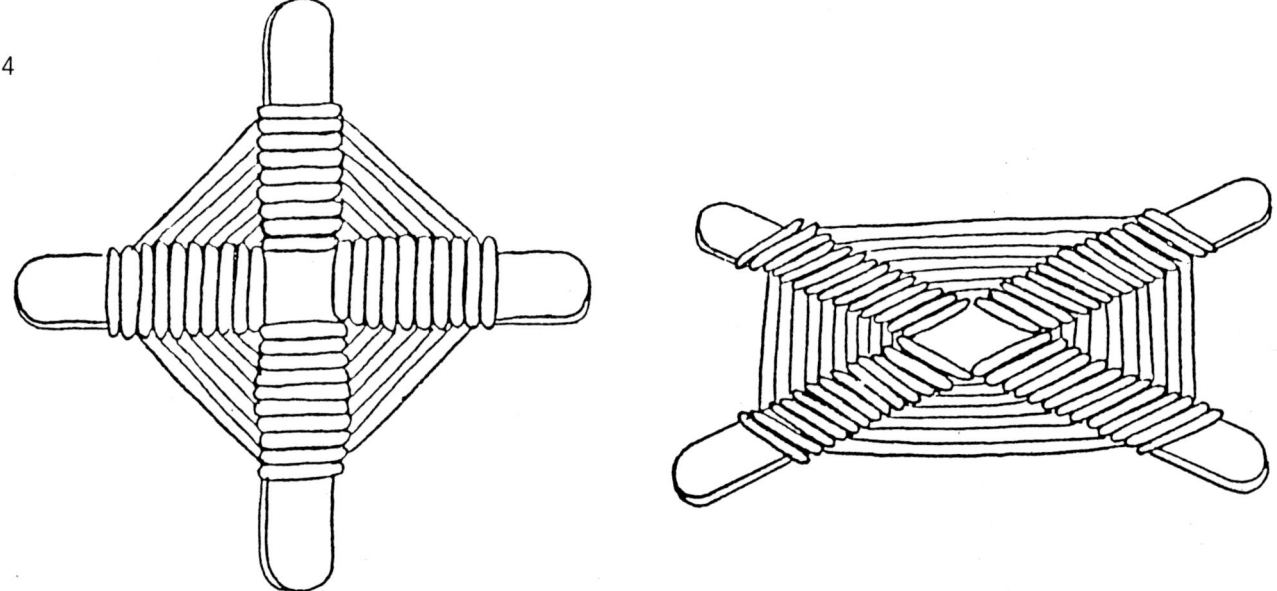

3. Once the basic weaving has been tried out, children can investigate other ways for fixing the sticks and try to predict what shape will result from the new arrangement. For instance, *"What happens to the woven shape if the sticks are not at right angles?"* (Fig. 4.) This could lead to the informal introduction to the special property of the square — the diagonals are equal and bisect each other at right angles. *"Can you weave a butterfly?"*

REFERENCES & RESOURCES
The Golden Hands Book of Crafts —
"Star Weaving" Marshall Cavendish
The Batsford Encyclopaedia of Crafts
— "God's Eyes" B T Batsford Ltd

RAINBOWSHAPES †

MATERIALS
PVA glue, spreaders, scissors, strips of tissue paper approximately 15 cm by 3 cm in three primary colours, 25 cm squares of black card.
For the teacher: 25 cm square of strong card, craft knife or sharp-pointed scissors, cutting board.

VOCABULARY
Hexagon, star, frame, sides, edges, along, top, below, overlap, upper, lower, half, vertex, tile, tessellation left, right.

Children are encouraged to decorate matching tiles with overlapping strips of tissue paper and to find different ways of fitting them together.

METHOD
Instructions for the teacher (fig. 1)
1. Draw a circle, radius 10 cm, on strong card and mark off the radius 6 times around the circumference at equal intervals.
2. Join up the arcs to form a regular hexagon.
3. Rule a line from the centre of the circle to one vertex of the hexagon.
4. Using the same centre, draw a second circle with radius 8 cm and, starting where the pencil line intersects the inner circle, mark off the radius 6 times around its circumference at equal intervals.
5. Join up the arcs to form an inner hexagon.
6. Cut out the hexagon frame using a craft knife or scissors.

This frame is now used as a master tile from which others can be traced by either teacher or pupil.

1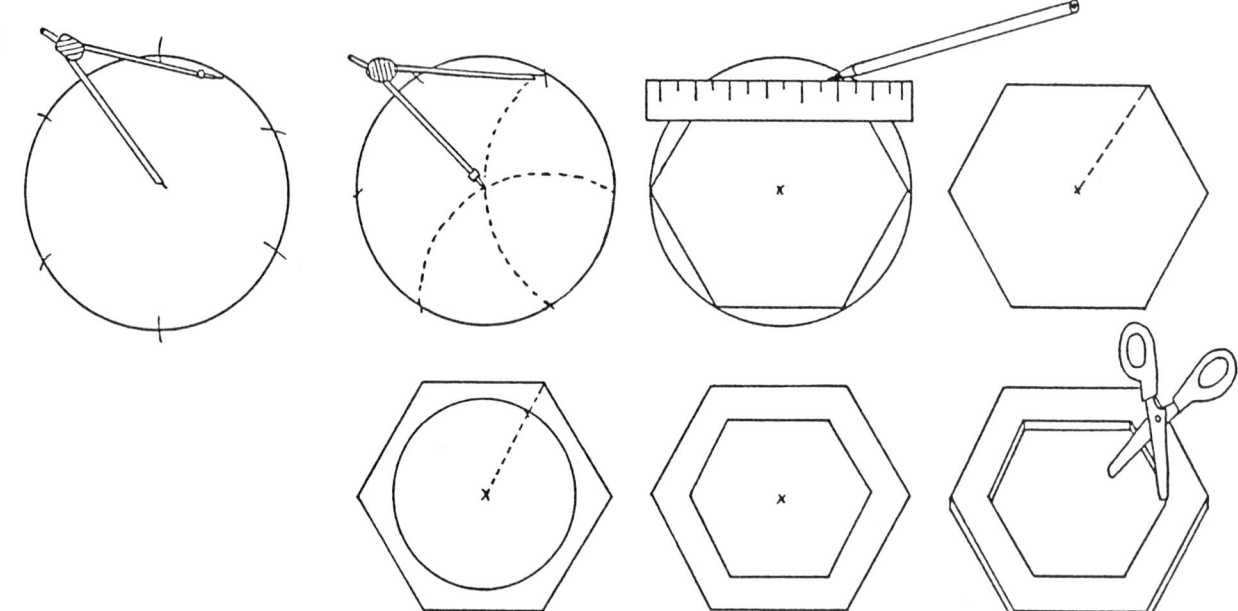

2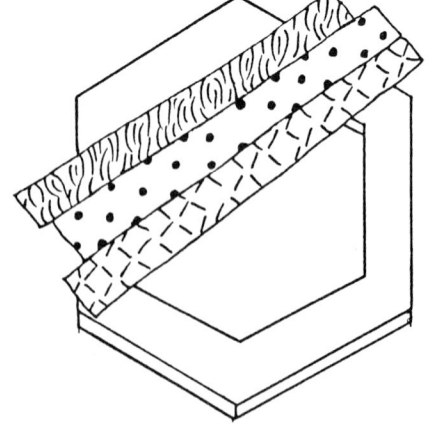

Instructions for the children
1. When you have made your own hexagon frame from the master tile, put a thin layer of PVA glue around the top half of the frame.
2. Lay a strip of tissue paper from left to right along the top of the frame so that it overlaps the top edge of the frame slightly. Press the strip down into the glue. Do not worry about the pieces of the tissue that stick out on either side of the frame.
3. Lay a contrasting strip of tissue below so that it overlaps the first strip. Press into position on the glue (fig. 2).
4. Continue in this way until the first half is completely covered.
5. Place a thin layer of glue around the bottom half of the frame.
6. Continue applying strips to the lower half of the frame until there are no gaps left.
7. Carefully trim away the surplus lengths of tissue paper.

22   RAINBOWSHAPES   † *Illustrated on page 1 of the first photograph section*

8. Place a small piece of *Blu-tack* on each vertex of the covered side of the frame.
9. Mount the hexagonal tiles on a large window to form a tessellating pattern.

TEACHING POINTS
1. By restricting the strips to two primary colours for each tile, discoveries can be made about secondary colours, allowing links with science to be exploited.
2. For very young children, it may prove easier to glue one large piece of tissue paper over the whole frame first, then glue strips of a contrasting colour over the top of the large sheet.
3. An attractive display results when adjacent tiles are rotated through part of a turn (fig. 3).

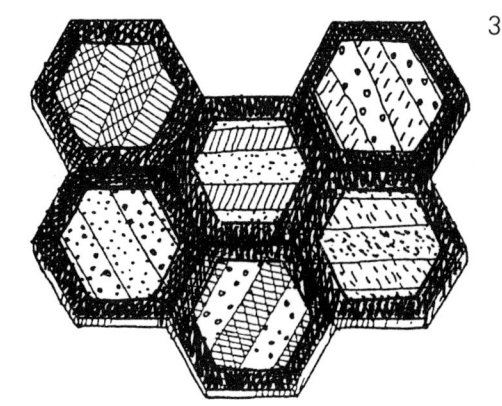

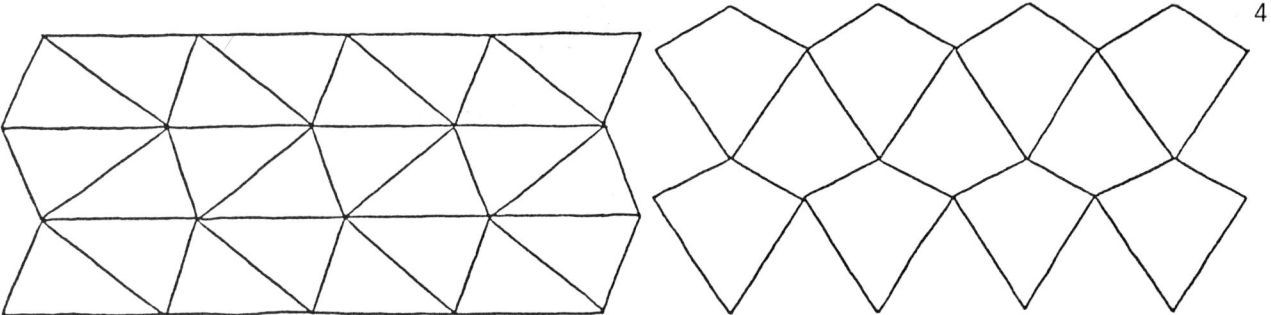

EXTENSIONS AND VARIATIONS
1. In place of hexagons, allow some experimentation with frameworks of other polygons that tessellate. For example, *all* triangles and *all* quadrilaterals tessellate (fig. 4).
2. By contrast, try shapes that do not tessellate on their own (circles, regular pentagons, etc) but may be arranged in a regular spatial pattern. If frames of these shapes are backed with one colour only, interesting patterns can be developed by overlapping so that the gaps are eliminated (fig. 5).

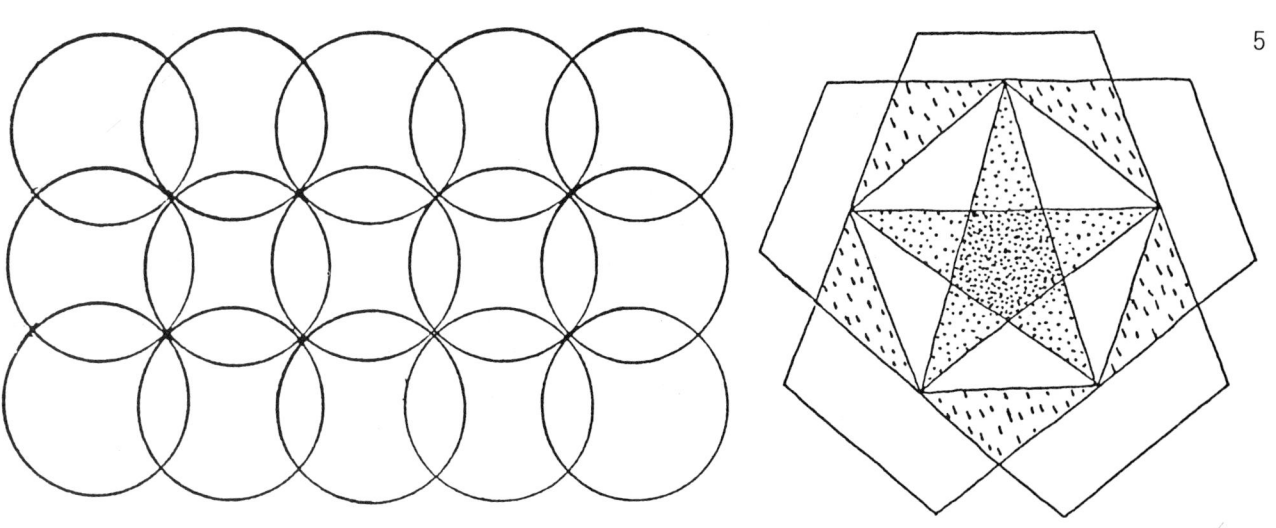

RAINBOWSHAPES

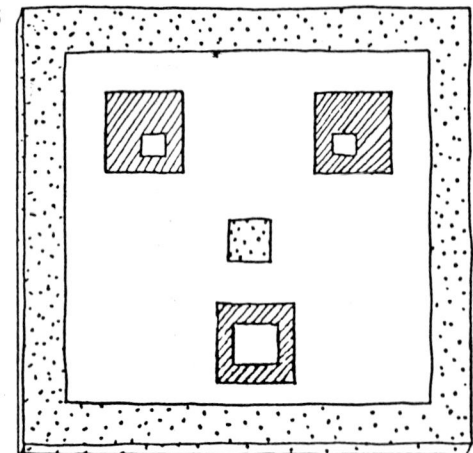
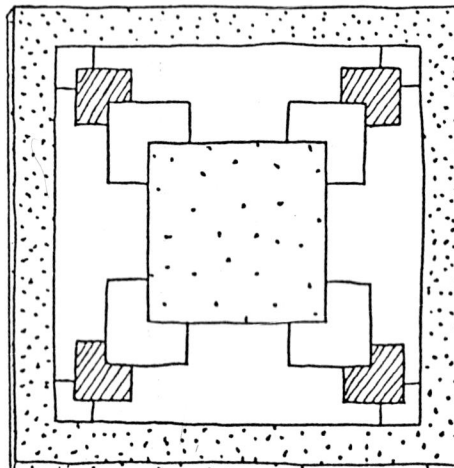

3. If one large piece of tissue is glued across the back of a frame, black sugar paper cutouts of the same shape as the frame can be glued on top of the tissue to make faces or pictures (fig. 6). In the example, a light-coloured tissue backing has been glued on to a square frame and a selection of smaller black squares has been superimposed. As the frame and picture are made entirely of squares, the varying sizes can be compared for similarities and differences.

4. Using the techniques outlined in *TESSELLATION 1*, page 25, and given assistance in cutting out a framework, children can design their own unique tiles.

5. Simple sequencing rules can be given for the strips. For example, *"Put a red strip first, a yellow strip second and a blue strip third. Repeat this pattern until you reach the bottom of the tile. How many strips of each colour did you use?"*

6. Attractive pseudo-weaving patterns can be made by using strips of different colours stretched in different directions and glued across the back of the framework.

7. *Rainbow Stars*

The teacher or an older child needs to prepare in advance a large star stencil in strong card from which further copies can be made. (If you make the star stencil for the children, demonstrate the construction with them and talk about what you are doing, using the appropriate language. Ask questions about the star — how many edges, corners, angles, etc, and discuss its symmetry.)

Star stencil (fig. 7)

(a) Draw a circle, radius 10 cm, on strong card and mark off its radius 6 times around the circumference at equal intervals.

(b) This time join up *alternate* points to form a six-pointed star.

(c) Use a narrow ruler or straight edge to draw a second star outline inside the first.

(d) Cut around the inner and outer perimeters of the star shape to make a star stencil. (A craft knife, ruler and cutting board give the most accurate results.)

(e) Larger and smaller star stencils can be made by varying the radius of the circle in step (a) and the width of the frame in step (c).

(f) Apply glue and 3 cm strips as for the rainbow hexagons. Trim any surplus tissue and attach a 'tail' if required. Mount on a window for best effect or, if there is not enough window area, use strips of foil or glittery paper as an alternative.

(g) Instructions for making a five-pointed star frame are given in the *TECHNIQUES AND MATERIALS* section on page 116.

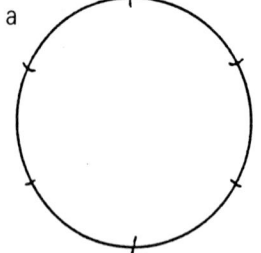
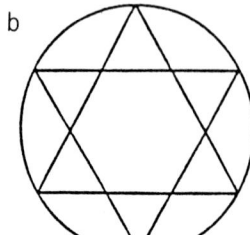
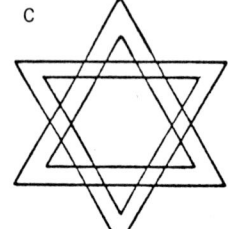
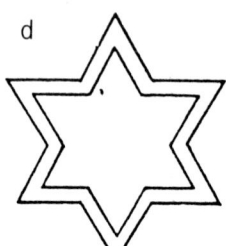

TESSELLATION 1 †

By a simple 'cut and slide' technique, children are encouraged to make their own tessellating unit tile to be used in creating a tiling pattern.

MATERIALS
Blank postcards or card cut to approximate postcard size, sellotape, backing sheets, pencil, scissors, colouring pencils, pens or crayons, collage scraps.

METHOD
1. Split the postcard into two pieces by cutting from one long edge to the opposite edge (fig. 1).
2. Slide the left-hand piece along until the two straight short edges line up with each other (fig. 2).
3. Sellotape the straight edges together. The resulting tile will tessellate.
4. Rotate the tile until the outline of its shape suggests a person, animal or object.
5. Trace the tile several times so that the outlines fit together with no gaps or overlaps.
6. Decorate by adding features with crayons, colouring pens, collage scraps, etc (fig. 3).

VOCABULARY
Long, short, straight, edge, opposite, slide, left, line up, together, tile, tessellate, shape, match, rotate, split.

TEACHING POINTS
1. These activities are intended to heighten the children's awareness of the many tiling patterns in the environment. As well as artwork, collections and displays can be made of wallpaper patterns, wrapping papers, tile samples, rubbings, etc that demonstrate the properties of tessellation. Sets of commercially produced tessellating tiles in wood or plastic can also provide useful experience. See how many examples of different tiling patterns children can find in and around the school — floor tiles, kitchen tiles, brickwork, squared paper, sheets of stamps, etc. (Fig. 4.)

Apart from helping young children to come to terms with the concept of *conservation of area*, work on tessellation has links with symmetry through the spatial patterns made by reflecting, rotating or translating the tiles. In later learning, links with angular measure can also be highlighted.

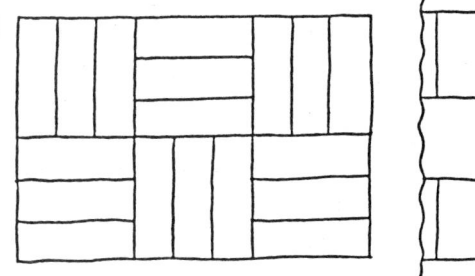
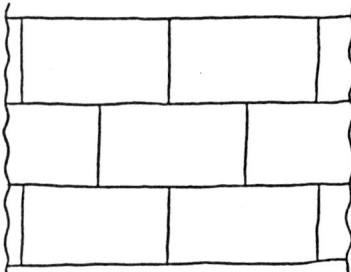
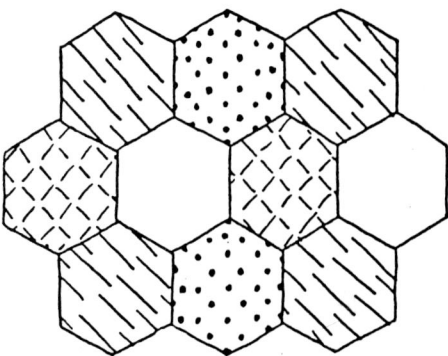

† Illustrated on page 4 of the first photograph section

2. A variety of approaches are needed to help children understand conservation of area, that is to appreciate that the same amount of surface may be covered in many different ways. This activity provides another means of presenting, or assessing the understanding of, the concept and is particularly effective if a group of children create a number of tiles generated from matching postcards. Discussion with the teacher follows along the lines of:

"How many of your patterns have an area of six postcards?"
"Which pattern covers the greater surface — John's six rockets or Sue's six dogs?"

The postcard tiles can be displayed to show the relation:

Has the same area as →

as a many-to-one mapping with the 'parent' tile as a reference (fig. 5).

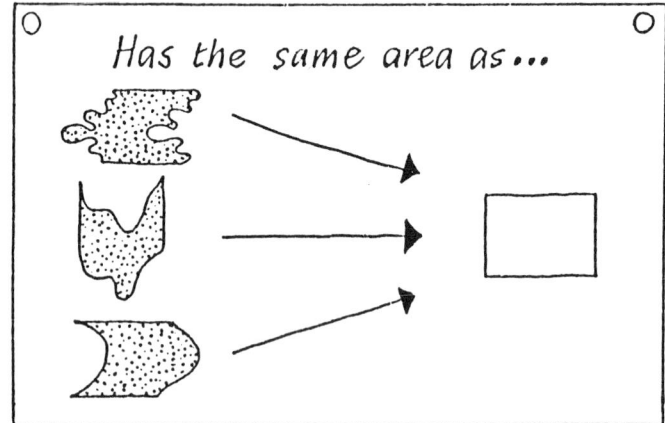

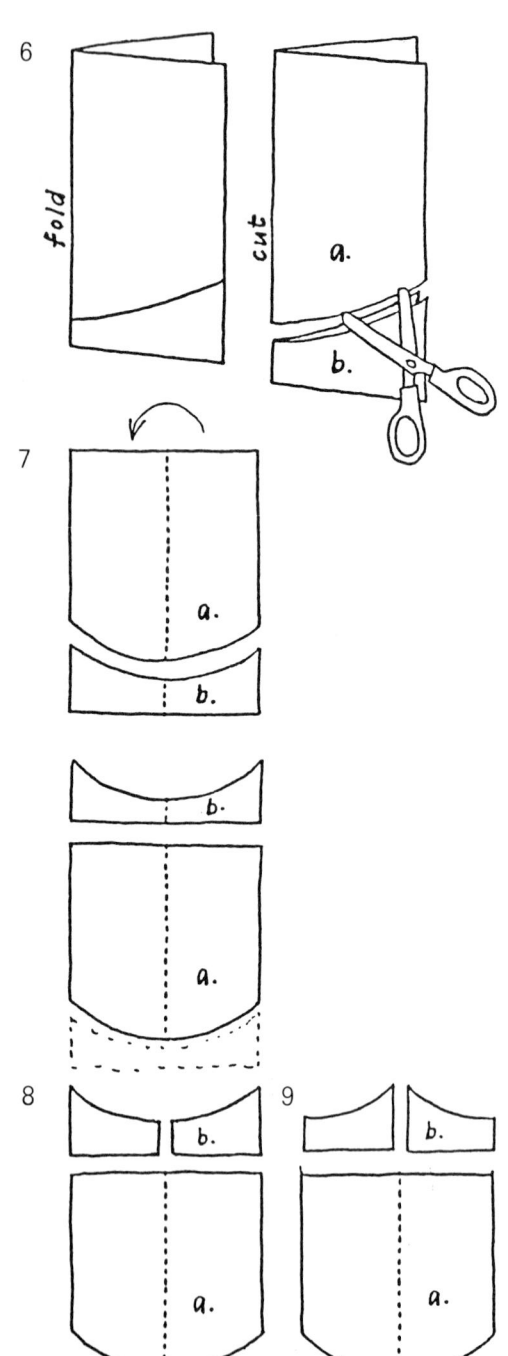

EXTENSIONS AND VARIATIONS

1. *Wax resist technique*
Follow the method through steps 1 to 3. Trace the outline of the tiling pattern heavily in black wax crayon. Apply a paint wash over the completed pattern using a small household paintbrush and thinned down poster paint. Individual tiles can also be painted in different colours more easily, as the wax crayon 'fence' resists the flow of paint over the edges.

2. *Gummed paper tiles*
Once the shape of a tessellating tile has been decided upon, cut out several exact copies from gummed coloured papers. (If two or three sheets are stapled together, they can be cut out from one template.) Arrange the tiles on the backing sheet to make quite sure they fit without overlaps or gaps. Using wallpaper paste to stick the tiles down on the backing sheet allows time for them to be manoeuvred into their correct positions before the paste sets.

3. *Symmetrical tiles*
(a) Fold the postcard along one of its axes of symmetry.
(b) Cut the folded tile into two pieces across the axis (fig. 6).
(c) Open out and press the pieces flat (fig. 7).
(d) Slide one piece across the other until the two straight edges align, then sellotape these edges together (fig. 8).
(e) (Optional) Cut one piece along the axis of symmetry and interchange these two pieces by sliding (fig. 9).

TESSELLATION 1

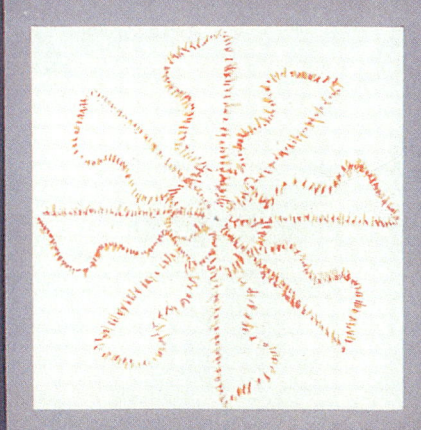

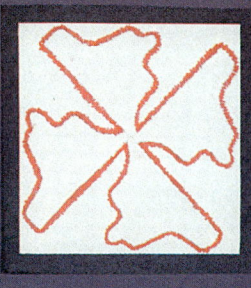

SHADOWSHAPES 1 (page 28)

RAINBOWSHAPES (page 22)

AREA 1 (page 4)

CYLINDERS (page 17)

BUBBLES AND CIRCLES (page 1)

LINE DOODLES (page 9)

CARBON COPYCATS 1 (page 6)

CLOWNS (page 14)

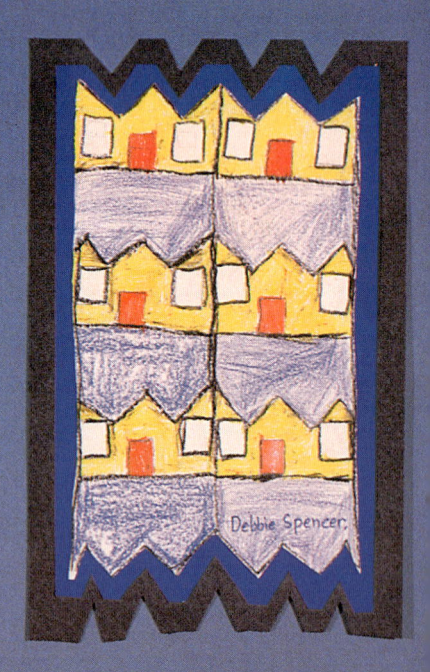

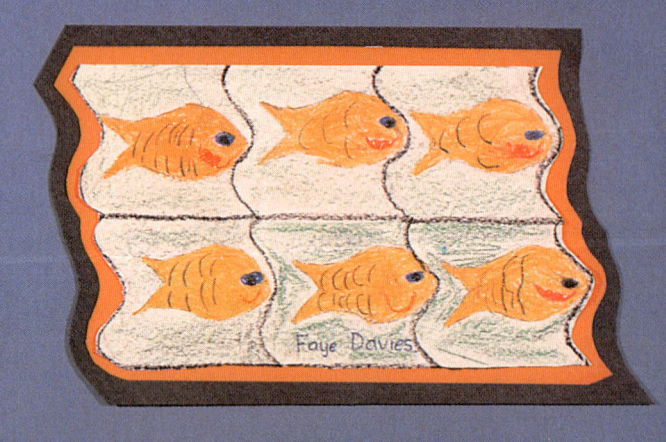

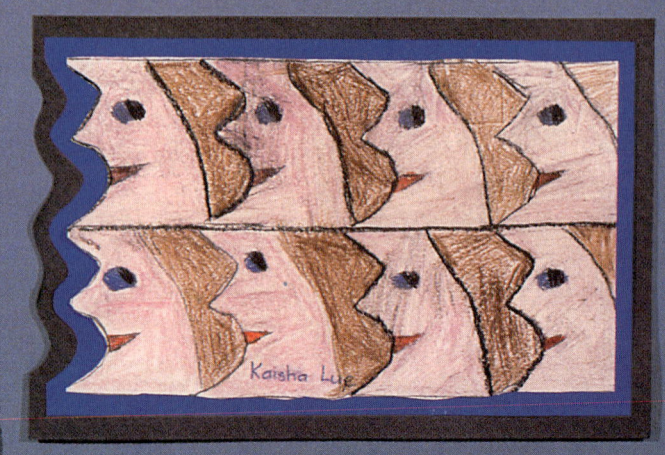

TESSELLATION 1 (page 25)

ROUNDABOUTS 1 (page 12)

STARWEAVING 1 (page 20)

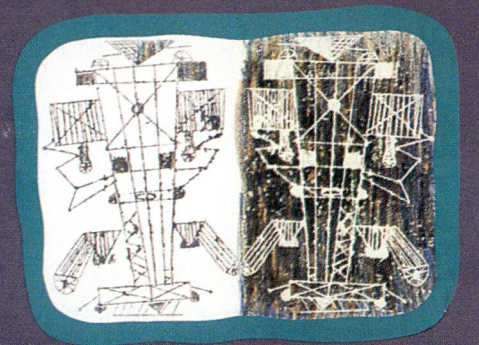

TETRALAND (page 42)

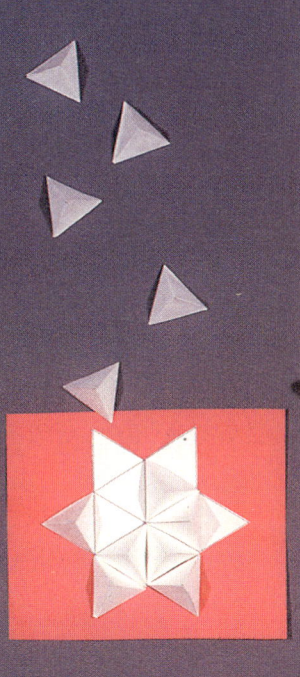

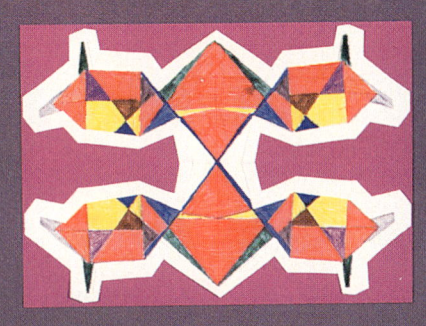

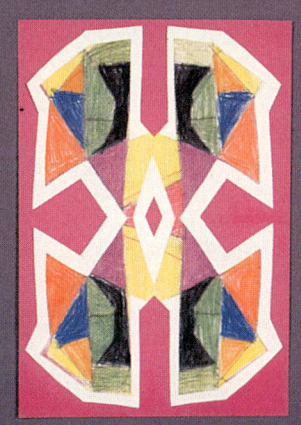

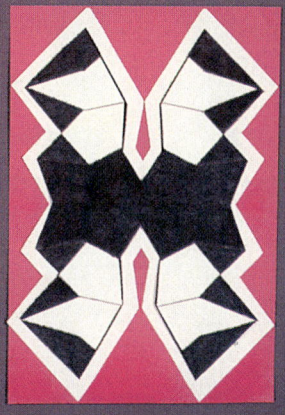

CARBON COPYCATS 2 (page 31)

EXPLODED SQUARES (page 46)

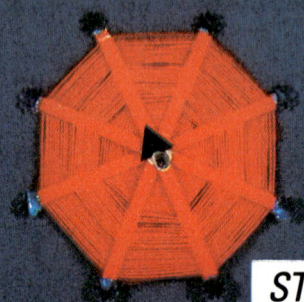

STARWEAVING 2 (page 48)

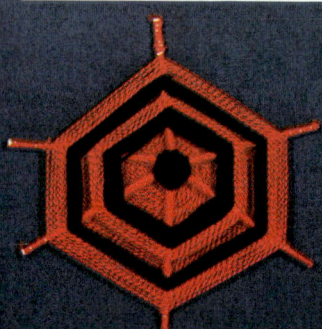

TESSELLATION 2 (page 50)

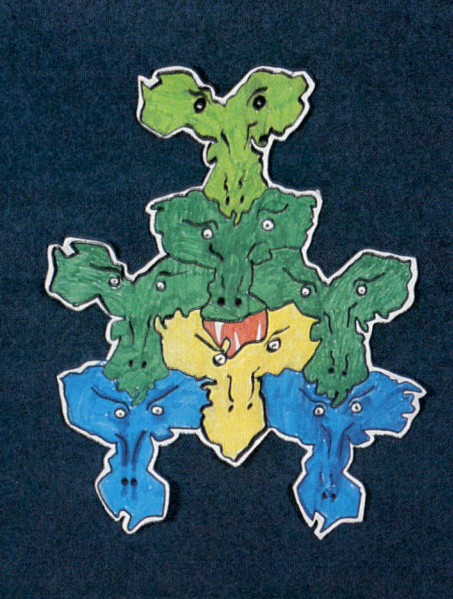

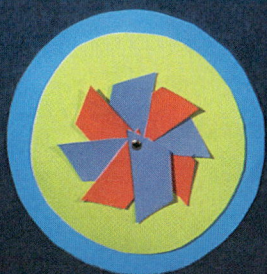

ROTASHAPES (page 33)

FABRIC SHAPES (page 35)

STRING PRINTS (page 40)

AREA 2 (page 37)

(f) Both of the shapes produced at steps (d) and (e) will tessellate. They differ in the way they fit together, as the shape from (e) tessellates in a diagonal arrangement (fig. 10).

4. Tessellations from tubes

A quick but foolproof method for making tessellating tiles is to use a toilet roll or kitchen roll tube and a pair of scissors. Simply make a fancy cut along the tube from one open end to the other, and press the card out flat. This shape will tessellate and can be used as a template for tiling patterns. (Fig. 11.)

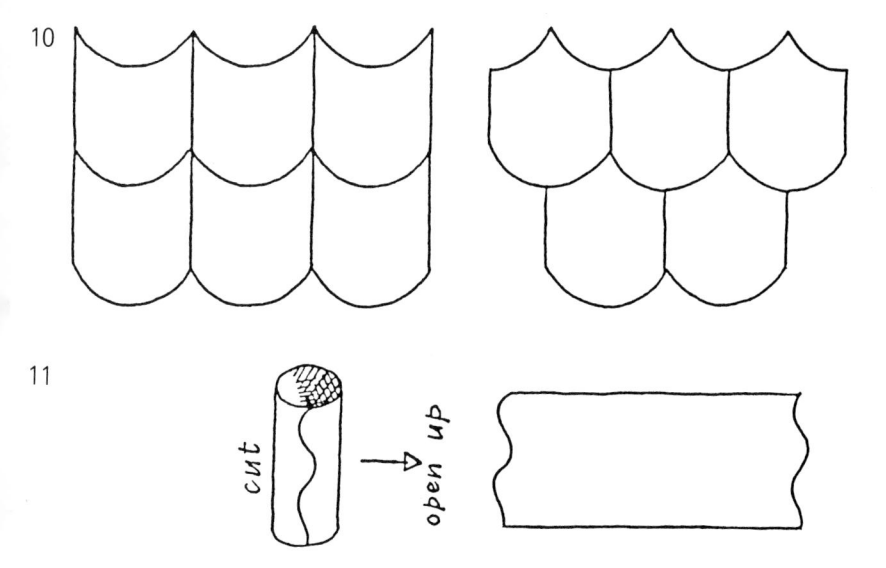

10

11

Investigations

1. Using a postcard and the basic 'cut and slide' method, what is the longest tile that can be made?
2. Investigate the perimeters of tiles made from matching postcards by putting a string 'fence' around them. Display the results by glueing down the length of string needed to surround each shape alongside the tile (fig. 12).

12

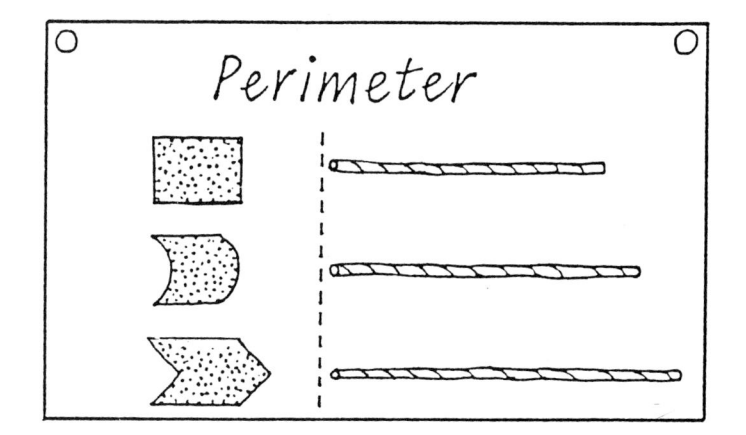

This activity highlights the fact that shapes with the same area do not necessarily have the same perimeter.

3. From a postcard, design a tile that looks like a rocket.

REFERENCES & RESOURCES
Nuffield Maths 5–11 Teachers' Handbook Longman; Book 2, chapter 8; Book 3, chapter 23; Book 5, chapter 17 and Book 6, chapter 13.
Do-it-yourself Tiles article in *Mathematics Teaching* number 66; Association of Mathematics Teachers
Tessellations Josephine Mold; Cambridge University Press

TESSELLATION 1

SHADOWSHAPES 1 †

MATERIALS
Squares of cartridge paper (approximately 30 cm square), rectangles of card in contrasting colours (approximately 15 cm by 8 cm), paper fasteners, piercing tool, pencil, crayons or paints, scissors, self-adhesive squares or circles.

VOCABULARY
Centre, fold, mirror lines (axes of symmetry), diagonal, edge, through, near, on top, turn (rotate), pattern, top, bottom, left, corner, complete turn (full rotation), around, outline.

The use of simple paper-folding techniques and the rotation of a template through quarter turns are combined to create a pattern with rotational symmetry. This is best demonstrated to a small group.

METHOD
1. Fold the square of cartridge paper along the two diagonals and flatten out (fig. 1a).
2. On a rectangular piece of card mark out a 'wandering line' from the bottom right-hand corner to the opposite edge and cut along this line. Children who have difficulty using scissors could tear along the line instead of cutting it. (Fig. 1b.)
3. Put aside the section with the uncut corners.
4. Pierce a hole through the card near one end of the uncut edge and through the centre of the cartridge paper.
5. Attach the card to the centre of the paper by using a brass paper fastener (fig. 1c).

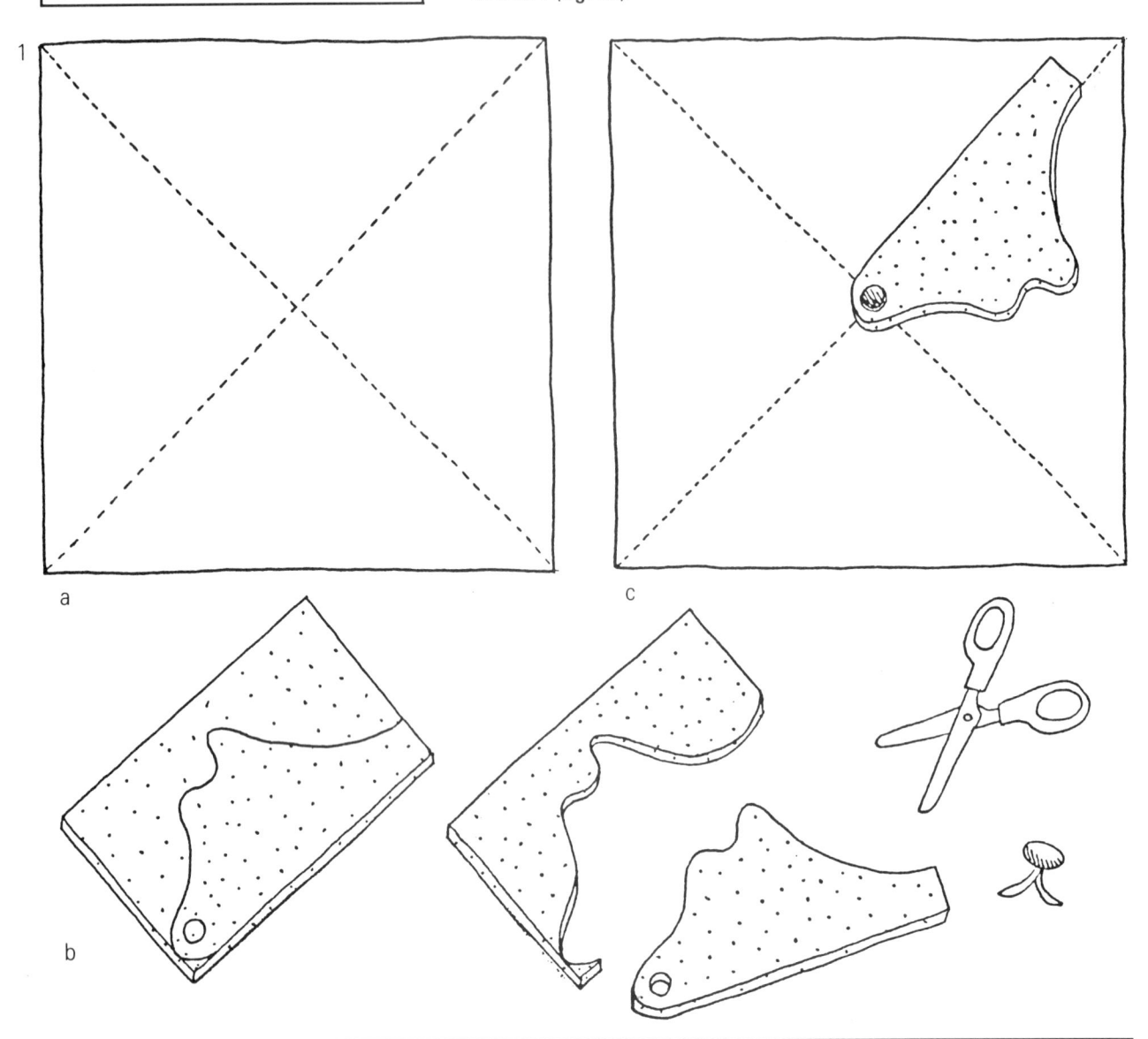

28 SHADOWSHAPES 1   † Illustrated on page 1 of the first photograph section

6. Rotate the card template until the corner farthest from the centre lines up on one of the 'spokes', i.e. one of the half-diagonals of the backing sheet.

7. Holding it in position, flick outwards around the edge of the template with a crayon to give a shadowy effect (fig. 2).

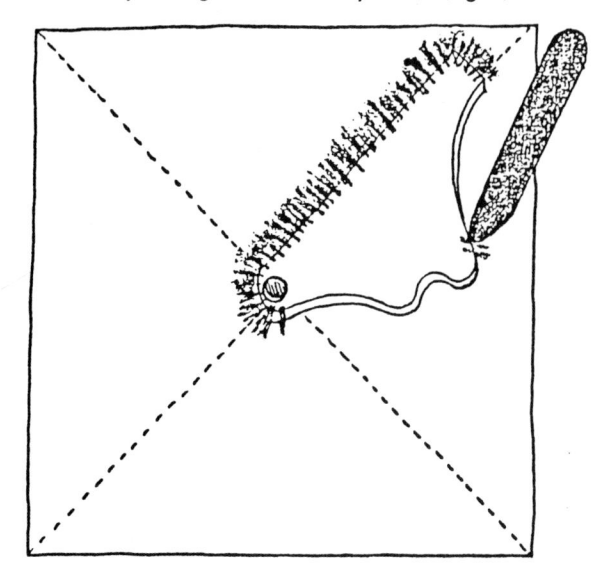

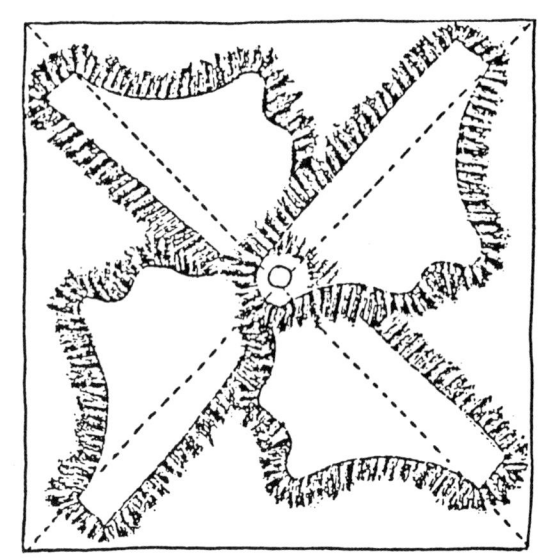

8. Rotate the template until the straight edge lines up on the next half-diagonal, and colour as before.

9. Repeat step 8 twice more so that there are four 'shadows' of the template equally spaced around the centre of the square backing sheet (fig. 3).

10. Remove the template carefully and conceal the hole with a paper sticker on the back.

The resulting pattern has *turning* or *rotational symmetry* (in this case of order 4) because the template will fit back on to the pattern four times in a complete turn.

TEACHING POINTS

1. This activity is particularly appropriate for younger children because
(a) the template cannot be inadvertently moved away from the centre of rotation;
(b) the template can rotate freely about the fixed centre, thus giving a good feeling for *symmetry about a point*;
(c) the flicking technique means that the problem of the crayon or pencil skidding off the edge of the template is avoided.

2. In the absence of split brass paper fasteners, the template can be secured temporarily with very small pieces of mastic adhesive such as *Blu-tack*, with the same corner always lining up with the centre.

3. This flicking technique works most effectively when large templates are used to produce bold patterns, but miniature versions can be made by scaling down the template and using colouring pencils for a more delicate effect. By overlapping two primary colours at the flicking stage, interesting colour blends are obtained. The new multicoloured crayons also give interesting results.

SHADOWSHAPES 1

4. Encourage the children to investigate how they can colour the arrangement so that a cyclic pattern occurs; for example, one colour repeated four times, two colours alternating, or four colours used once each.

5. Before the template is detached, the children can check the 'fourness' of the pattern by rotating it to see how many times it fits back on to its outline in one complete turn. This will give its *order* of rotational symmetry. The notion of a *quarter of a turn* can also be considered.

6. If a selection of patterns and the templates used to make them are mounted on separate displays, children can be asked to map each template on to its related pattern using lengths of string.

EXTENSIONS AND VARIATIONS

1. By folding the square sheet in step 1 along its four axes of symmetry, eight 'spokes' are formed (fig. 4). A pattern with rotational symmetry or order 8 can now be made and suitable colouring sequences can be investigated. (See teaching point 4.)

"How many different possibilities are there for this framework?"

2. For children who are able to trace around a template by holding a crayon or pencil vertically, there is no reason why the resulting pattern cannot be enhanced by using paints, collage, paper mosaic, pasta, etc. Some children may enjoy making hard-edged and shadowy-edged versions of the same template.

3. If pairs of children work together using the same template, each could use a different point about which to rotate it. The patterns could then be compared for similarities and differences. Alternatively, one child could use the template while the other uses the section put aside in step 3 of the method, so that both 'outside' and 'inside' shadows are produced.

4. Depending on the size of the template, children could investigate the patterns obtained by varying the amount of overlap between one outline of the template and the next (fig. 5).

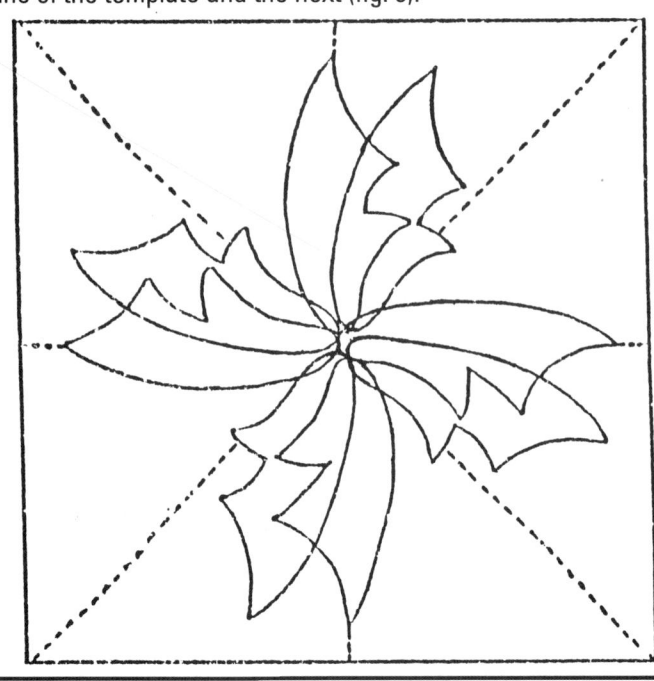

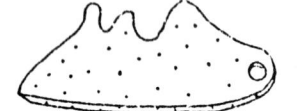

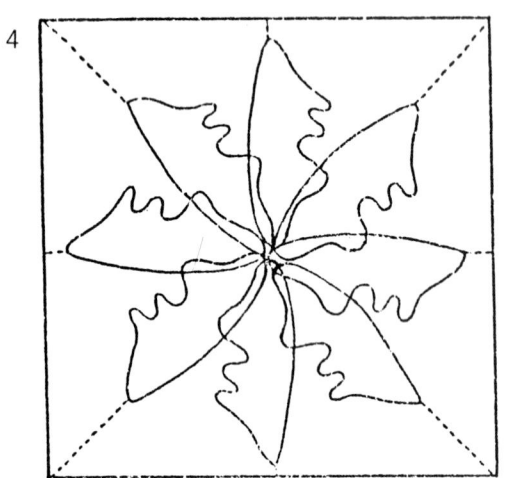

30 SHADOWSHAPES 1

CARBON COPYCATS 2 †

This activity takes the use of carbon paper a stage further by folding the paper into quarters so that, when unfolded, there is reflection in two axes of symmetry.

MATERIALS
Sheets of A4 paper, sheet of A4 carbon paper, ball-point pen, colouring materials, safety mirrors.

VOCABULARY
Axis (axes) of symmetry, reflection, rotation.

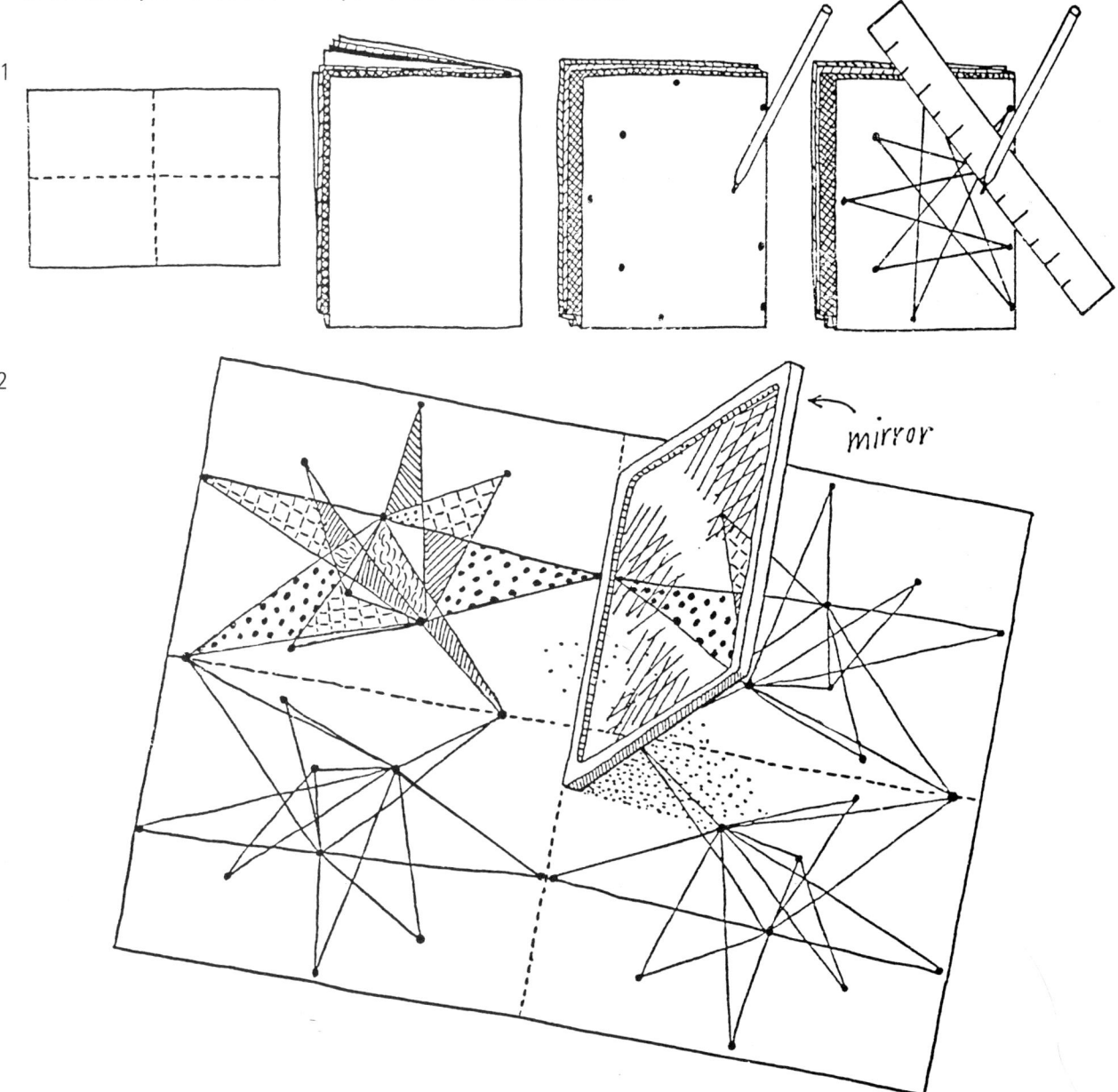

METHOD
1. Fold a sheet of A4 paper along both axes of symmetry and crease the fold lines firmly.
2. Flatten it out and refold it with a sheet of carbon paper tucked inside, with the glossy side facing the paper.
3. On the uppermost quarter, mark about eight or nine dots with two or three of them on a folded edge.
4. With a ruler, join up the dots to make a pattern (fig. 1).
5. Unfold the paper and check the reflections with a mirror (fig. 2).
6. What do you notice about the points that were on the folds?

† Illustrated on page 8 of the first photograph section

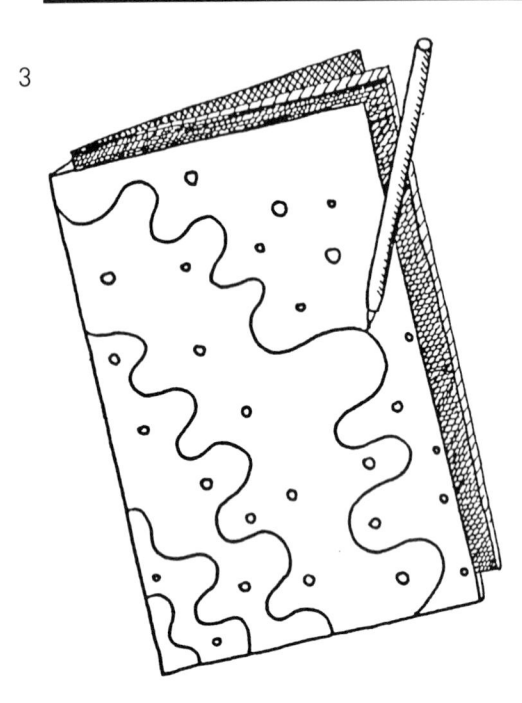

7. Experiment with different patterns (fig. 3).
8. Take a new sheet of paper and design a symmetrical pattern so that, when the paper is unfolded, you can see four people in a ring with their hands joined.
9. Work out a symmetrical colouring arrangement. What kind of symmetries does your pattern have?

TEACHING POINTS

1. The images transfer more effectively when thin paper is used, and a ball-point pen is better than a pencil. (Different writing materials could be tried to see which are most efficient.)
2. When complete, if the paper is refolded with the pattern facing outwards, cutting around the edges gives a symmetrical shape. Alternatively, some children may enjoy designing a carbon paper border around the edges.
3. The children will find that the images are not equally clear — bottom layers will be much less distinct. To overcome this problem, go over all the carbon lines with a black felt pen so that they all have the same thickness and clarity.

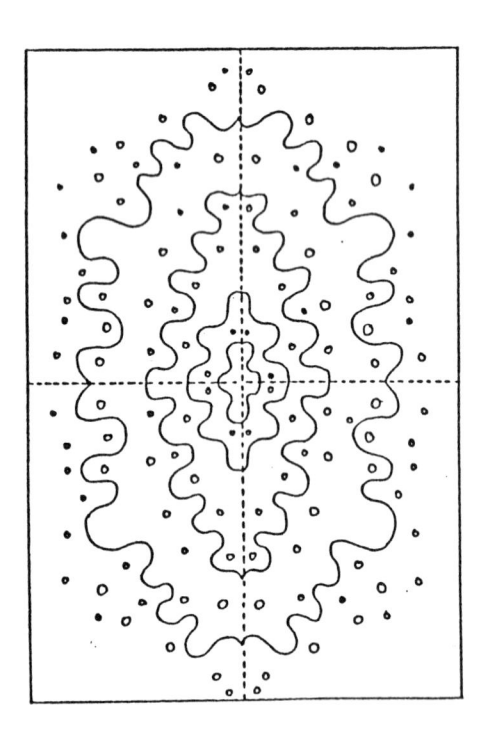

EXTENSIONS AND VARIATIONS

1. Experiment with different starting shapes — square, circle, octagon, etc. Can the children find some shapes that do not fold into four equal (*congruent*) parts?
2. "Using A4 sheets, how many ways are there of folding it into four equal parts all the same shape?"
"What effect do different folds have on the carbon paper images?"
"Are all the images equally clear?"
"How can you make parts of the images connect or not connect?"
3. "What about folding into eight equal parts, or six; how well do the images come out then?"
"What would be the best way to fold the sheet into five equal parts?"
Experiment with unusual folds and see what happens.
4. Think of some more specific design restraints, or ask a child to write a task for a partner; for example: using an A4 sheet of paper folded into four equal parts, make two butterflies fly towards each other, or fly alongside each other; make them fly in opposite directions to each other; make four butterflies meet at the centre of the paper.
5. Provide an example of a simple paper cutout pattern with two axes of symmetry and challenge the children to recreate it using the carbon paper technique. *"What clues are there to help?"*
6. Make a simple carbon symmetrical pattern and see if the children can recreate it using a different technique.

REFERENCES & RESOURCES
Mirror Resource Pack (Safety)
E J Arnold

ROTASHAPES †

Children cut out a set of congruent shapes and, with the aid of a paper fastener, use them to create patterns with rotational symmetry.

METHOD
1. With the backing sheets, prepare two strong circular mounts of card of contrasting colours, one with radius 20 cm, one with radius 22 cm. Pierce the centres and reinforce them well.
2. From card or strong patterned paper, cut out a set of congruent shapes, either creating your own shape or using a commercially produced template or stencil.
3. Hold the set of shapes so that they fit exactly on top of one another (this illustrates the meaning of the word *congruent*) and punch a hole through them all in exactly the same place, near one edge.
The example (fig. 1) shows one of the chosen shapes with the hole punched in.
4. Align the centres of the two backing sheets with the larger one at the back.
5. Push a brass paper fastener through the set of shapes, then through the centres of the backing sheets, and secure the fastener at the back.
6. Rotate the shapes in different ways until you get a pleasing pattern. If the shapes are equally spaced, a pattern with rotational symmetry is made, the order of rotational symmetry being determined by the number of shapes in the set.
The example (fig. 2) shows 8 congruent shapes cut out; 4 of each of two contrasting colours.
7. Make several different sets and store them in polythene bags for future use. Vary the number of shapes in a set and try out a variety of shapes and colour combinations.

MATERIALS
Brass paper fasteners, assorted colours and textures of card, hole punch, reinforcing tabs, two large rigid backing sheets, scissors, commercially produced stencils or templates (optional).

VOCABULARY
Circle, centre, rotate, half turn, quarter turn, template, stencil, congruent (same shape and size), angle, rotation of order ___.

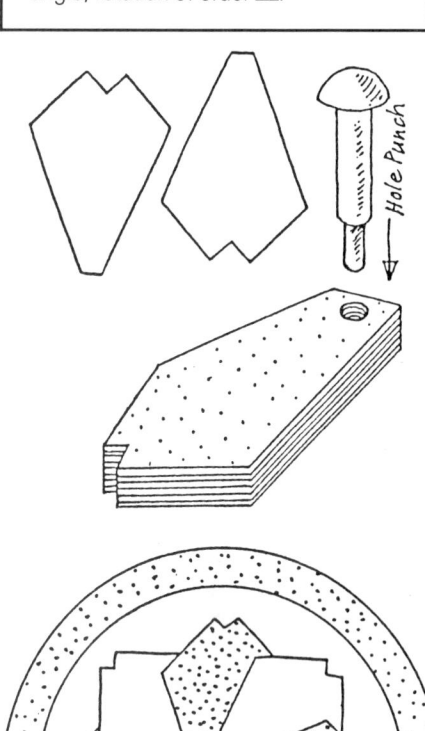

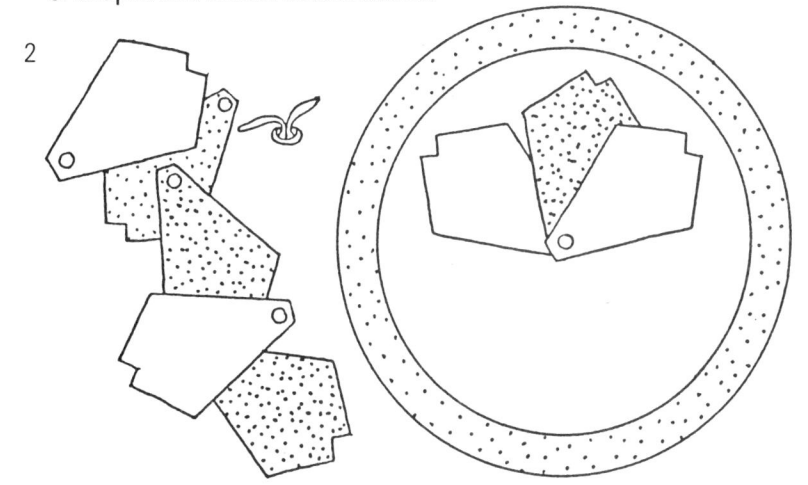

TEACHING POINTS
The advantage of this activity is that the mounts can be used many times for different sets of shapes. Allow the children to experiment freely with shapes and colours and to vary the number of shapes in a set to make patterns with different orders of rotation. Discussion should be encouraged so that reasons for pattern choices are given.

† *Illustrated on page 6 of the first photograph section*

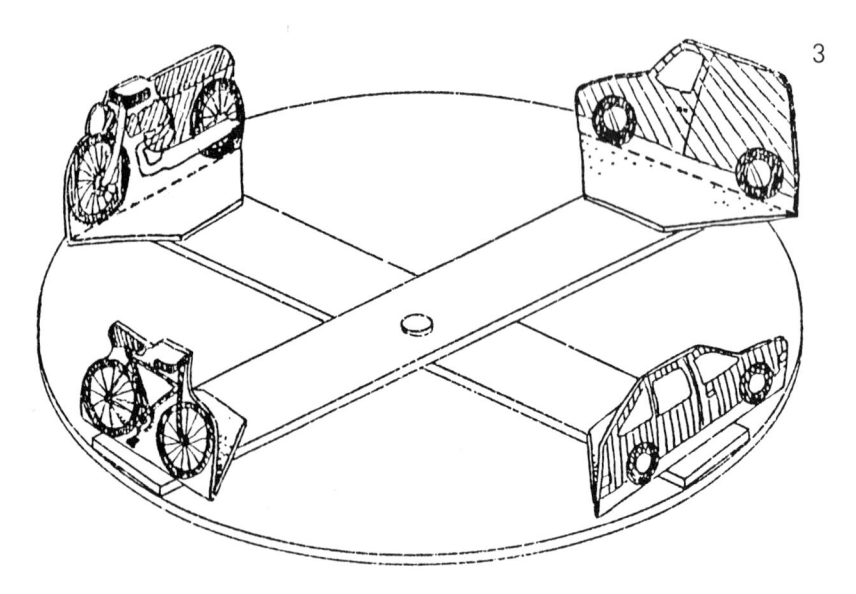

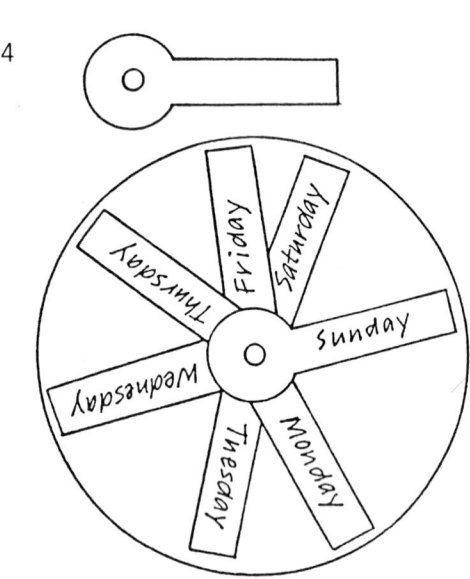

EXTENSIONS AND VARIATIONS

1. If a second matching mount is made, children can be asked to copy patterns made by the teacher, who can then provide alternative ways of sequencing according to number, shape or colour.

2. Make sets of people, transport, animals, etc chase each other round in a circle by standing them on card spokes secured to the centre by a paper fastener (fig. 3).

3. If seven simple shapes are cut out, they can be labelled with the days of the week before they are fixed on the circular mount. Children can then be asked to arrange the days in the correct order (fig. 4). This idea can be extended for any cyclic pattern — seasons, months of the year, figures on a clock face, etc.

4. The rotashape can also be used to record early grouping activities. The example (fig. 5) shows how a group of eight children were sorted according to eye colour.

If the teacher carefully chooses a shape that approximates the appropriate size of a sector (in the example, one-eighth of a circle), this idea could be used as a gentle introduction to pie charts, with all the necessary calculation and measurement of angles being done in advance by the teacher.

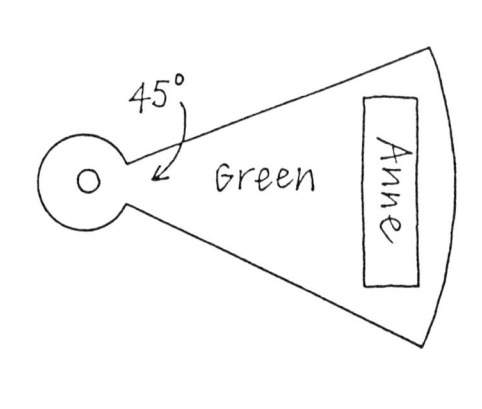

34 ROTASHAPES

FABRIC SHAPES †

Arrangements of cut out shapes are explored using transfer fabric crayons to create a positive and negative image. Note that the final part of this activity requires the use of an iron at cotton setting. *This needs direct supervision.*

MATERIALS
Fabric transfer crayons, scrap paper, thick pad of newspaper, scissors, backing sheet and white synthetic fabric of the same size, iron.

VOCABULARY
Surface, reflect ('flip over'), rotate (turn), translate ('slide'), transfer, texture.

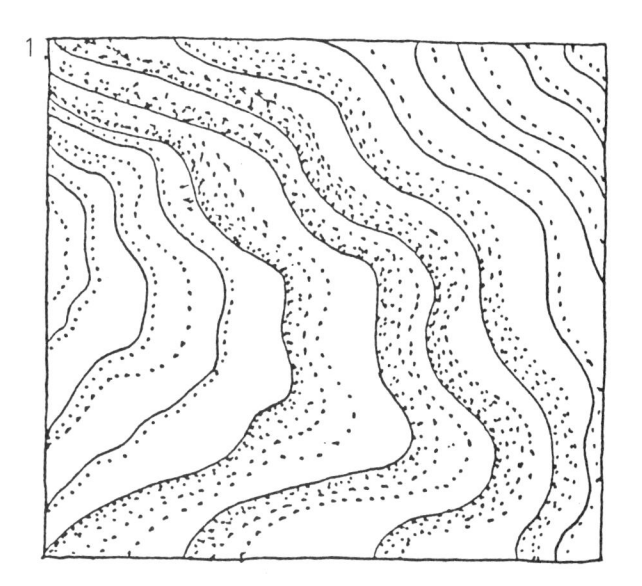

METHOD
1. Using the fabric crayons, cover the entire surface of the backing sheet with an all-over design, doodle pattern or rubbing (fig. 1).
2. Centre the piece of fabric on a thick pad of newspaper and place on it a selection of rectangles of different sizes cut from scrap paper.
3. Move the shapes around on the fabric until you have a pleasing arrangement.

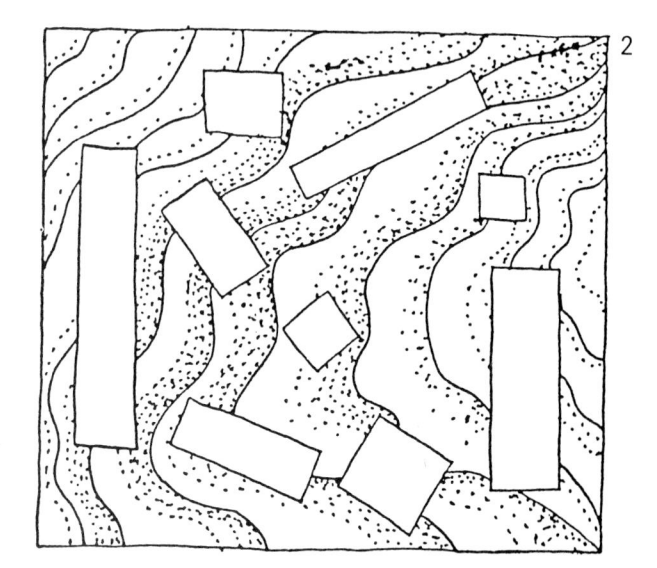

4. Place the crayon design face downwards over the top of the fabric and carry the work carefully on the pad to the ironing area.
5. Iron off the design following the manufacturer's instructions.
6. Remove the crayonned paper, shake of the loose rectangle shapes to reveal the finished design (fig. 2).

TEACHING POINTS
1. It is important that children are given experiences that allow them to reflect, rotate and translate shapes. Free manipulation of a variety of shapes and related discussion are needed if children are to appreciate and learn about *conservation of shape*, a concept often neglected in mathematics schemes.
2. In preparation for the activity, get the children to collect as many samples of white fabric as they can — different weaves, textures, thicknesses, etc — and plan a 'fair test' to find out which samples give the best results. The actual test would have to be done by an adult, but the results could be put in order from the best to worst transfer. Synthetics give the best results, but natural fabrics also work, so for the test allow any white fabric to be used. One fabric that gives good results and does not fray is dressmaker's interfacing, which can be bought cheaply in markets.

† *Illustrated on page 5 of the first photograph section*

3

3. Discuss with the children different ways of making a selection of rectangles: marked out on squared paper, drawn freehand, templates, stencils, tracing round the faces of solids or commercially produced tiles.

4. For more interesting results, allow the children to experiment with different types of paper, such as doylies, tissue and 'J-cloths', and different thicknesses of card for their templates. Surprising things can happen with different textures and thicknesses.

5. If appropriate, impose certain rules on the way in which the rectangles (which includes the family of squares) should be arranged on the backing sheet, for example:
should overlap/should not overlap each other,
sides parallel/not parallel to the edges of the backing sheet.

EXTENSIONS AND VARIATIONS

1. Once they have been transferred, the loose shapes can be matched back on to their outlines and then reused to make a negative pattern, that is a plain background with coloured shapes. The new pattern can be
(a) a repeat of the original pattern,
(b) either a horizontal or vertical reflection of the original,
(c) an entirely different pattern.
All three options allow for discussion of the conservation of area and shape.

2. Cut out the shapes for the crayonned sheet in step 1 and place them face downwards on the fabric. Place a blank sheet on top to secure the shapes and iron as in the basic activity.

5

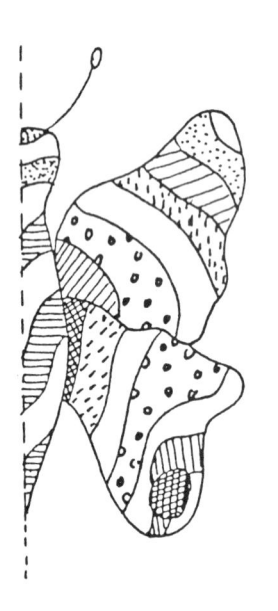

4

3. The activity as described uses rectangles but the idea can be used to explore other shapes and concepts (fig. 3). For example, straight lines, shapes with curved edges, shapes with axes of symmetry, etc. Torn shapes can be used by children unable to manipulate scissors. The technique can also be used to produce tangram pictures (see *TANGRAM 1*, page 64).

4. Since the transfer process gives a reflection of the original shapes, some children may enjoy experimenting with their names (fig. 4). Can they design their names in crayon so that, when ironed off, it is in the correct orientation?
(Cf. *NAME GAMES* on page 58.)

5. Can the children work out a design for a half-image, a butterfly perhaps, so that when it is ironed off the two halves can be put together to make a complete picture? (Fig. 5.)

REFERENCES & RESOURCES
Finart Fabricrayons Binney and Smith Ltd
Schola Di-stix Playaway Supplies Ltd
Transfer Printing Guy Scott; B T Batsford Ltd

36   FABRIC SHAPES

AREA 2 †

Nowadays many different types of grid (square, isometric, hexagonal, etc) are readily available. These can be used for experimental work as a prelude to more formal work on area. This activity makes use of isometric grid as a medium for design in order to help with the understanding of the concept of area, although it would relate equally well to work on tessellation.

MATERIALS
Equilateral triangle tiles all the same size, in plastic or card; a sheet of 3 cm isometric grid; ruler; pencil; scissors; colouring materials.

VOCABULARY
Isometric grid, equilateral triangle, hexagon, hexagonal, rhombus, rhombic.

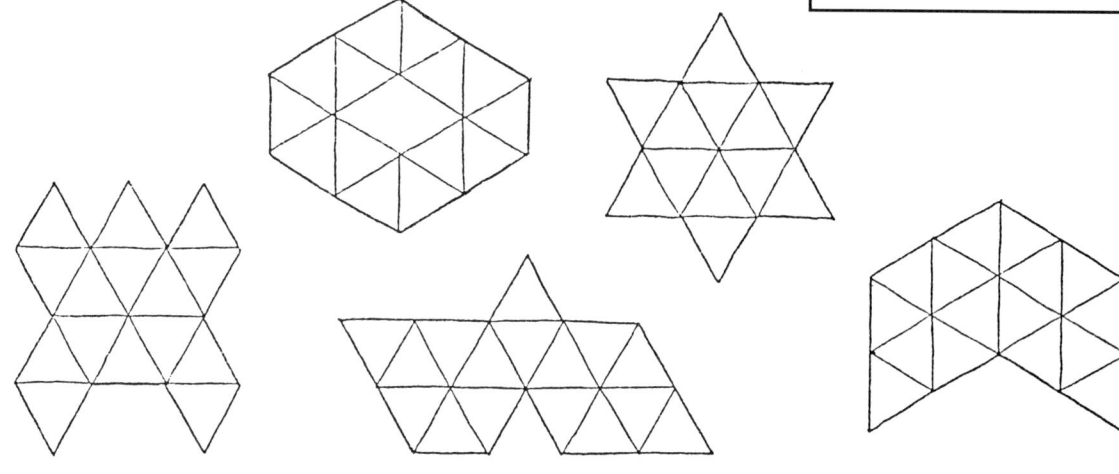

METHOD
1. Experiment with the triangular tiles to make shapes and patterns. When you create a design you like, transfer it on to a sheet of isometric grid by drawing lines *on the printed grid lines only*. (Fig. 1.)

2. On another sheet of isometric grid, design a creature that could live in the sea. Colour your design and cut it out carefully. (Fig. 2.)

† *Illustrated on page 5 of the first photograph section*

AREA 2   37

TEACHING POINTS

1. *Clixi, Polydron, Tactile Tessellation sets,* and *Activity Mats* all contain equilateral triangle tiles that can be manipulated and fitted together quite easily and will allow children to alter their designs without having to erase lines.

2. If a variety of sea creatures is produced, with appropriate background, they can be displayed as a group or class aquarium. Ask questions about the display:

"Which sea creature has the largest/smallest area?"

"Which one has an area of 18 triangles?"

"Do you think equilateral triangles are the best shapes to use for the calculation of area?" (See *Extensions and Variations* 1 also.)

3. Other themes could be isometric gardens, zoos, snakes and Christmas motifs — especially stars (fig. 3).

4. It is possible to use 1 cm isometric grid, but should this prove too fiddling for the less dextrous child, use it as a guide to make your own 'master' sheets in other dimensions. (See page 120 for a master for isometric grid.) Place a blank sheet of paper over the 1 cm grid and go over every third line to make a 3 cm grid. *Clixi* is based on a 5 cm edge length so you can make your own 5 cm grid to correspond to this.

5. A worthwhile game to support the learning at this stage is *Cover-up*, consisting of geometric shapes and inset boards based on the equilateral triangle module (fig. 4).

4

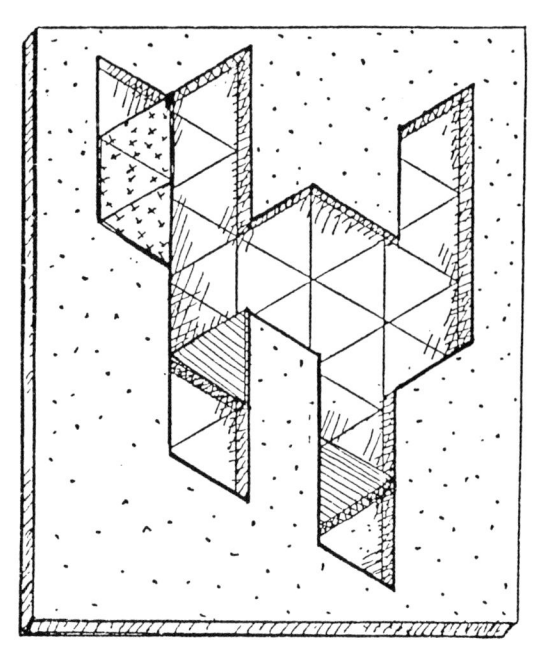

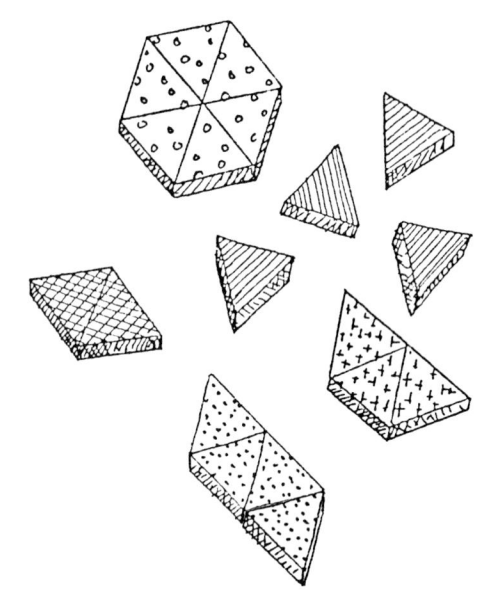

EXTENSIONS AND VARIATIONS

1. Allow the children to investigate other repeating units for establishing area — hexagonal, rhombic, square, circular, etc (fig. 5). Can they come to some conclusion about which is the most sensible shape to use and why?

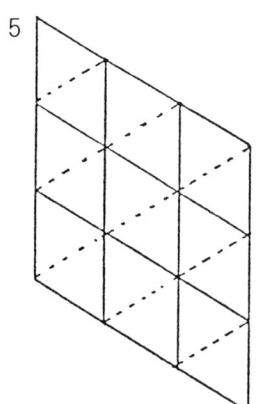

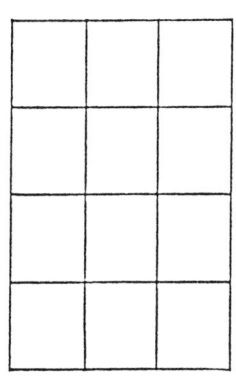

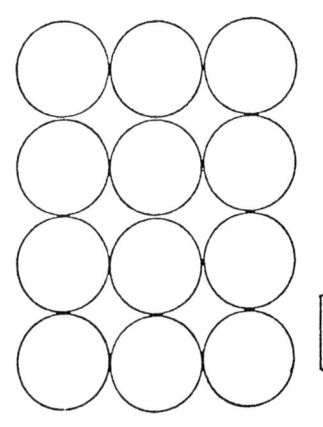

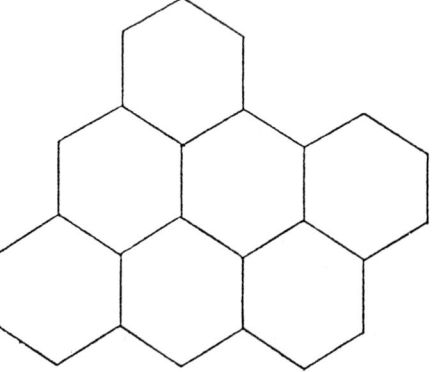

5

2. Using stencils or templates, congruent equilateral triangles can be cut out from old greetings cards, etc, and reassembled to make a variety of Christmas motifs and decorations such as stylised trees and stars.

3. If designs worked out on the grid are coloured with fabric crayons, they can be transferred to fabric without showing the reference lines, which can sometimes dominate the design. (See *FABRIC SHAPES*, page 35.)

REFERENCES & RESOURCES
Polydron E J Arnold
Clixi E J Arnold
Cover-up E J Arnold
Isometric Grids E J Arnold
Gummed Equilateral Triangles (variety of sizes) Playaway Supplies Ltd
Activity Mats Association of Teachers of Mathematics

STRING PRINTS †

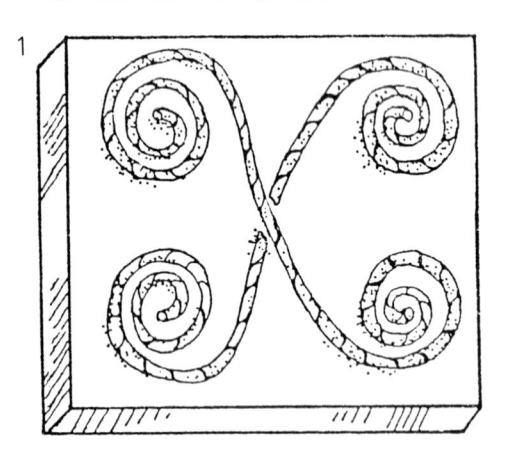

This activity is divided into two parts. Part 1 deals with the making of a string print block, which must be allowed to dry before proceeding to part 2, the actual printing process that creates a repeating pattern.

MATERIALS
Part 1: Soft string; rectangular offcuts of wood, hardboard, chipboard or thick strong card; PVA glue; scissors; scrap paper; pencil.
Part 2: Printing ink or substitute (see teaching points 1); roller; printing tray or a smooth, flat, washable surface; backing sheet; printing block prepared in part 1. (See page 3 for homemade printing pad.)

VOCABULARY
Rectangle, rectangular, block, surface, coiling, twisting, strip pattern, repeat pattern, horizontal, vertical, oblique, mirror image.

METHOD
Part 1
1. Trace round the perimeter of the rectangular offcut several times on scrap paper and sketch out some patterns or objects in them.
2. Generously cover one surface of an offcut with neat PVA glue.
3. Using lengths of string, make a likeness of one of your design sketches on the glued surface, coiling and twisting the string into position, and pressing it firmly into the glue (fig. 1).
4. Allow your printing block to dry thoroughly.

Part 2
1. On the reverse side of the printing block, make a mark to remind you which is the top edge.
2. On the printing tray, roll out the printing ink or paint to give a thin, even surface.
3. Press the printing block into the ink and transfer the inked design on to the backing sheet, pressing the block down firmly.
4. Print the design as many times as you like, taking care to space each of them out evenly in straight lines without rotating the block, i.e. keeping the 'top' mark at the top (fig. 2).

TEACHING POINTS
1. In the absence of commercial printing ink, a good substitute can be made with a mixture of PVA glue and poster paint. You will need to experiment to find the most satisfactory proportions. This mixture also adheres well to fabric, which can be used instead of paper. Smooth paper is by no means the only suitable backing material. Some children may enjoy trying out the printing block on backings of different materials, surfaces and textures before selecting the 'best' medium.

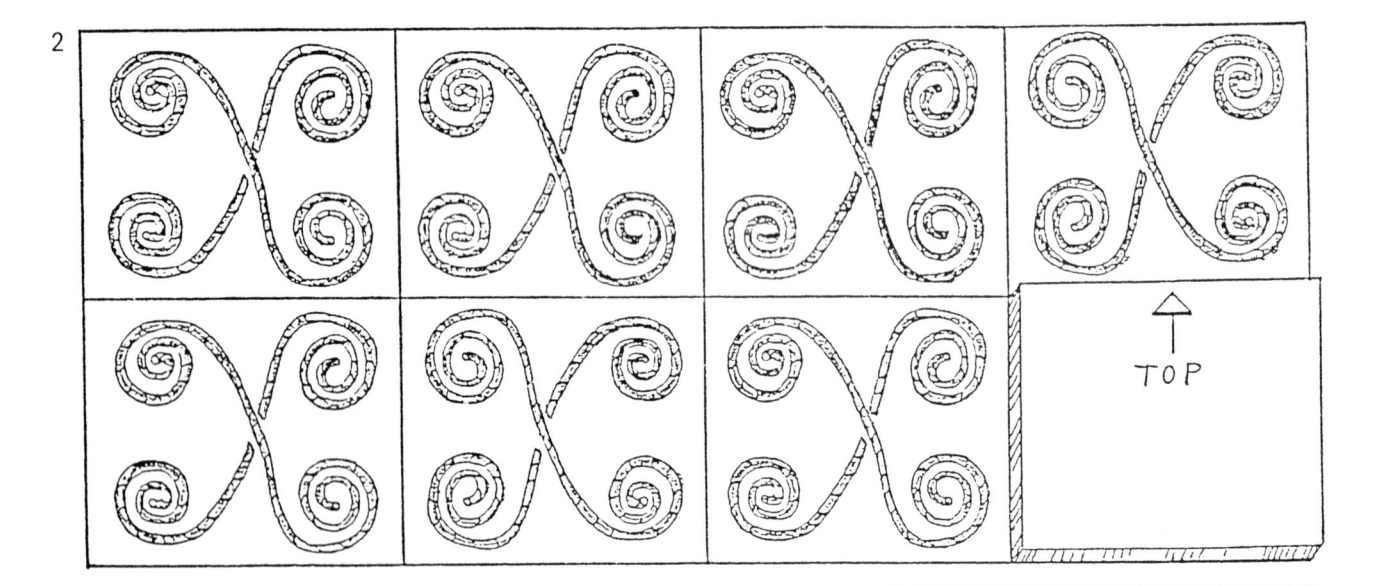

† Illustrated on page 5 of the first photograph section

2. This method relies on eye judgment, but some children may be able to suggest more accurate methods such as:
(a) marking off equally spaced points on a line, every 10 cm, for instance, and using these marks to assist with the spacing; the lines can be orientated in different ways — horizontal, vertical or oblique;
(b) folding a band of paper into equal divisions and using a segment for each repeat;
(c) using ruled lines spaced so that they are related to the size of the block and marking out a grid pattern over the backing sheet;
(d) using squared paper.
(a) and (b) will give a strip pattern; (c) and (d) will give an all-over repeat pattern. If desired, the motifs can overlap, provided that the spacing is kept regular. Alternatively, they can be used for half-drop patterns.
3. The only criterion for a repeat pattern is consistency of approach for each motif. The string prints can be:
(a) overprinted, or printed in a different orientation, with a second colour;
(b) combined with other string print blocks, which could be used by two or three children on a mix and match basis;
(c) combined with other materials such as corks which print off well.
4. The prints will give a mirror image of the block design, and a useful exercise is to get children to match up a set of blocks to their corresponding repeat patterns.
5. Bands of overlapping tissue paper, ink or paint washes, applied to the backing sheet before the printing process, add interest.

EXTENSIONS AND VARIATIONS
1. If the children are asked to use the same length of string for their different designs, the teacher can then use the opportunity to introduce questioning related to the conservation of length as a diagnostic tool.
2. Commercially produced printing sets such as *Geometric Motifs* and the *Picture and Pattern Printing Sets* can provide a quick method for investigating different types of printed patterns, including repeat patterns.
3. There are many other printing techniques, which can be used by pupils of all ages. One that complements the string block is the use of compressed polystyrene, such as *Press-Print*, which is easy to cut with scissors to the same size as the original printing block. Unlike lino, this indents easily without sharp cutting tools. Children can be encouraged to make facsimiles of their string prints, but this time *indenting* their chosen designs. When applied to the backing sheet, it is the *background* that prints off, not the motif. This negative image can be compared with the original positive print (fig. 3). Methods for transferring the motif accurately could be discussed and tried out.
4. *"Can a printing block be designed so that it not only makes a repeating pattern but also tessellates?"*
5. The printing block can be used to 'mass produce' twenty or thirty greetings cards. Children could be encouraged to design a block of a suitable size to fit available card, and more able children may also enjoy the challenge of designing an appropriate envelope.

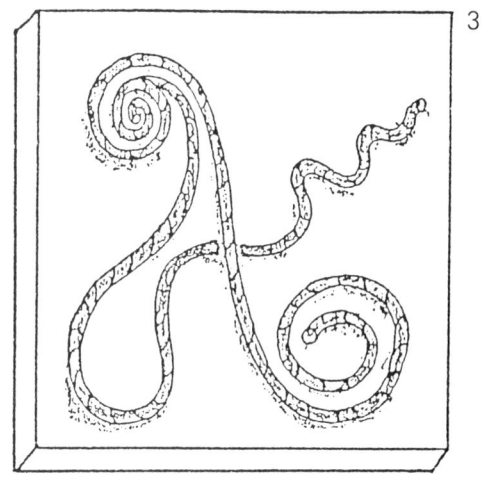

3

REFERENCES & RESOURCES
Pattern Printing Set James Galt & Co Ltd
Picture Printing Set James Galt & Co Ltd
Geometric Motifs Philip and Tacey
The Know How Book of Print and Paint Usborne Publishing Ltd
Creative Print Making B T Batsford Ltd
Prints (Leapfrog Series) Tarquin Publications
Printing Inks Berol Ltd
Rollers Berol Ltd
Press-Print Berol Ltd

TETRALAND †

MATERIALS
Two different tetrahedron nets, on card or card-backed paper, with edge lengths of 5–8 cm; PVA glue; paper springs; collage materials such as buttons, oddments of fabrics or paper; wool; string; gummed paper; strips of coloured activity paper; ruler; ball-point pen.

VOCABULARY
Net, tetrahedron, triangular, rotate, mobile, faces, fold, fit together, opposite.

There are two possible nets for the tetrahedron (fig. 1). The first net is more popular but both are featured in this activity. Before starting, the children should ideally have had experience of making tetrahedra and discovering the two net designs by using materials such as *Polydron* or *Clixi* unit triangles.

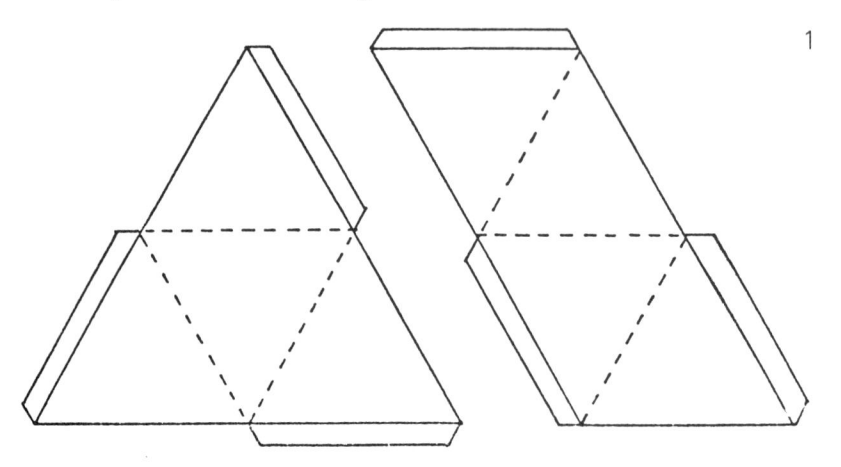

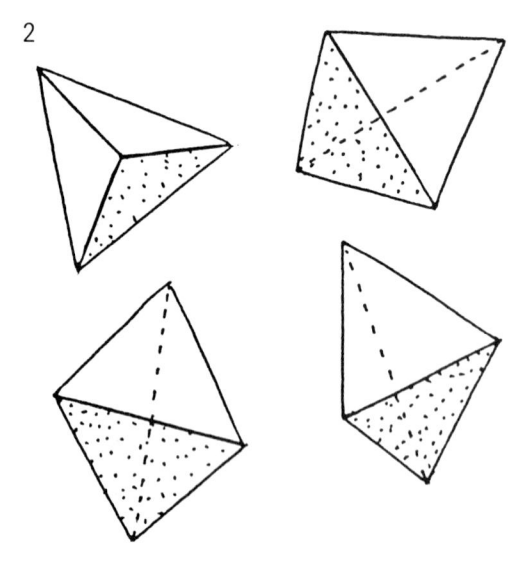

1

2

METHOD
1. Score the lines of one of the nets with a ruler and ball-point pen, then fold up the faces to check how they fit together.
2. On the opposite side of the net, put a thin layer of PVA glue on each tab. Fold up and secure the net to form the tetrahedron.
3. Rotate and view the tetrahedron from all directions and decide how you would like to decorate it (fig. 2).
4. Using the second net design, construct another tetrahedron and design a person with paper springs for limbs (fig. 3). You may like to draw some sketches first to make your character interesting and different to everyone else's. (Instructions for making paper springs are in *TECHNIQUES AND MATERIALS* on page 115.)
5. When finished, try to think of a way to display your 'tetra-person'.

3

42 TETRALAND   † *Illustrated on page 8 of the first photograph section*

4

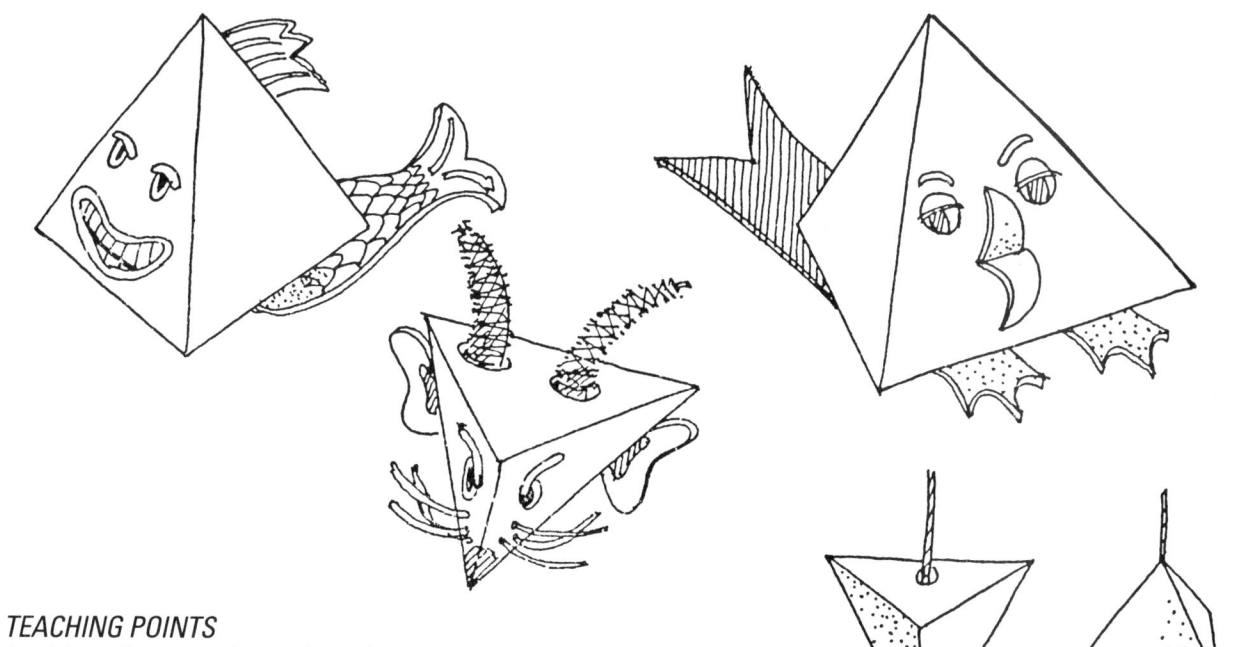

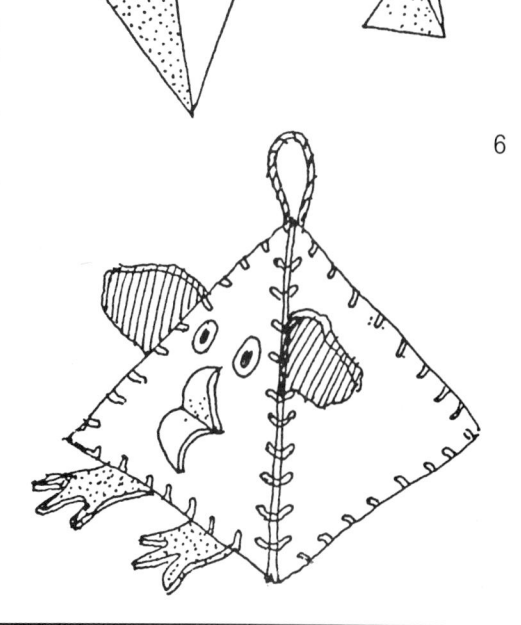

TEACHING POINTS
1. Ideas for experimental work with springs are suggested in *CLOWNS*, teaching point 2 on page 14.
2. You may like to discuss with the children possible ways of displaying the completed models — suspended as a mobile, propped up with soft wire embedded in a block of polystyrene packing, sitting, wall-mounted, or used to make a simple puppet which could feature in a group production.
3. Other possible themes for the models are animals, birds, robots, fish or forms of transport (fig.4).

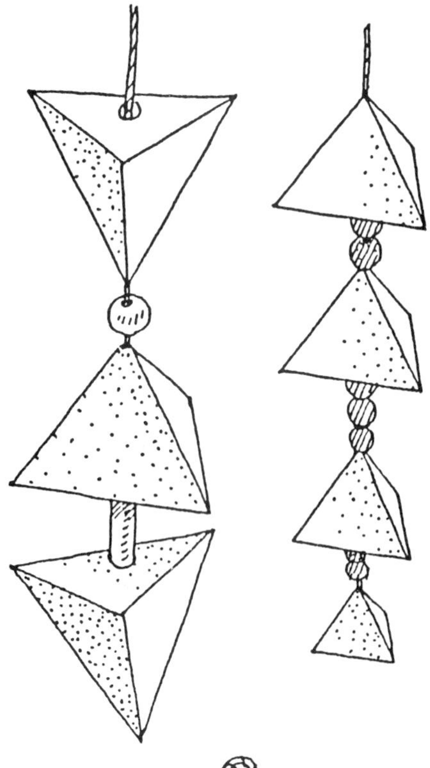

EXTENSIONS AND VARIATIONS
1. The tetrahedron is a pleasing shape in its own right but its appearance can be enhanced by different techniques of which a few are suggested here.
(a) Cover in advance with marbled paper (see page 114) or bubble prints (see page 1), gift wrap paper or gummed paper mosaic (see page 17).
(b) Make a printing block to decorate each face before assembly (see *STRING PRINTS*, page 40).
(c) Pattern each face using the technique described in *ROUNDABOUTS 1*, page 12.
(d) Use aerosol sprays, including metallic colours, and small adhesive stickers.
(e) If the net is designed directly on to isometric grid paper, it can be coloured and assembled so that the grid pattern is on the outer faces.
(f) Display tetrahedra in columns threaded on to thin wire or thread, with beads as spacers (fig. 5). Columns can be ordered by size, use shades of the same colour or consist of congruent models in different orientations. (A mattress needle *for the teacher only* and buttonhole thread are useful for this.)
(g) Make up tetrahedra in felt by oversewing four equilateral triangles along their edges (fig. 6).

5

6

TETRALAND

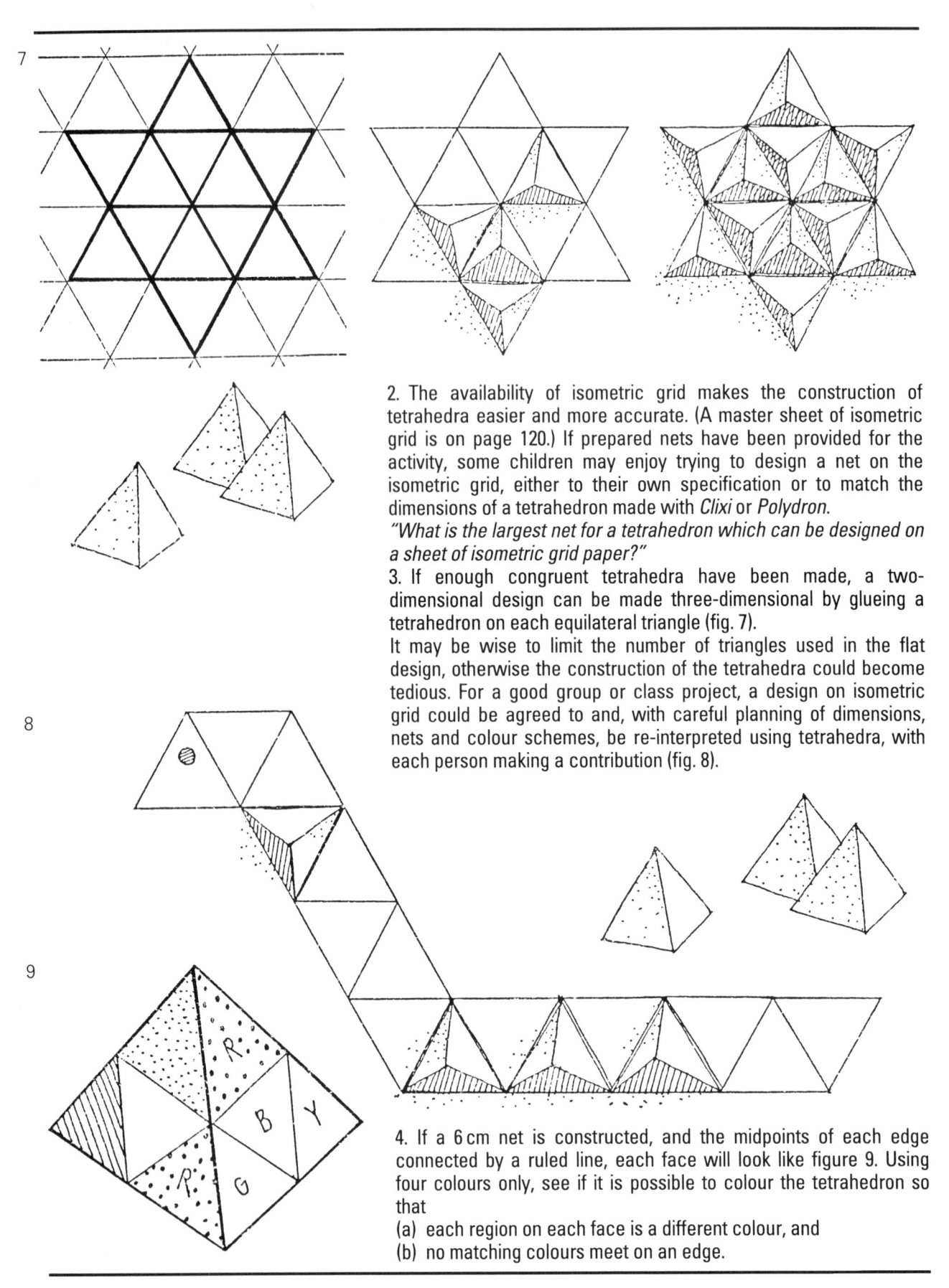

7

2. The availability of isometric grid makes the construction of tetrahedra easier and more accurate. (A master sheet of isometric grid is on page 120.) If prepared nets have been provided for the activity, some children may enjoy trying to design a net on the isometric grid, either to their own specification or to match the dimensions of a tetrahedron made with *Clixi* or *Polydron*.

"What is the largest net for a tetrahedron which can be designed on a sheet of isometric grid paper?"

3. If enough congruent tetrahedra have been made, a two-dimensional design can be made three-dimensional by glueing a tetrahedron on each equilateral triangle (fig. 7).

It may be wise to limit the number of triangles used in the flat design, otherwise the construction of the tetrahedra could become tedious. For a good group or class project, a design on isometric grid could be agreed to and, with careful planning of dimensions, nets and colour schemes, be re-interpreted using tetrahedra, with each person making a contribution (fig. 8).

8

9

4. If a 6 cm net is constructed, and the midpoints of each edge connected by a ruled line, each face will look like figure 9. Using four colours only, see if it is possible to colour the tetrahedron so that
(a) each region on each face is a different colour, and
(b) no matching colours meet on an edge.

44   TETRALAND

5. Tetrahedra make a good introduction to the idea of composite models — those made from more than one polyhedron. For example, if two tetrahedra are glued together, a hexahedron, which looks rather like a three-dimensional diamond, is formed (fig. 10). These look particularly attractive as a collection suspended at different heights from a ceiling or hanging from a branch. Try to design a one-piece net for this shape. This theme is developed more fully in *ROUNDABOUTS 3*, page 93.

6. Two congruent tetrahedra, glued together after one has been rotated through 60°, make an attractive structure. When viewed from above or below, it looks rather like a three-dimensional star. (Fig. 11.)

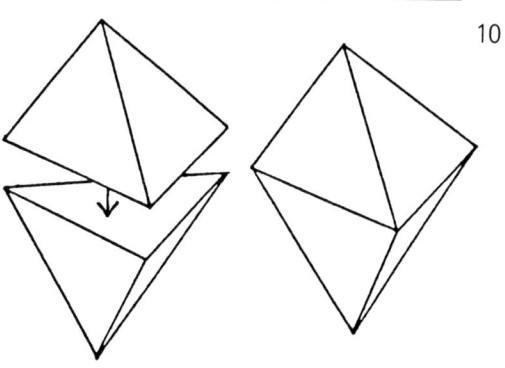

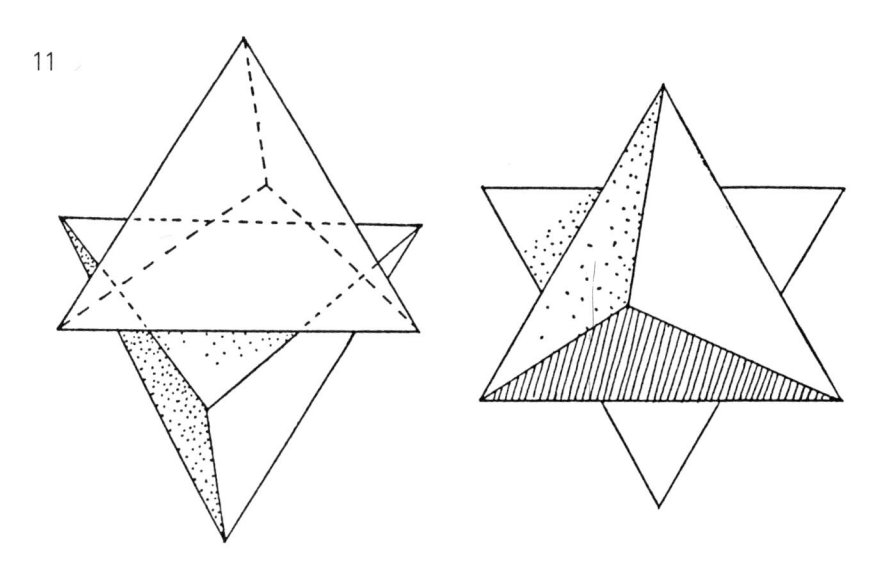

7. Suitable reference books could be made available to find out about other polyhedra, including the stellated variety, which have faces made up entirely or partially from equilateral triangles (fig. 12).

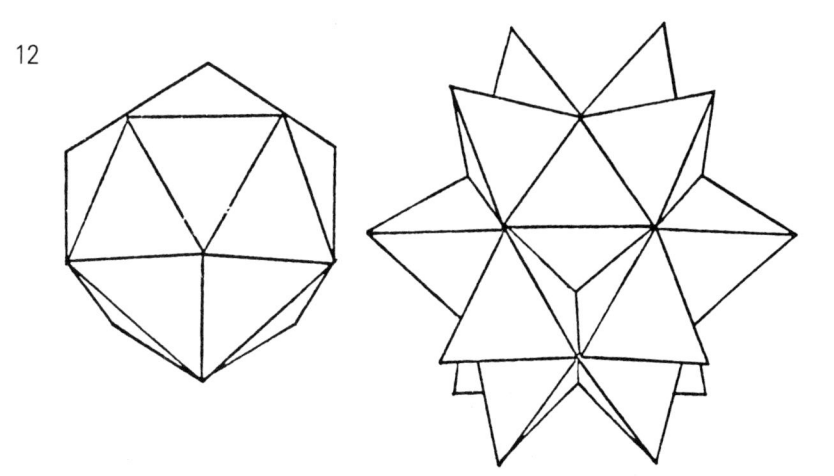

REFERENCES & RESOURCES
Make Shapes Books 1, 2 and 3; Tarquin Publications
Polyhedra Posters and Postcard Set Association of Teachers of Mathematics
Activity Mats Association of Teachers of Mathematics
Polydron E J Arnold
Clixi Hestair Hope Ltd

EXPLODED SQUARES †

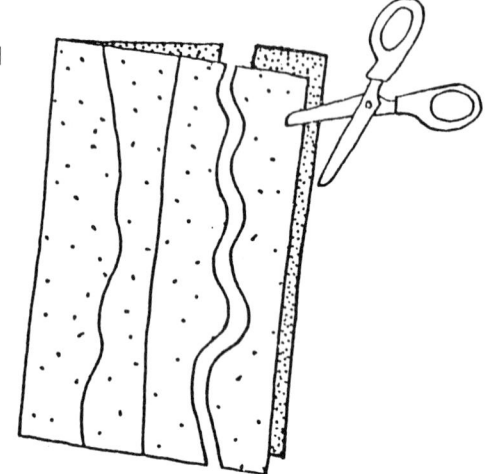

Bilateral symmetry and the conservation of area are explored using paper-cutting skills to create patterns.

MATERIALS
15 cm gummed squares, scissors, pencil, backing sheet.

VOCABULARY
Fold, half, axis or line of symmetry, squares, top, bottom, section, edge, centre-fold, coincide, adjoining, mirror image.

METHOD
1. Fold the square in half along an axis of symmetry.
2. Keeping the square folded, cut through both layers from top to bottom near the open edges (fig. 1).
3. Repeat this three or four times, laying down in order the sections you cut out. The last piece should still have a folded edge.
4. Mark the centre-fold of the backing sheet.
5. Open out the gummed section with the folded edge and paste it so that its fold coincides with the fold on the backing sheet.
6. Take the pairs of adjoining sections in turn and space them out on the backing sheet so that they form mirror images of each other.
7. When you are sure that the pieces have been positioned correctly, glue them down (fig. 2).

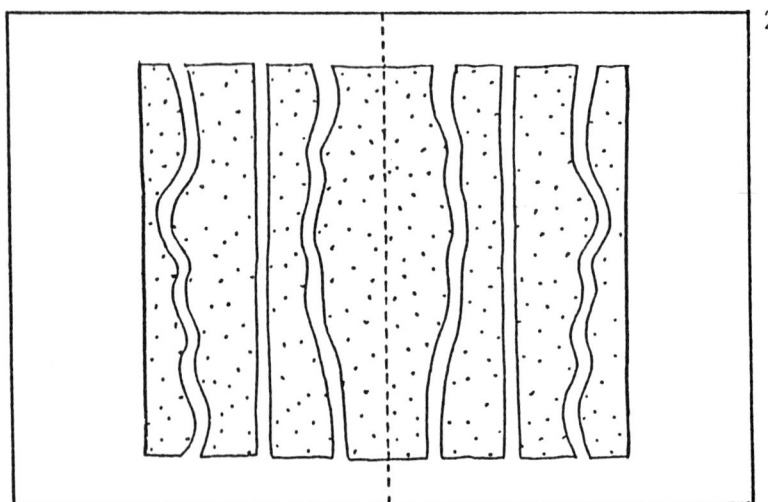

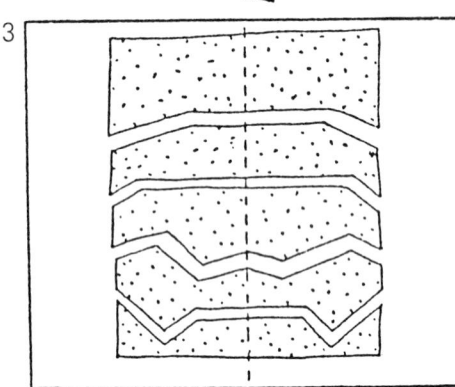

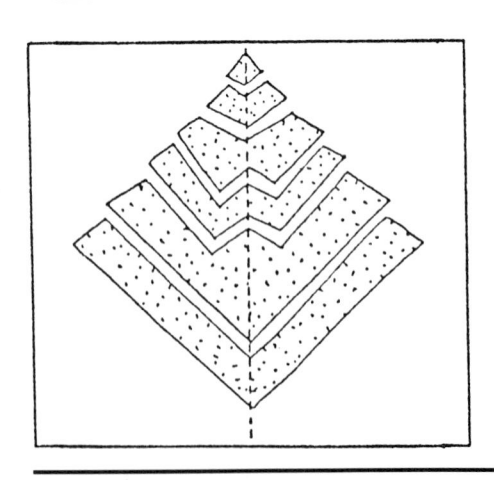

TEACHING POINTS
1. Apart from reflective symmetry, which should be checked with the use of mirrors, this activity provides an opportunity to discuss the conservation of area, since the area of the separate 'exploded' pieces is still the same as the area of the original uncut square.
2. You will probably find that some children prefer to mark out their cutting lines in pencil first.
3. Encourage the children to position all the pieces first without glueing, to avoid disappointment if a piece is wrongly glued.
4. Depending on how the children wish to display their work, distinctions can be made between horizontal, vertical and oblique axes of symmetry, and classified accordingly.

EXTENSIONS AND VARIATIONS
1. There are many alternative ways of exploding squares. Cuts can be made through the fold each time, giving a different overall effect, or the fold can be a diagonal axis of symmetry (fig. 3).

46 EXPLODED SQUARES   † Illustrated on page 7 of the first photograph section

2. If two squares are folded and cut out simultaneously with matching cuts, the two patterns, both with reflective symmetry, can be arranged differently (fig. 4).

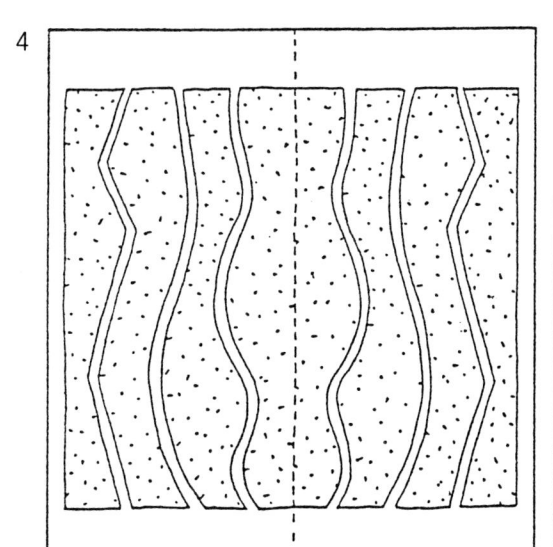

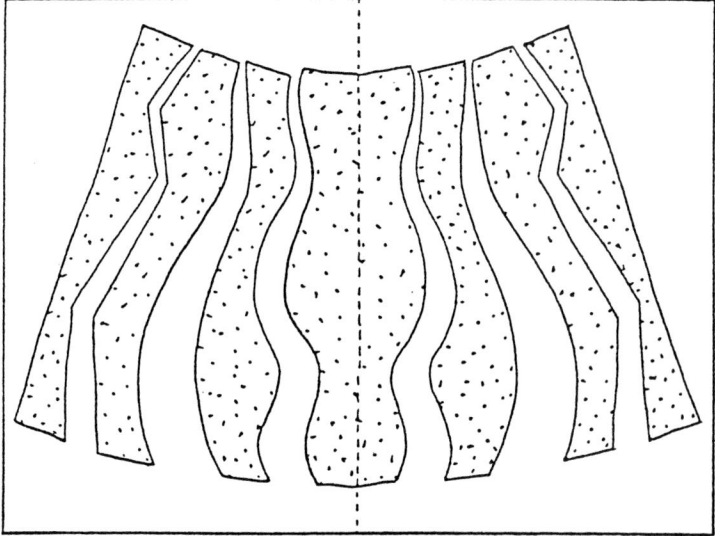

4

3. Allow children to experiment with multiple folds. In figure 5, the square has been folded along two axes of symmetry before the standard procedure was followed. It is amazing what children will design if encouraged to experiment.

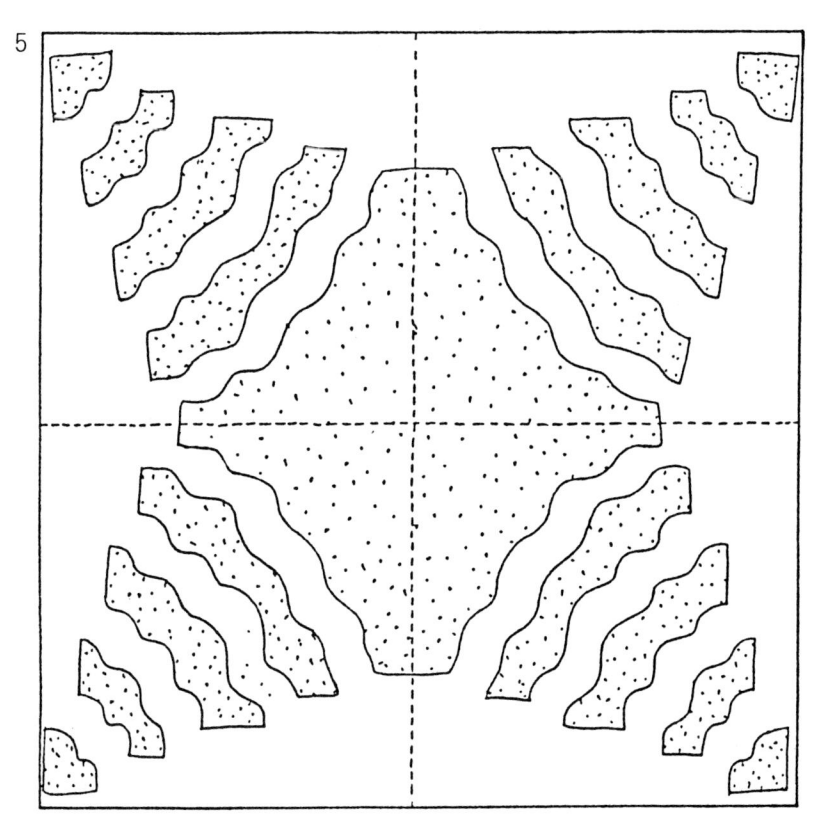

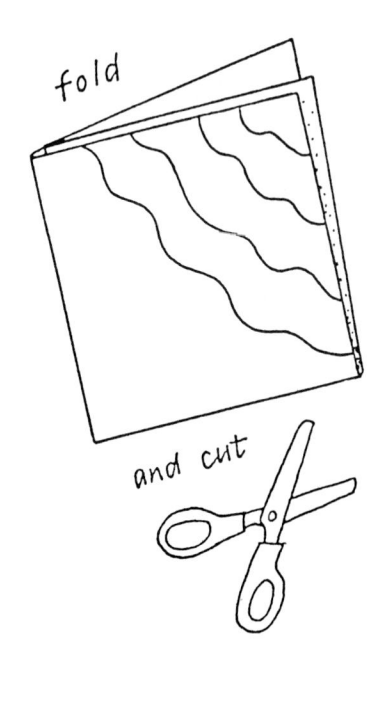

5

fold

and cut

STARWEAVING 2 †

MATERIALS
Wools of assorted colour, thickness and texture; 2 garden canes about 20 cm long; PVA glue.

VOCABULARY
Right angles, centre, figure of eight, repeat, over, under, close to, loop, around, top, anticlockwise, next, across, finish, square, diagonals.

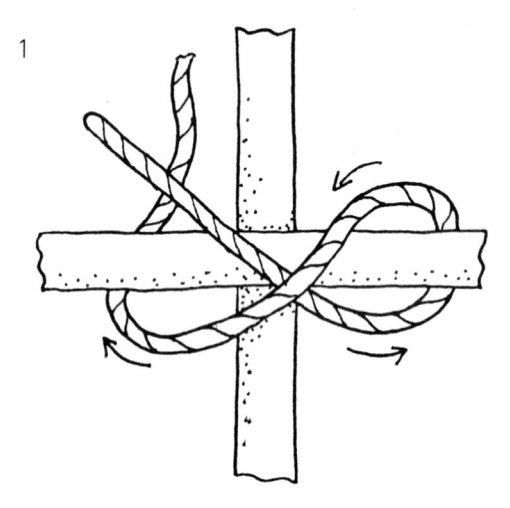

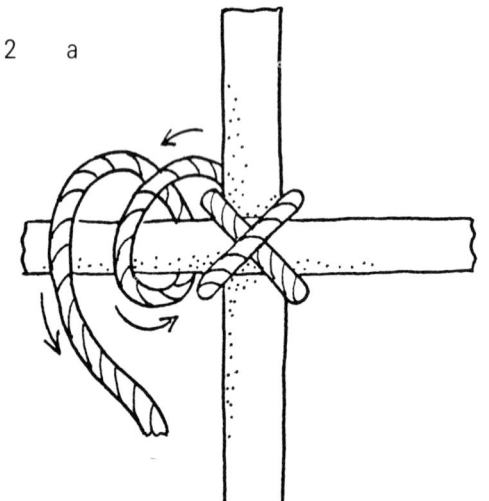

This chapter extends the ideas and weaving skills introduced in *STARWEAVING 1*.

METHOD

1. Lash the canes together firmly by placing them at right angles to each other at their centres and securing them with strong wool wound in a figure of eight movement (fig. 1). This is the most difficult part and is best done by one person holding the canes while the other lashes them together.
2. Tie a knot at the back of the sticks and trim the short end off, leaving the ball of wool attached.
3. At all times, work with the 'right' side of the starweaving towards you, holding the wool in one hand and the diagonals of the star in the other.
4. Bring the wool *over* the top of one arm of the cross, close to the lashing, then loop the wool *under* the same arm and back around the top, keeping the wool taut (fig. 2).

This is known as the 'raised method', as the finished star will lie above the level of its diagonal framework.

5. Move the wool anticlockwise to the next arm of the star. Lay the wool across the top of the stick, close to the lashing, then wind it under and around the top. Keep the wool taut at all times.
6. Repeat step 5 twice more and you will come back to where you started, having moved through four quarter turns.
7. Continue in this way until you wish to change colours by breaking off the wool, leaving about 10 cm with which to tie on the next colour.

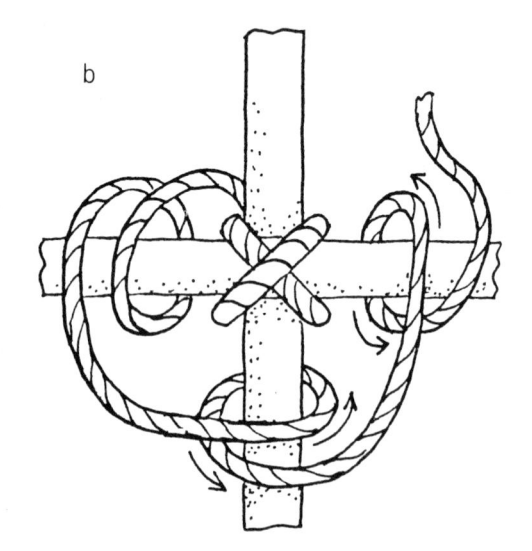

8. Once the new colour has been knotted on, carry on weaving in the same way until you wish to change colours again.
9. To finish off the weaving, either make an overhand knot on the back of the sticks or secure the end of the wool with a very small blob of PVA glue. If the raw ends of the canes are exposed, they can be bound with wool and wooden beads or sequins glued to the ends. Alternatively, buttons or woollen tassels can be attached.

† *Illustrated on page 7 of the first photograph section*

TEACHING POINTS

1. This simple weaving technique can be mastered by young children and has the advantage that it can be finished off at any stage, depending on the patience of the weaver. As the technique is mastered, you will notice that, in order to speed up the process, the children automatically start to rotate the sticks a quarter of a turn each time. This makes the concept of rotational symmetry a practical reality. The movement of the hands is also repetitive — a pattern of movement.

2. The stars look effective if displayed as mobiles, either singly or in groups. For a Christmas display, glittery wool and fine tinsels can be woven into the design. The ends of the canes can be bound with foil to add to the sparkle.

3. If you look at the back of the star, you will see the effect of weaving by the 'recessed method' (see below) in which the finished star will lie in the recesses between its diagonals.

EXTENSIONS AND VARIATIONS

1. By altering steps 4 and 5 only, the 'recessed method' can be achieved.
(a) Vary step 4 by bringing the wool *under* the cane, close to the lashing. Loop the wool around the cane and back *under* the star (fig. 3).
(b) Vary step 5 by moving the wool anticlockwise to the next arm of the star, lay the wool *under* the cane, close to the lashing, then loop it around the cane and back *under*.
(c) Follow through from step 6.

2. As the children become more confident, they can be encouraged to alternate between the recessed and raising methods on the same piece of weaving. This gives an interesting textural effect.

3. Although the lashing is more difficult, it is possible to bind together three canes to give a six spoke framework. The weaving method follows the same pattern as before and, if the canes are spaced out evenly at 60° to each other, a regular hexagon will be woven. Silver and white wools will produce attractive snowflake patterns. Another idea is to weave with gaps between the strands to give a spider's web which can be suitably decorated (fig. 4).

4. A construction kit called *Kugeli* contains junction pieces and rods for making skeletal solids. These provide a rigid and versatile framework on which to weave stars with up to eight spokes. The junction pieces can be used instead of beads to finish off the ends, and lengths of wool or ribbons can be threaded through the holes. Several identical stars built on this kind of framework can be slotted together to make a large display.

5. As an alternative to lashing the canes together, use PVA glue to fix them into polystyrene spheres of the type used for flower arranging. This allows large models to be constructed.

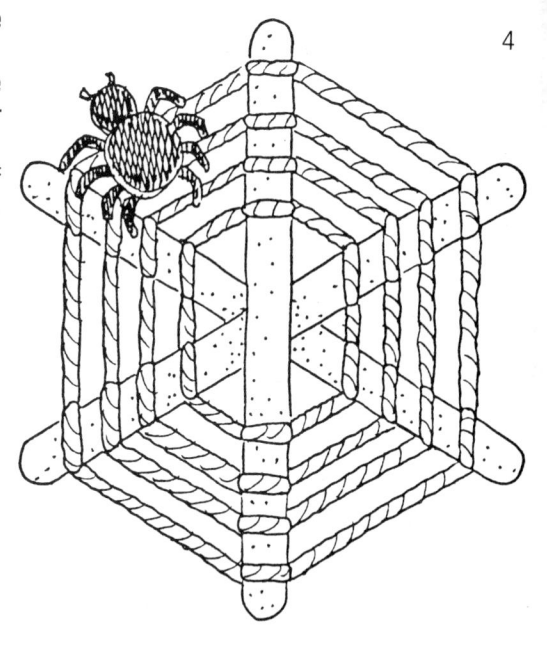

REFERENCES & RESOURCES
The Golden Hands Complete Book of Crafts — "Star Weaving" Marshall Cavendish
The Batsford Encyclopaedia of Crafts — "God's Eyes" B T Batsford Ltd
Kugeli E J Arnold

STARWEAVING 2

TESSELLATION 2 †

MATERIALS
Blank postcards or card cut out to approximate postcard size, sellotape, backing sheets, pencil, scissors, colouring pencils, pens or crayons, collage scraps.

VOCABULARY
Long, short, straight, edge, opposite, slide, left, line up, together, tile, tessellate, shape, match, rotate, split, corner.

This chapter takes the work of *TESSELLATION 1* (page 25) a stage further by introducing more intricate tessellating patterns using 'cut and slide' techniques.

METHOD

A slightly more sophisticated technique which produces more interesting tiles follows the first three steps of the basic method described in *TESSELLATION 1*, then proceed as follows:

3a. Cut out a second piece from corner to corner along one of the uncut edges.

3b. Slide this piece over the tile until it lines up with the opposite matching edge. Sellotape the pieces together.

Now follow steps 4, 5 and 6 of the basic method.

This shape will interlock both in rows and in columns (fig. 1).

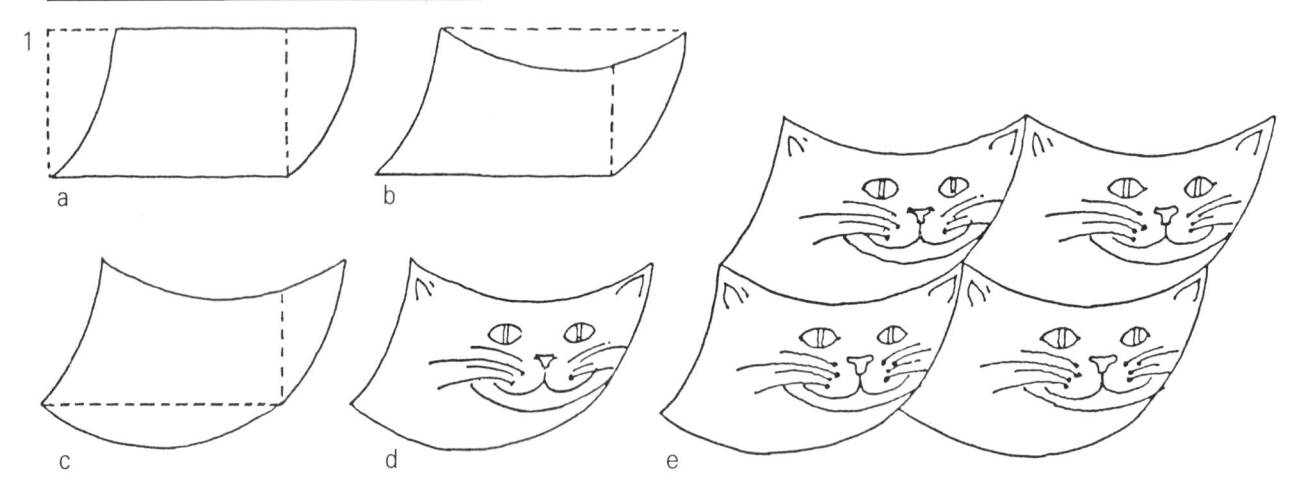

Some further suggestions for variations on the basic tile are given in figure 2.

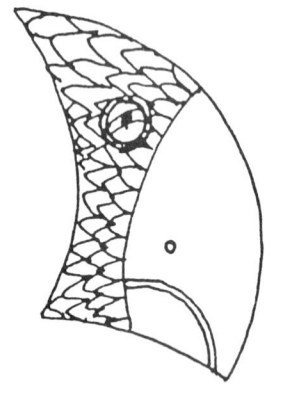

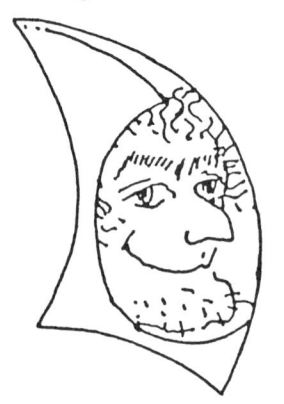

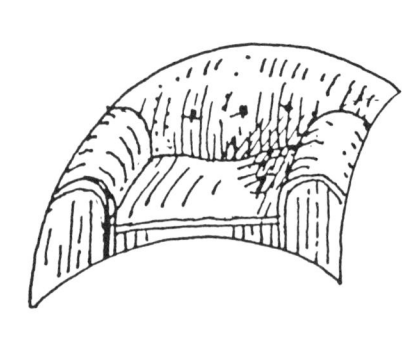

TEACHING POINTS

1. Prepare a wall display of different tessellations and a set of master tiles from which the patterns were generated. Can the children match the master tiles to the patterns? Alternatively, each master tile could be matched to its pattern using a length of string.

2. Make sure the children appreciate that taking a piece from one side of the starting tile and adding it to the opposite side, alters the *shape* of the tile but keeps the *area* the same (*conservation of area*).

50 TESSELLATION 2   † *Illustrated on page 6 of the first photograph section*

EXTENSIONS AND VARIATIONS
1. (a) Starting with a rectangle, design a tile that has two straight edges and two curved edges.
(b) Starting with a square, make a tiling design in which all the lines are curved.
2. Investigate the 'cut and slide' techniques on other quadrilaterals such as squares, rhombi, parallelograms, etc, or even on regular hexagons (fig. 3).

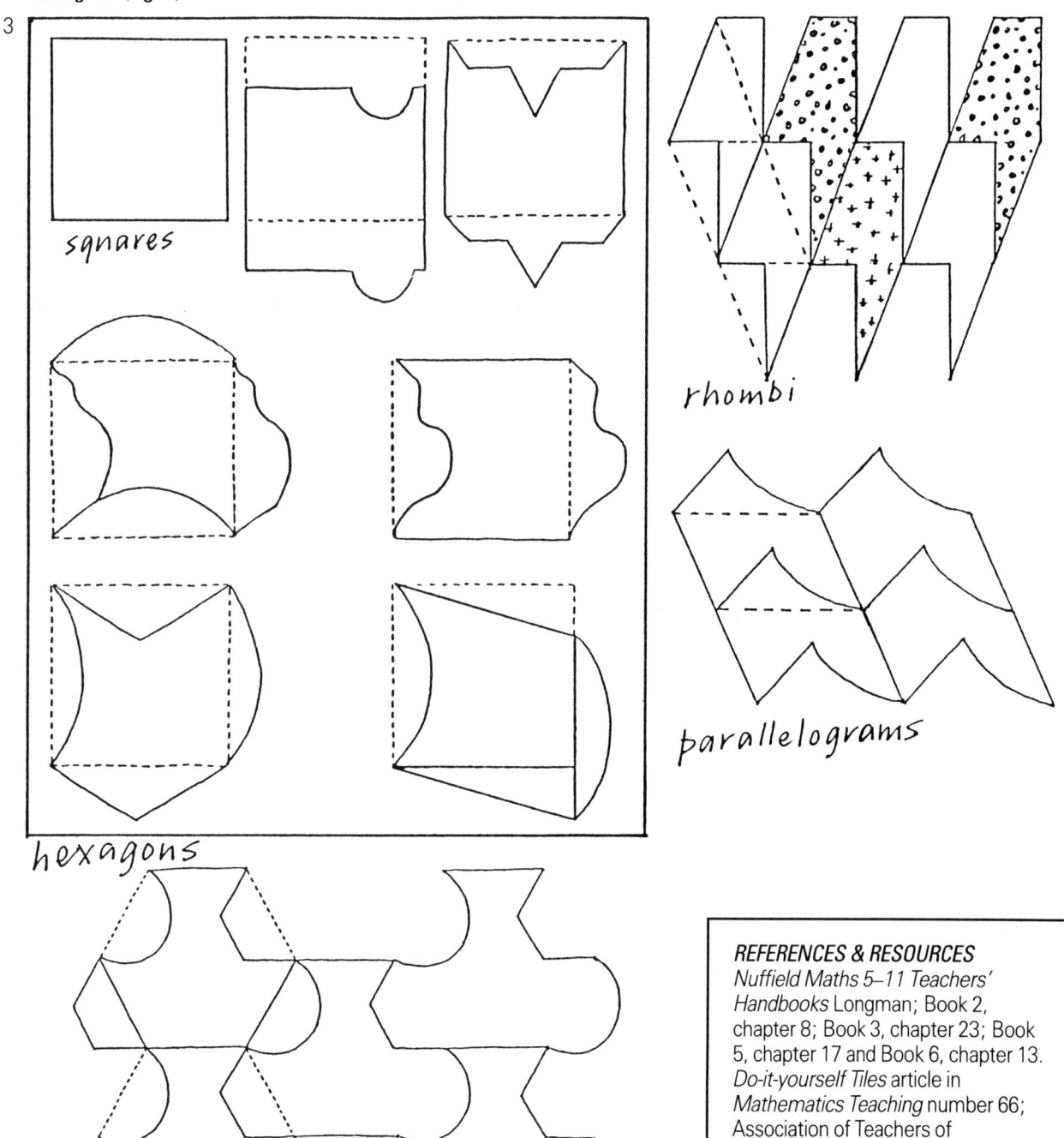

3

squares

rhombi

parallelograms

hexagons

REFERENCES & RESOURCES
Nuffield Maths 5–11 Teachers' Handbooks Longman; Book 2, chapter 8; Book 3, chapter 23; Book 5, chapter 17 and Book 6, chapter 13.
Do-it-yourself Tiles article in *Mathematics Teaching* number 66; Association of Teachers of Mathematics
Tessellations Josephine Mold; Cambridge University Press.

ROUNDABOUTS 2 †

MATERIALS
Templates or stencils of regular polygons, card scraps, backing sheets, pencil, ruler, scissors, colouring materials.

VOCABULARY
Rotate, regular polygon, perimeter, outline, template, edge, vertex, vertices, position, coincide, vertically, clockwise, rotational symmetry, reflect ('flip over'), line symmetry, one revolution (360°).

The work of *ROUNDABOUTS 1* (page 12) is taken a stage further by using a wider range of regular polygons and developing more intricate patterns created by taking cuts out of templates and rotating them in a systematic way.

METHOD
These steps are similar to those given in *ROUNDABOUTS 1* but this time they apply to *any regular polygon* rather than to just a square.
1. Trace round the perimeter of the chosen regular polygon on the centre of the backing sheet.
2. Trace out the same outline on a piece of firm card and cut it out carefully to use as a template.
3. Cut out a simple shape from one edge of the card template.
4. Position the card template on top of the outline drawn on the backing sheet so that the edges coincide.

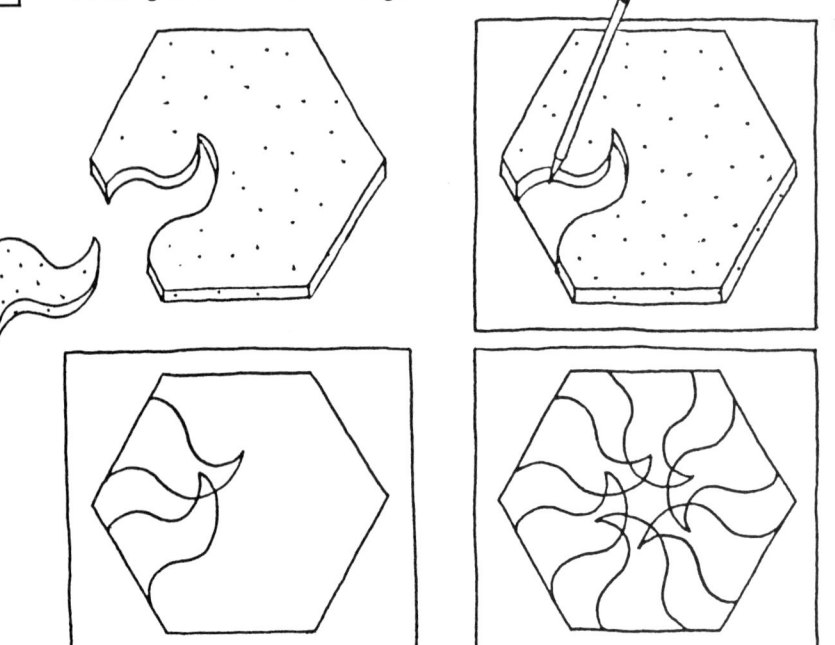

5. Trace out the section removed, holding the pencil vertically (fig. 1).
6. Rotate the template clockwise until it fits back on to its outline and trace round the cutout section again.
7. Repeat step 6 until the cutout section has been traced out on each edge (fig. 2).

The pattern constructed will have *rotational symmetry*. The *order of rotational symmetry* the pattern has will depend upon the number of sides of the regular polygon chosen.

TEACHING POINTS
1. This activity provides excellent opportunities to reinforce understanding of regular polygons. The children can experience for themselves that, as the template is rotated, its edges and corners (vertices) fit into the outline on the backing sheet. If a selection of different regular polygons is provided (equilateral triangles, squares, regular pentagons, hexagons, octagons, etc) then, before the activity starts, a list can be drawn up as follows:

---

52   ROUNDABOUTS 2   † *Illustrated on page 4 of the second photograph section*

Regular Polygon	number of sides	number of times polygon fits	Fraction of one revolution	Angle turned (optional)*	Order of Rot. Symm.
Equilateral triangle	3	3	1/3 of 360°	120°	3
Square	4	4	1/4 of 360°	90°	4

2. Encourage children to spot the relationships within the table of results. For example, can the children spot the link between the number of sides and the number of times the polygon fits back into its outline? In other words can they appreciate the *order of rotational symmetry* of the shape?

3. Is it possible to predict results for other regular polygons not shown in the table — for example, a regular decagon (10 sides), a regular duodecagon (12 sides) or even a regular icosagon (20 sides)?

4. Let the children work out colouring sequences to highlight the symmetry within the patterns.

EXTENSIONS AND VARIATIONS

1. Design the cutout section so that the finished pattern will have line symmetry as well as rotational symmetry.
One example is given in figure 3.

2. Experiment with sections cut out from other semi-regular shapes — for example, a star shape (fig. 4).

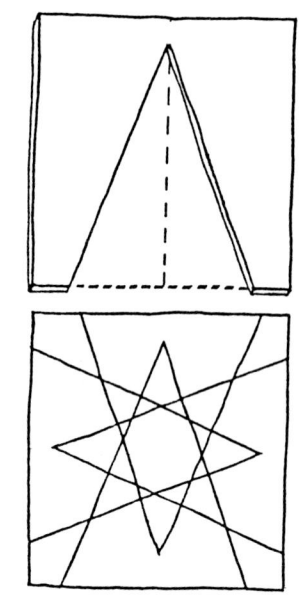

ROUNDABOUTS 2   53

5

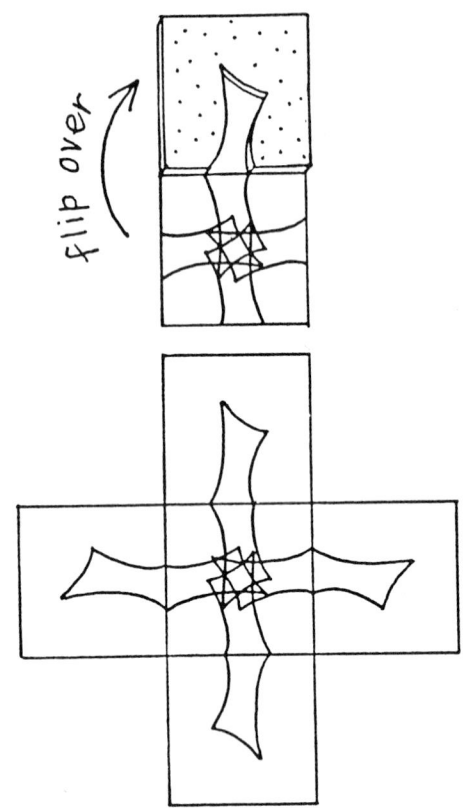

flip over

3. A more sophisticated pattern can be constructed by extending the procedure in this way:
(a) Design the basic pattern in the usual way.
(b) After drawing the final outline of the cutout section, reflect or 'flip over' the template using the edge as the axis of symmetry (fig. 5).
(c) Proceed to mark out the outline of the cutout on each outer edge in turn.
Encourage children to try out other variations.
4. Get a group of children to investigate the effect on the designs if:
(a) the same shape cutout section is used but applied to different regular polygons;
(b) the same regular polygon is used but with different cutouts;
(c) a 'graded' cutout is used — that is, first a small cutout section is used to create a pattern, then the cutout area is enlarged and a new pattern drawn.
5. If black felt pen outlines are drawn on greaseproof or tracing paper and the patterns coloured with felt pens, they can be displayed on a window to give a 'stained glass' effect.
6. If the cutout area is planned so that it is removed from the centre of the edge of the regular polygon, it is possible to apply the design to the faces of solid shapes so that the pattern links up on each face. (The photograph shows the faces of a cube designed in this way.) Tessellating units can also be designed using this technique (fig. 6).

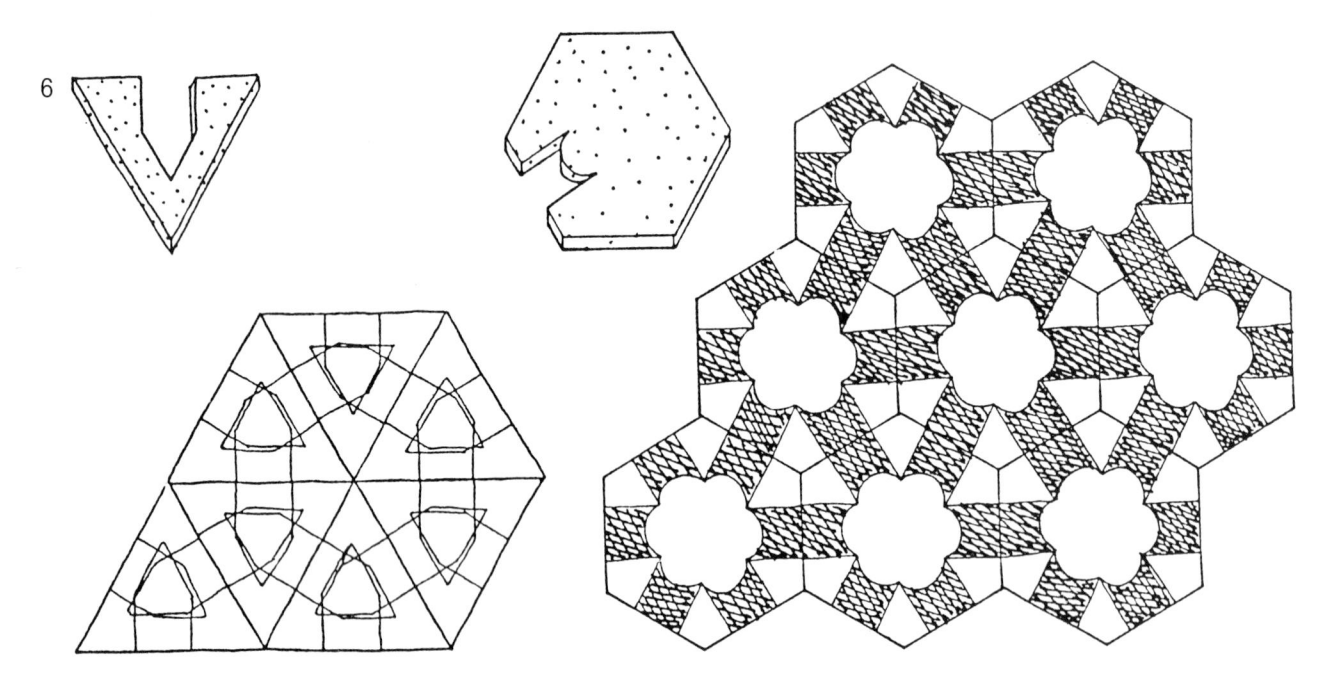

6

REFERENCES & RESOURCES
Activity Mats Association of Teachers of Mathematics

7. Collect examples of kitchen or floor tiles that are designed so that the patterns link up when assembled. Catalogues often have photographs of whole areas tiled in this way.

54   *ROUNDABOUTS 2*

HORIZONTAL AND VERTICAL †

Patterns using strips of paper are created to emphasise the words *horizontal*, *vertical* and *parallel* and the ideas behind them.

METHOD
1. Cut lengths of coloured paper into strips 15–20 millimetres wide. A safety guillotine will do this quickly and accurately; otherwise use a ruler and pencil to mark out the strips and cut them out with scissors.
2. Before applying any glue, space out coloured strips of different lengths on the backing sheet, parallel to the vertical edges of the paper (fig. 1).
3. Now overlap these strips with others placed parallel to the horizontal edges of the backing sheet (fig. 2).

MATERIALS
Assorted coloured papers, backing sheets approximately 40 cm square, glue pen or glue and small spreader, safety guillotine or scissors, ruler, pencil.

VOCABULARY
Horizontal, vertical, perpendicular, parallel, at right angles, intersection, edge, lengths, widths, millimetre.

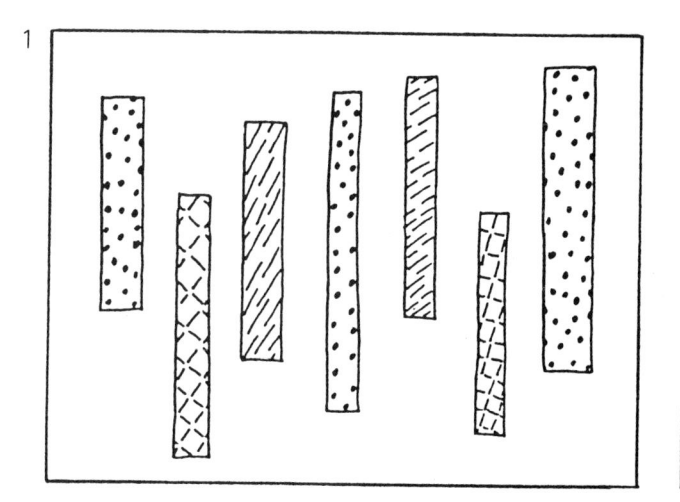

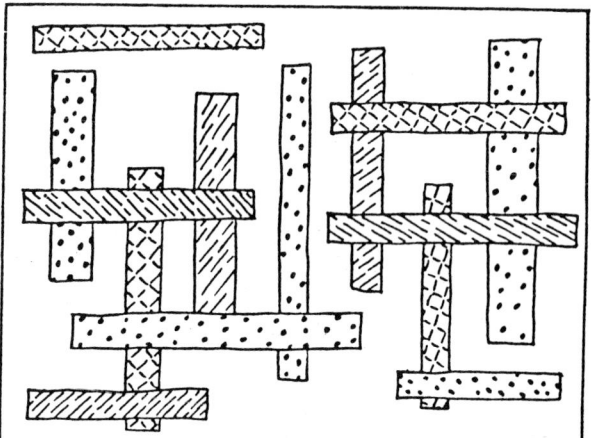

If positioned correctly, the two sets of strips will be perpendicular (at right angles) to each other.
4. When this can be done successfully, remove all the strips and then re-apply the vertical strips, glueing them down one at a time. Make sure they are parallel to the vertical edges of the backing sheet.
5. Do the same with the horizontal strips.

TEACHING POINTS
1. Older children should be able to cut their own paper strips using the safety guillotine. The ruled top guide edge and the cutting edge make this a perfect example of a tool specially designed to give accurate right-angled cuts. If available, *gummed paper strips* and the perforated edging from computer print-out paper give an interesting effect.
2. Make a class collection of environmental examples — objects, photographs, sketches, or lists of items that demonstrate and make use of the properties of
(a) *parallelism*, for example motorways, railway lines, Venetian blinds, lined paper, combs, stratified rock formations, etc;
(b) *horizontal/vertical alignment*, for example plumb lines, spirit levels, T-squares, drawing boards, set-squares, architectural plans, tartans, weavings, square grids, scaffolding, stalagmites, etc.

† *Illustrated on page 2 of the second photograph section*

3. Encourage children to learn to use as many as possible of the tools mentioned so that they can appreciate the purpose behind their design. In the initial activity, eye judgment only was used. Can the children now develop a more accurate method of creating a similar 'horizontal–vertical' design using either their own choice of materials or alternative ones suggested by you? For example, a quick and effective method is to use tracing paper over squared paper. Black pen lines can be drawn using the printed lines as guides and the regions coloured to give a 'stained glass window' effect. Logo graphic designs could also be used.

4. What generalisation can be made about the shapes created by the intersection of the strips?

5. Obtain books or prints depicting the work of artists who have used geometric precision to great effect. For instance, suitable examples of the work of Mondrian may support this area of learning.

EXTENSIONS AND VARIATIONS

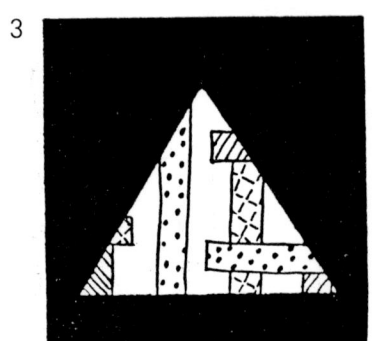

1. Experiment with different shaped overlays to display the designs — circular, triangular, off-set squares, etc. (fig. 3). Which do the children like best?

2. Can the children suggest a way of creating a three-dimensional 'horizontal–vertical' design?

3. Examine examples of woven fabrics with a magnifying glass or under a microscope. Can the weaving patterns be re-created using horizontal and vertical strips? The relationship between *weft* (horizontal) and *warp* (vertical) threads can be highlighted here.

In the example (fig. 4), the vertical strips were glued to the backing sheet only at the very top. Horizontal strips were then woven in and out of the vertical strips, suitably positioned and then glued down. Finally, the bottom ends of the vertical strips were glued into position to give a random weaving effect.

5. How could strips be applied so that:
(a) only squares appear in the pattern,
(b) only non-rectangular parallelograms appear in the pattern?

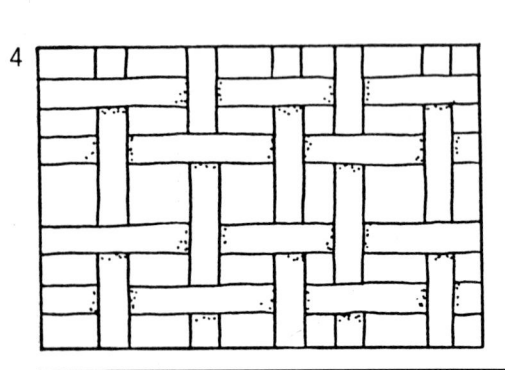

56   HORIZONTAL AND VERTICAL

6. Make a collection of patterns or symbols that make use of horizontal and vertical lines only. Use the examples in figure 5 to encourage children to make their own designs, using squared paper to ensure accuracy.

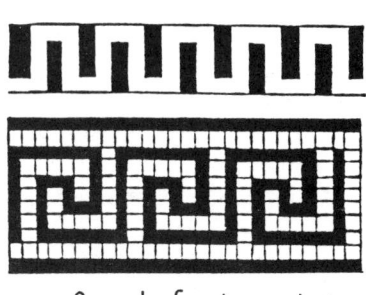

5

Greek fretworks

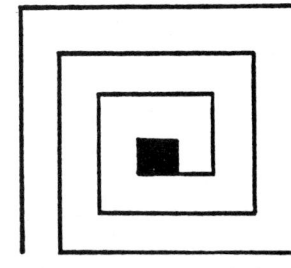

Square spiral

Trade mark

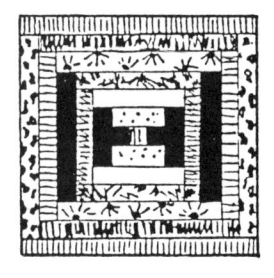

Patchwork

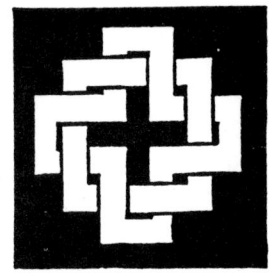

Interlacement

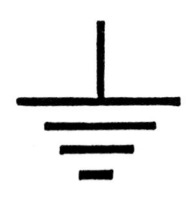

"Earth" Symbol

7. Get the children to use different shaped backing sheets, some rectangular and some irregular, and to 'take a line for a walk', that is to draw a freehand continuous line starting from a point chosen at random, with the rule that only horizontal and vertical line segments should be used (fig. 6).

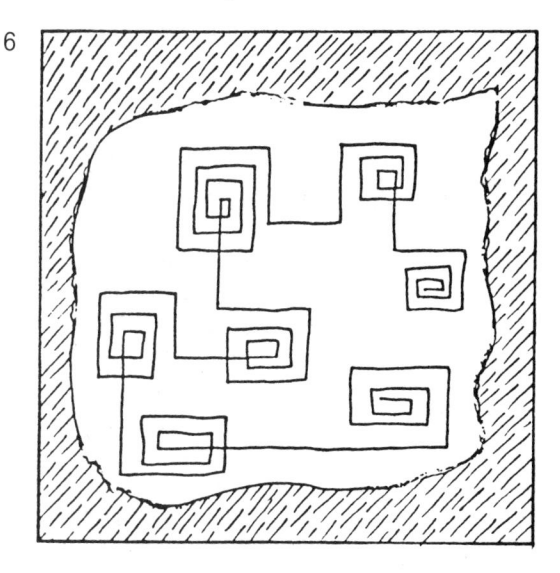

6

"Which shapes of backing paper give the best results and why?"
Ask the artist to find out why this kind of diagram or network is *traversable.*

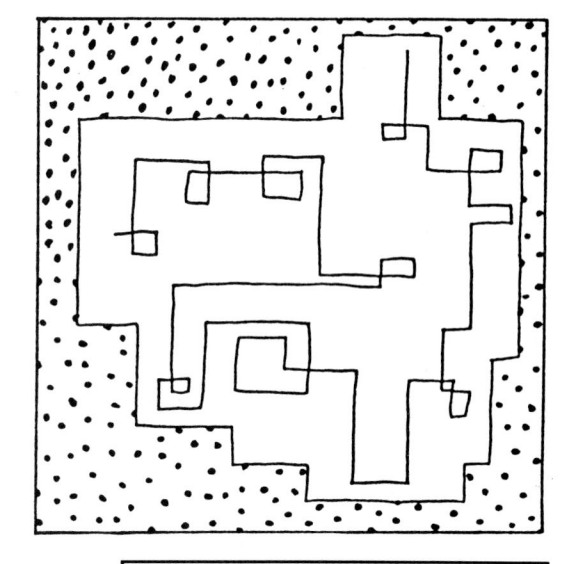

REFERENCES & RESOURCES
Gummed Paper Strips E J Arnold

HORIZONTAL AND VERTICAL 57

NAME GAMES †

MATERIALS
Two rectangles of contrasting activity paper (at least A4 size), scissors, wallpaper paste and small brush, pencil, ruler.

VOCABULARY
Rectangle, horizontal, vertical, axis of symmetry, reflection, parallel, fold, equal space, approximately, perimeter, inner, outer, coincide.

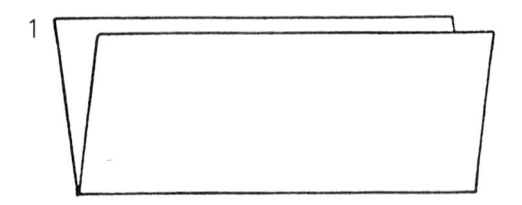

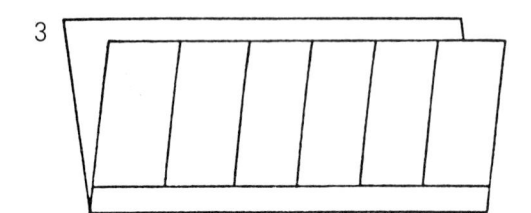

Paper-cutting skills and the use of letter forms combine to create patterns with bilateral symmetry, extending to more than one axis of symmetry.

METHOD
1. Place both sheets of paper in the 'landscape' position and fold them along their horizontal axis of symmetry (fig. 1). Put one sheet aside.
2. On the remaining sheet, rule a line about 1 cm from the fold and parallel to it (fig. 2).
3. Think of a word with a maximum of six letters — a name perhaps — and plan how much space there will be for each letter.
[It helps to mark out dividing lines for each letter in pencil (fig. 3).]
4. Plan your word in capital letters so that each letter makes a good contact with the pencil line. Make the strokes of the letters between ½ cm and 1 cm thick. Space the letters out carefully so that the gaps between them are approximately equal.
5. With the paper still folded, cut around the perimeters of the letters, *making sure that you do not detach them from the part where they adjoin the pencil line*. Some letters will have an inner and an outer perimeter (fig. 4).
6. Open up the folded word carefully to reveal the reflected word on the other side of the horizontal axis of symmetry (fig. 5).
7. Carefully paste the cutout on the 'wrong' side — that is, the side with the pencil markings — and position it on the uncut sheet of contrasting paper so that the foldlines coincide.

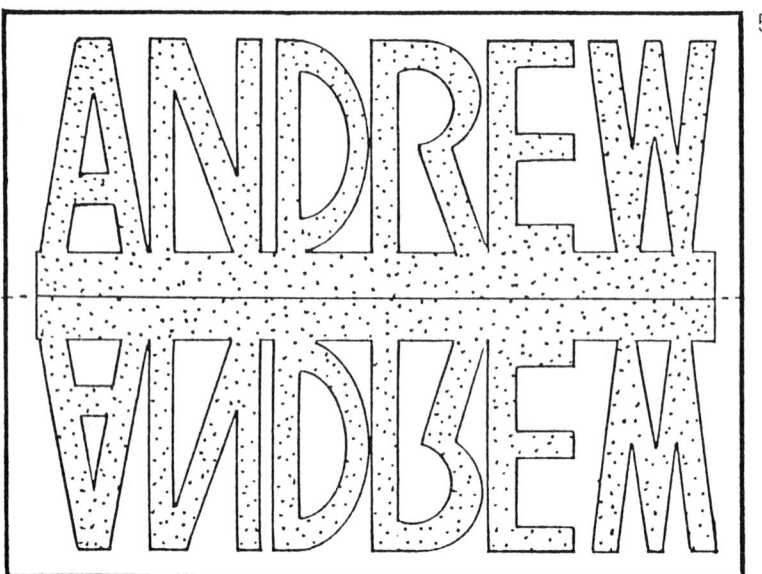

58   NAME GAMES   † *Illustrated on page 2 of the second photograph section*

TEACHING POINTS

1. If the words are displayed vertically, they are more difficult to read and offer an interesting activity. Ask the designer to write a cryptic clue to display alongside his or her word. Someone else can then try to guess the word before being allowed to read it sideways. Alternatively, make a collection of cryptic clues on a separate sheet of paper, number the mirror words on display and see if the children can match the words to the clues.
2. If the words are mounted on card, it is possible to display them propped up by flexing them along the foldline, rather like a greetings card.
3. Some children may prefer to cut away the letters instead of the surrounding area. This is done much more easily if the letters are extended to the open edges of the paper opposite the foldline (fig. 6).

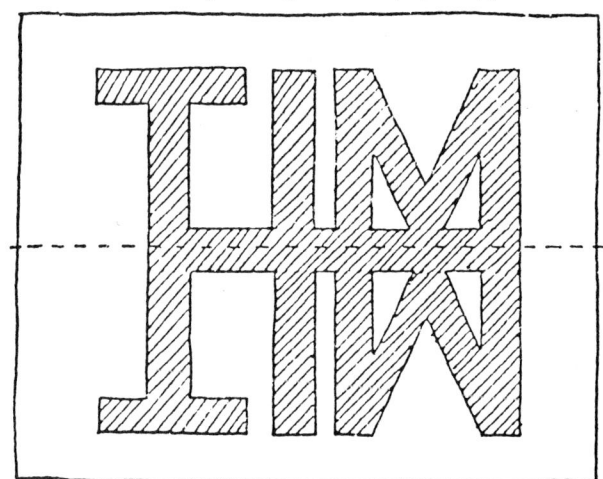

Cut out the shaded pieces and stick onto the backing sheet

EXTENSIONS AND VARIATIONS

1. If a simple word is chosen, the cut-away area can be removed carefully and reconstructed on a separate backing sheet so that two mirror-words are produced — a *positive* and a *negative* (fig. 7).
2. Encourage the children to think of words that suggest a particular style of lettering, for example, *fat* and *thin* (fig. 8). Other suitable words might be *spiky, bent, smooth, zig-zag, broad, wiggly, curvy, flash*, etc.
3. Instead of an 'upside-down' word, the technique can be adapted to make a 'back-to-front' word with a vertical axis of symmetry (fig. 9).

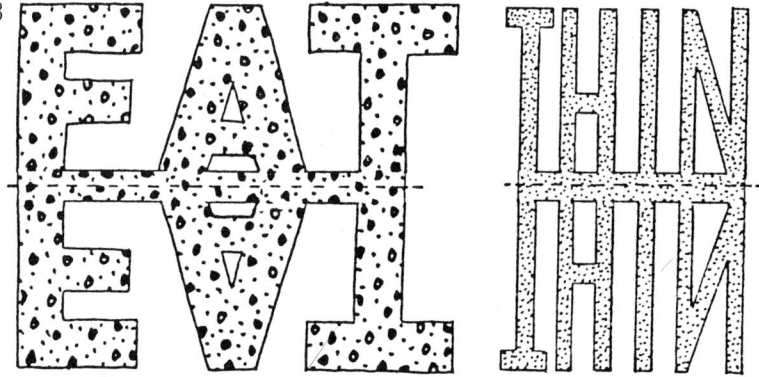

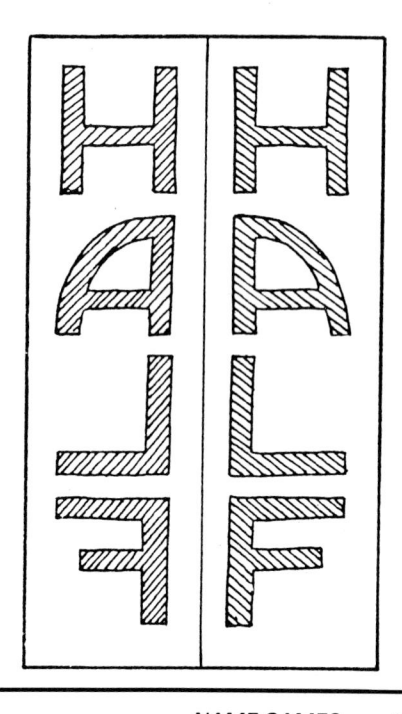

NAME GAMES

11

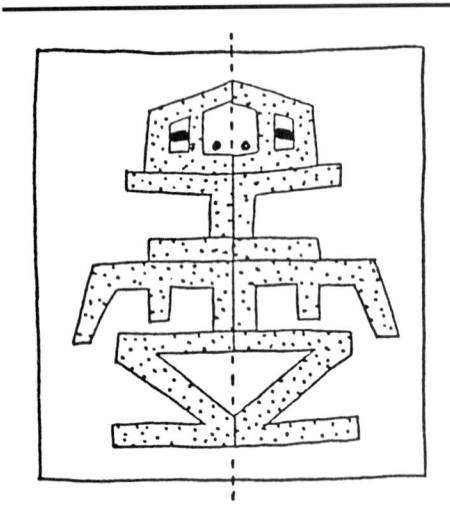

4. Encourage free experimentation by:
(a) varying the shape of the backing sheet — children can think of a suitable shape to complement their choice of word;
(b) trying multiple folds — the mirror-word in the example (fig. 10) was made by using a square sheet and two diagonal axes of symmetry;
(c) using different letter forms and handwriting styles — perhaps mounted on marbled paper;
(d) varying the overall shape of the word and the letters to give an imaginative representation of the word (fig. 11).

10

12

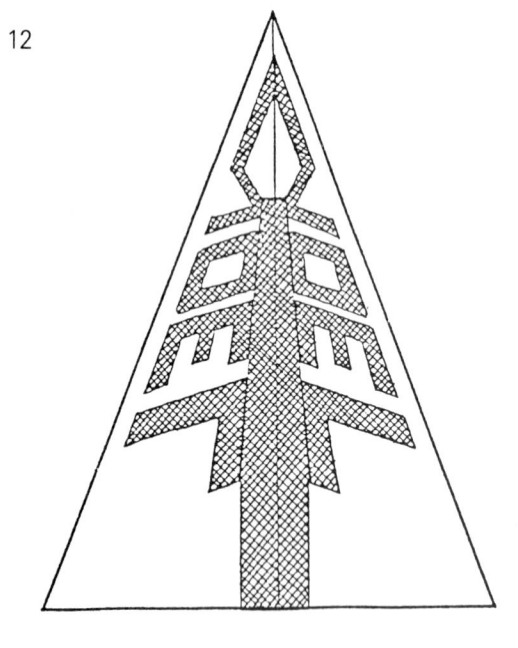

5. The mirror-word in figure 12 makes an appropriate design for a Christmas card. Ruled lines were used to give the letters a more geometric form.

6. By selecting those capital letters that have a horizontal axis of symmetry or a vertical axis of symmetry, half words can be designed on folded paper so that the complete word is revealed when the paper is opened out (fig. 13).

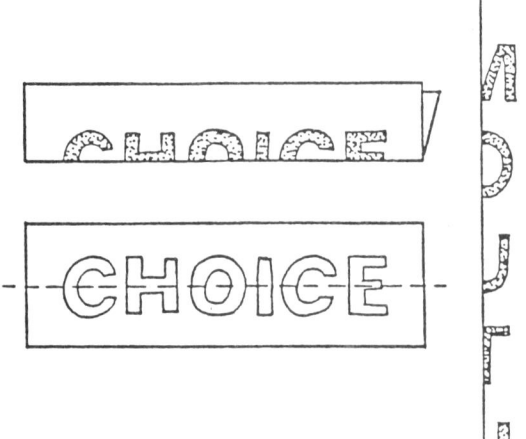

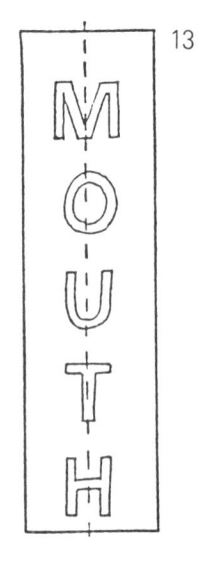

13

REFERENCES & RESOURCES
Lettercraft Tony Hart; Heinemann

Challenge the children to find the longest word with
(a) a horizontal axis of symmetry,
(b) a vertical axis of symmetry.

60 NAME GAMES

CROSS-STITCH PATTERNS †

Children are encouraged to design a blueprint or plan for a symmetrical pattern which is then interpreted on binca canvas.

METHOD
1. On the squared paper mark out in pencil a square measuring 15 cm × 15 cm.
2. Mark in the horizontal and vertical axes of symmetry to give four square quarters or quadrants.
3. With a pencil, mark in about 30 or 40 crosses in one of the quarters. To make stitching easier, arrange the crosses in blocks rather than lots of single, unattached crosses. You could decide that each cross should touch at least one other cross. (Fig. 1.)
4. When you are happy with the pattern of crosses, choose two coloured pencils or pens to match the colours you wish to use for the embroidery.
5. Go over some of the crosses with one colour and the rest with the second colour.

MATERIALS
5 millimetre squared paper approximately 20 cm by 20 cm, binca square at least 15 cm by 15 cm, tapestry needles, assorted smooth wools or soft cotton embroidery thread, tacking thread, pencil, ruler, scissors, coloured felt pens or pencils, mirror.

VOCABULARY
Symmetry, reflection ('flip over'), rotation ('turning'), translation ('sliding'), binca, quarter or quadrant.

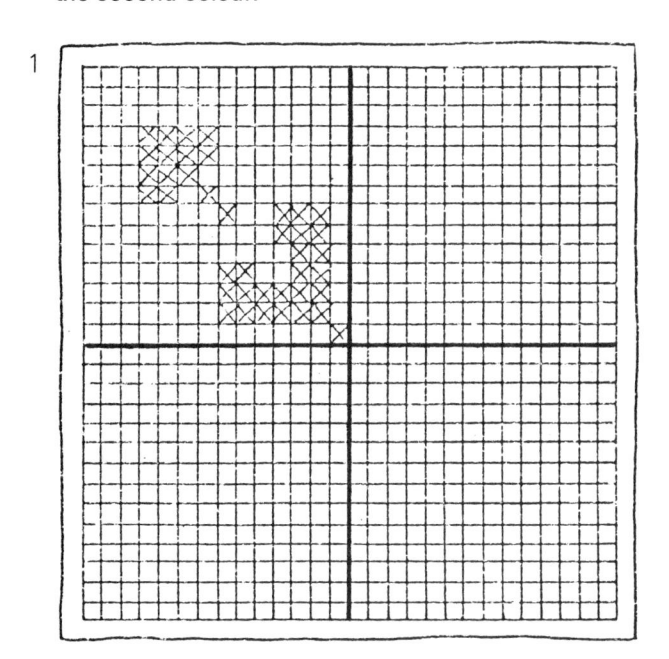

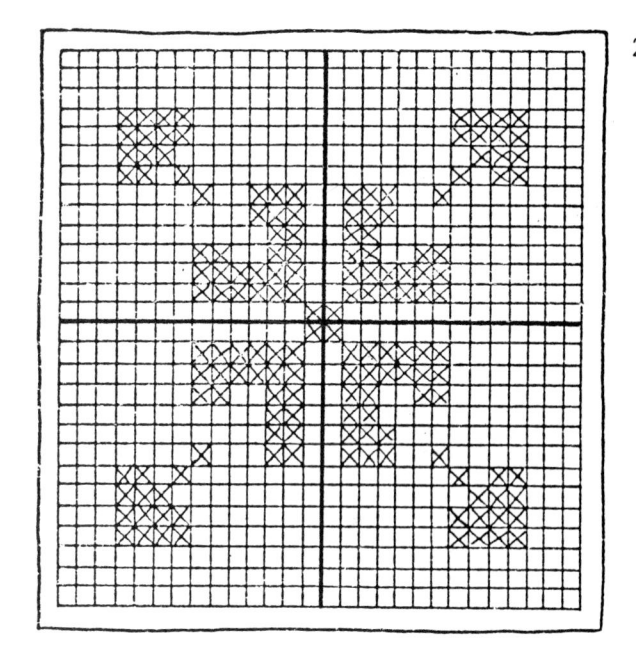

6. Reflect the design into the other quarters, first in faint pencil and then in colour. Use a mirror to check your reflected pattern as you work. The example (fig. 2) has both line and rotational symmetry.
7. When the paper pattern is complete, start transferring it to the square of binca. The points where the horizontal and vertical lines meet on the paper pattern represent the holes in the binca.
8. On the binca square, tack the axes of symmetry in running stitch to help you place the crosses correctly (fig. 3).
9. Thread a tapestry needle with one of your chosen colours of wool or soft cotton.
10. Start working the design in cross stitch in one quarter at a time. Try to make sure that the top threads of the crosses all go in the same direction.
11. Change to the second colour and complete the pattern.
12. Remove the tacking stitches.

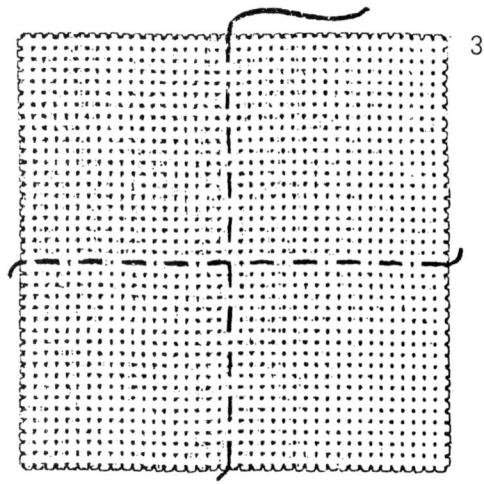

---

† Illustrated on page 1 of the second photograph section

13. Finish off the design by working a border around the perimeter. A simple hanging loop will complete the work. (Fig. 4.)

4

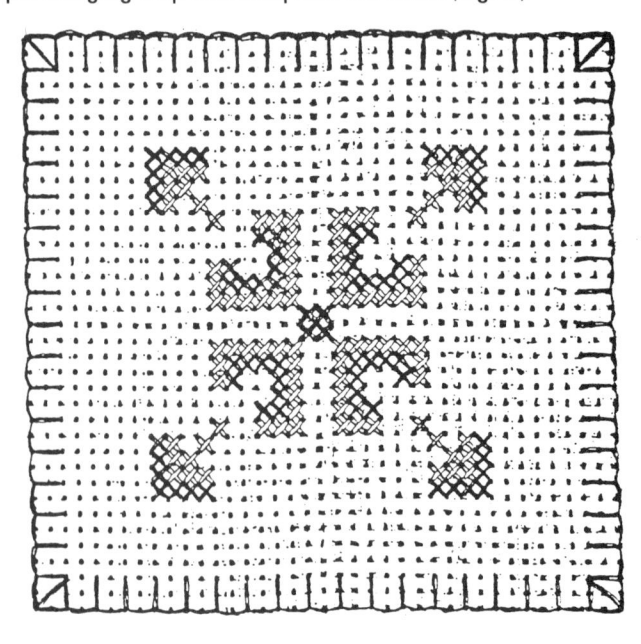

TEACHING POINTS

1. Some children may prefer to experiment initially by creating patterns on pegboards or *Centicube* or *Unifix* baseboards. Rubber bands can be used to indicate the axes of symmetry. There is also some computer software that allows patterns of this type to be designed and printed before starting the cross-stitching. (See *References and Resources* section at the end of this chapter.) Both these techniques allow modifications to be made to the design very easily.
2. Encourage children to finish off strands of wool or cotton by weaving them in and out of the threads at the back of the binca rather than by tying knots.
3. As an alternative to binca, embroidery canvas, plastic canvas or gingham can be used. To prevent gingham from puckering when stitching is applied, strengthen it with heavy iron-on interfacing or by glueing a light card backing using wallpaper paste. This would have to be done the day before it is required.
4. Tapestry wool, acrylic and pure wool are the best to use, but try to avoid nylon wool as it snarls badly. Experimental work could be attempted with synthetic raffia or lurex thread.

EXTENSIONS AND VARIATIONS

1. Some of the more enthusiastic children could be set the problem of designing a pattern that has rotational symmetry only (fig. 5). One of several ways to do this is to make sure that the design in the first 'quarter' is *asymmetrical*, i.e. lop-sided; and the more lop-sided the better. If this design is then rotated through a quarter of a turn each time it is moved to an adjoining quarter, the final pattern will have rotational symmetry of order four but no line symmetry.
2. Translation, i.e. sliding, of the design in the first quarter to each of the other quarters can also be investigated (fig. 6).

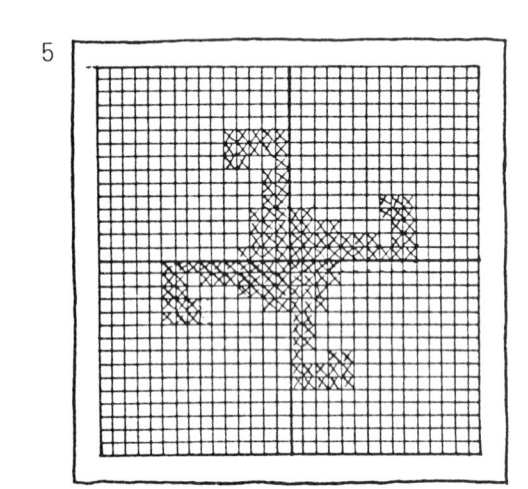

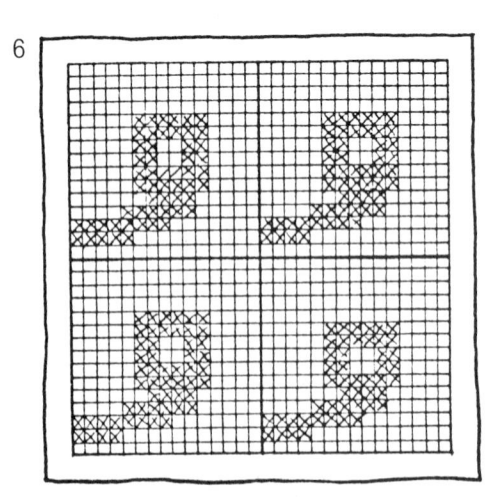

5

6

CROSS-STITCH PATTERNS

7

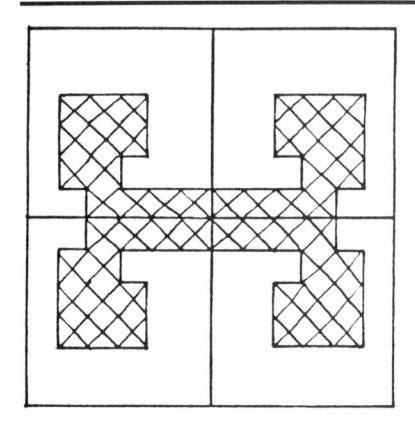

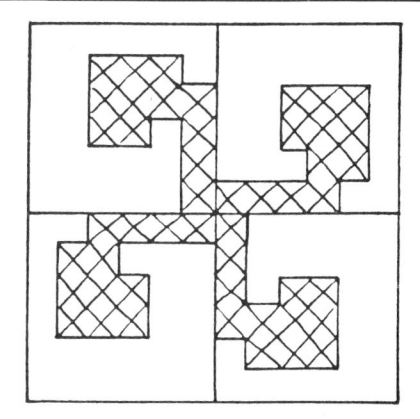

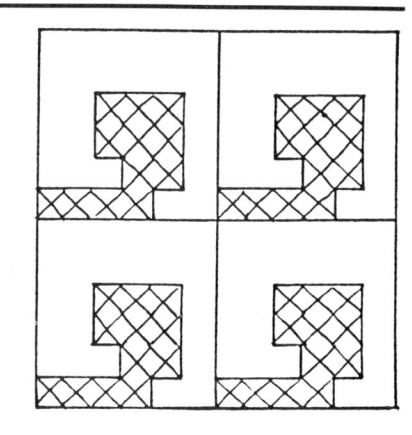

3. An interesting activity for a small group arises when they design and agree upon a motif which is then *reflected*, *rotated* and *translated* by three different 'artists' so that the effects can be compared (fig. 7).
4. A computer design package such as *Mosaic* offers an alternative way of creating a plan for cross-stitching, allowing many examples to be tried without it becoming tedious.
5. Design, or get a child to design, a simple computer graphic motif using Logo, for example, which could be interpreted by cross-stitching.
6. There is no reason why designs should not be created with only one axis of symmetry — horizontal or vertical (fig. 8). Some children may enjoy using either one or two diagonal axes of symmetry.

8

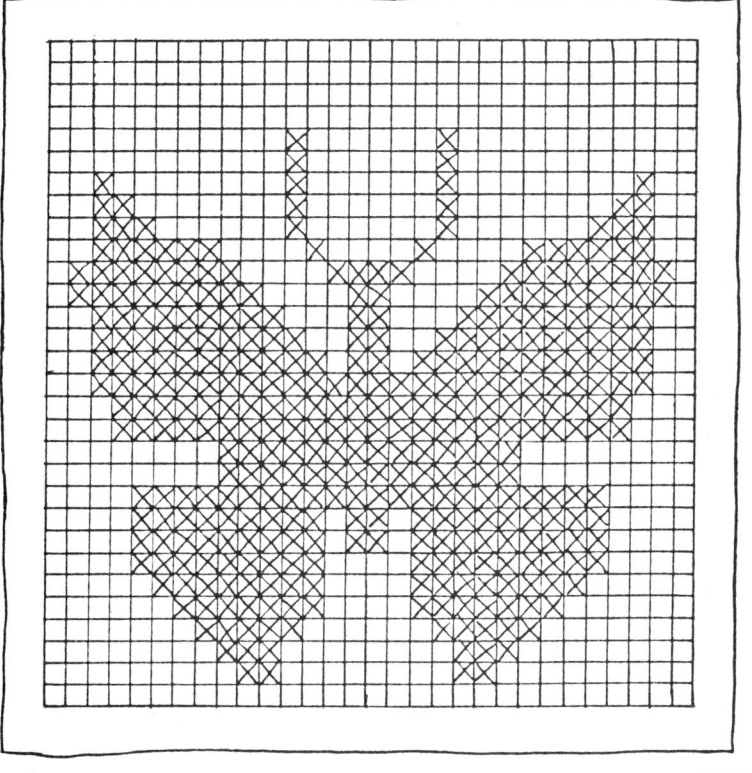

REFERENCES & RESOURCES
Mosaic A computer program by Paul Spurgeon/AUCBE, Herts Local Education Authority.

TANGRAM 1 †

MATERIALS
Tangram master, backing sheet, scissors, wallpaper paste, small brush or spreader.

VOCABULARY
Square, parallelogram, quadrilateral, polygon, triangle, isosceles, right-angled, small, medium, large, area, surface, match, dissect.

Although the basic activity uses the popular Chinese Tangram in a conventional way as a means of considering the conservation and redistribution of area, many ideas, both mathematical and artistic, are suggested for further development later in the chapter.

The tangram puzzle was invented in China over 4000 years ago. The puzzle requires the seven pieces to be used to create an arrangement according to these simple rules:

(a) all seven pieces must be used,
(b) no pieces should overlap.

METHOD

1. Look at the tangram carefully and try to name all the different shapes that go to make up the large square (fig. 1).
2. From your tangram sheet cut out the seven pieces along the cutting lines.
3. Jumble the pieces up and then try to re-arrange them back into the square you started with. (If you find this difficult, look at the starting diagram.)
4. Experiment with arranging pieces on the backing sheet (remember the rules!) until you make a design you like. A few examples are given in figure 2.
5. Glue down the pieces using wallpaper paste.
6. Think of a name for your design and label it.

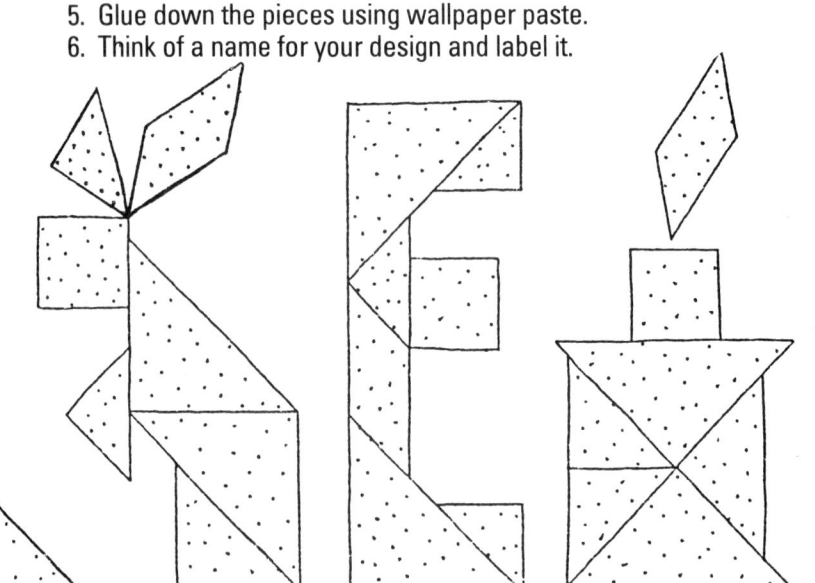

TEACHING POINTS

1. Before tackling this activity, have available some 'heavy duty' tangrams made of stout card or plastic. (It may be possible to get a sympathetic craft teacher, parent or older pupil to make some tangram kits out of wood.) Tangrams provide an excellent source of investigational material which can be linked with several mathematical topics such as symmetry, angles, polygons, fractions and area. It is up to the teacher to extract as much mathematics as possible from the puzzle whilst at the same time encouraging the creative aspect of the activities.

2. Ensure that the children learn the names of all the polygonal pieces and allow opportunities to investigate their properties. This can include classifying the shapes in as many ways as possible.

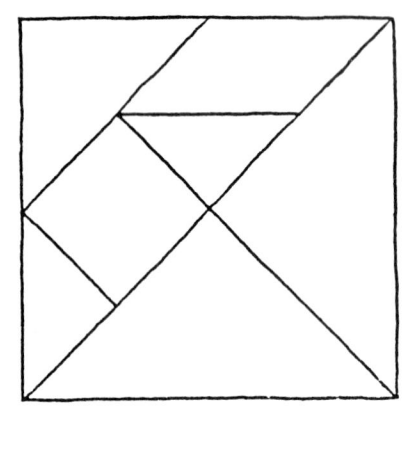

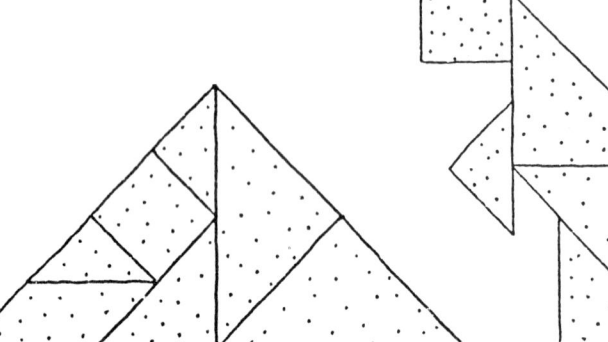

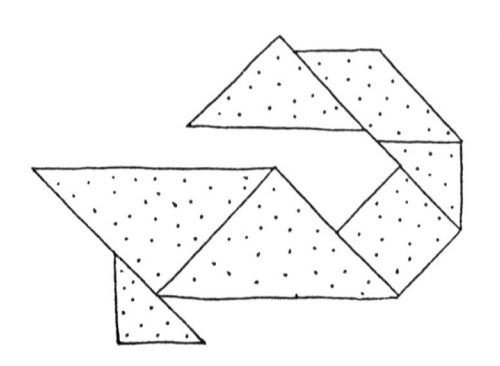

† *Illustrated on page 3 of the second photograph section*

3. An interesting and useful activity is to sort the seven pieces into 'Yes' and 'No' categories using such criteria as *"Is the shape a triangle?"*; *"Does the shape have an axis of symmetry?"*; *"Does the shape have parallel sides?"*; *"Are all the sides of the shape equal?"*; *"Does the shape have a right angle?"*; etc. A simple Carroll diagram makes an effective display for this activity (fig. 3).

This type of activity is best carried out by small groups working co-operatively so that there is a rich interaction of mathematical language.

Alternatively, one person in the group decides secretly on a form of classification, displays it on the Carroll diagram and asks the rest of the group to say how the pieces have been sorted.

4. The dissection of the tangram provides a perfect opportunity to discuss and demonstrate *conservation of area*. The tangram patterns can be displayed to reinforce the concept.

EXTENSIONS AND VARIATIONS

1. How quickly can a jumbled tangram be re-assembled into a square
(a) copying from another diagram, or
(b) relying on memory?
Hold a friendly competition to find the 'Tangram Champion', using a timer and a results board.

2. Make an overhead projector transparency of the tangram, dissect it and use it for some memory games. For example, in its 'square setting' remove one piece before switching on the OHP and ask which piece is missing, or jumble up six of the pieces and ask for the missing piece to be named. It is important to encourage correct, unambiguous language such as 'small triangle', 'medium triangle', 'large triangle', 'square' and 'parallelogram' when playing these games.

Alternatively, a set of 'heavy duty' tangram pieces can be placed in a 'feelie bag' and classified by touch.

3. There are several ways to enliven tangram diagrams.

(a) If the tangram picture is mounted on a backing sheet of marbled paper, additional interest and atmosphere are created. See the *TECHNIQUES AND MATERIALS* section for instructions for marbling paper (page 114).

(b) A simple line drawing in character with the tangram design can enhance it (fig. 4).
(The books by Susan Johnson listed in the *References and Resources* section at the end of this chapter use this technique to good effect.)

(c) If the pieces of the tangram are positioned on a plain backing sheet, then sprayed with an aerosol spray, an interesting effect is achieved. This is particularly striking if black paper is used with a gold or silver spray. If you use a tangram cut from light card you may have to secure the pieces temporarily with some plastic adhesive, otherwise the spray will blast the pieces out of position! Alternatively, use a spray diffuser or paint stippling.

(d) Fabric crayons can also be used to 'iron on' the tangram shapes. (See page 35.)

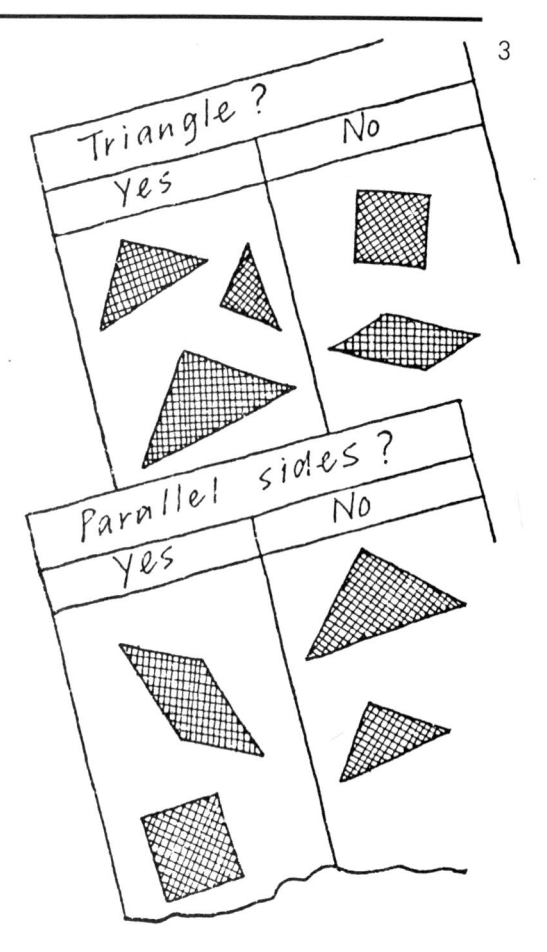

(e) The exotic parrot in the photograph section was created by colouring each piece of the tangram a different colour before cutting it out. A simple cloze procedure can be linked with this variation to reinforce the names of the polygons (fig. 5). (No connection with the parrot!)

5

```
I have coloured:
the small triangles _ _ _ _ _ _ _ and _ _ _ _ _ _ _ _
the medium triangle _ _ _ _ _ _ _
the large triangles _ _ _ _ _ _ _ and _ _ _ _ _ _ _ _
the parallelogram _ _ _ _ _ _ _
the square        _ _ _ _ _ _ _
```

4. Some children may enjoy constructing large and small tangrams for themselves. The construction lines can be worked out using a 4-unit square. If an example of figure 6 is provided as a master, and square grids of different dimensions are available, a variety of tangrams can be made, requiring measuring skills and the accurate use of a ruler. Perhaps a 'tangram family' could be made.

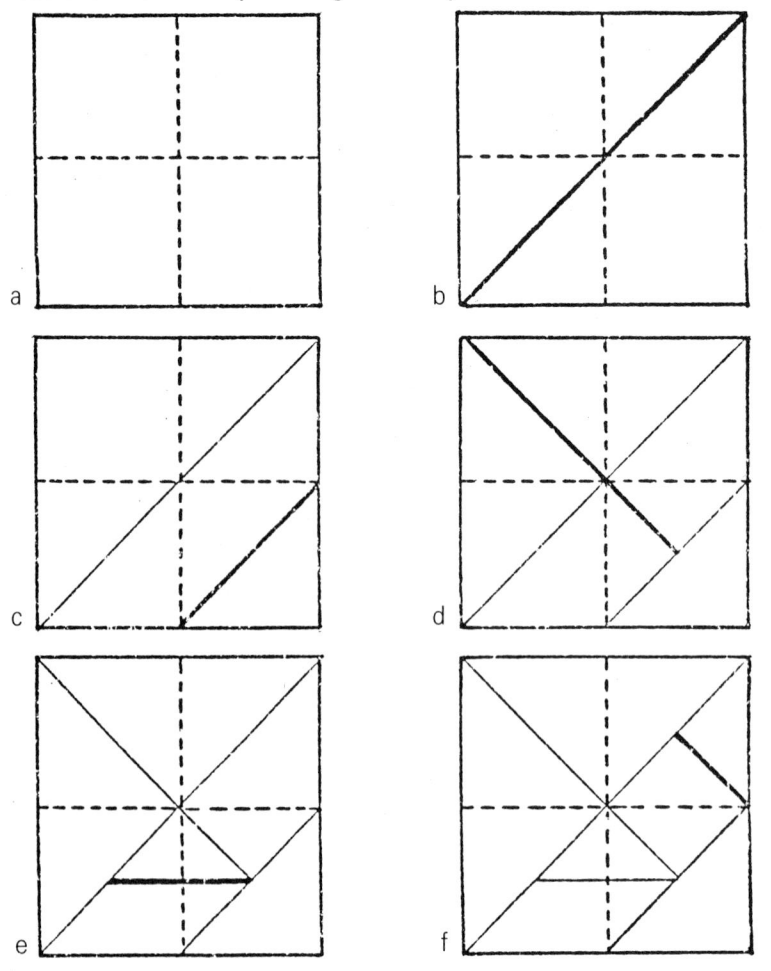

6

a b

c d

e f

REFERENCES & RESOURCES
Tangrams — 330 puzzles Ronald C Read; Dover Publications
Tangram Joost Elffers; Penguin Books
The Tangram Tree Poster The Mathematical Association
Tangram Puzzles 2 plastic tangrams and 20 graded workcards; Hestair Hope Ltd
Tangrams ABC Kit Susan Johnson; Dover Publications
The Fun with Tangrams Kit Susan Johnson; Dover Publications
Tangram Boxed Game plastic tangram and 70 playcards; Creative Toys
Tangram Shapes precut tangrams; Philip and Tacey.

AREA 3 †

By encouraging children to colour the same amount of surface of paper but in different designs, this chapter concentrates on the redistribution and conservation of area using different types of grids.

MATERIALS
Squared and isometric paper, coloured crayons, pens or paint; ruler, pencil.

METHOD
1. On squared paper, draw several rectangular 'flags' four squares long and three wide.
2. Design as many different flags as you can where half of the flag is one colour and the other half is a different colour. Make sure that the two colours each cover the same amount of surface. (Fig. 1.)

VOCABULARY
Isometric grid, equilateral triangle, surface, half, equal area, rectangle, rectangular, rhombus, rhombic, parallelogram, symmetrical, asymmetrical, polyhedron, polyhedra.

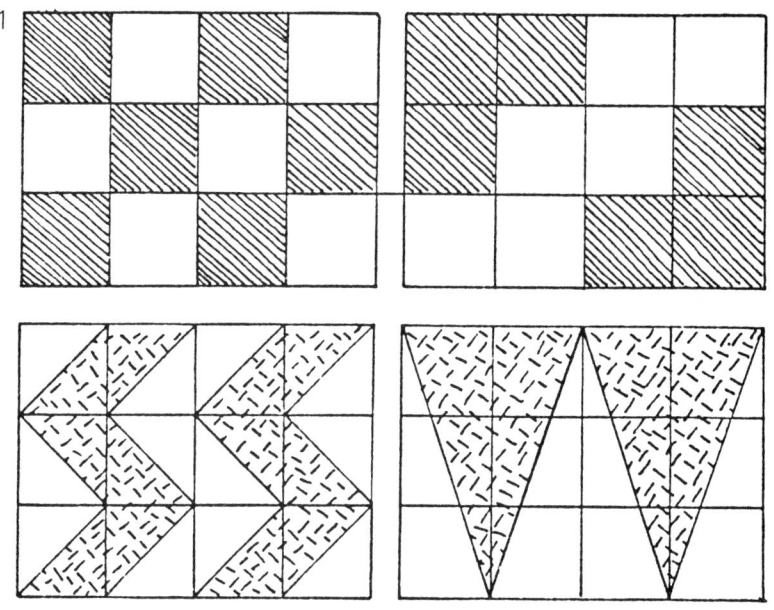

3. Now use isometric grid paper to design triangular flags in two colours, each covering the same amount of surface (fig. 2).

† *Illustrated on page 1 of the second photograph section*

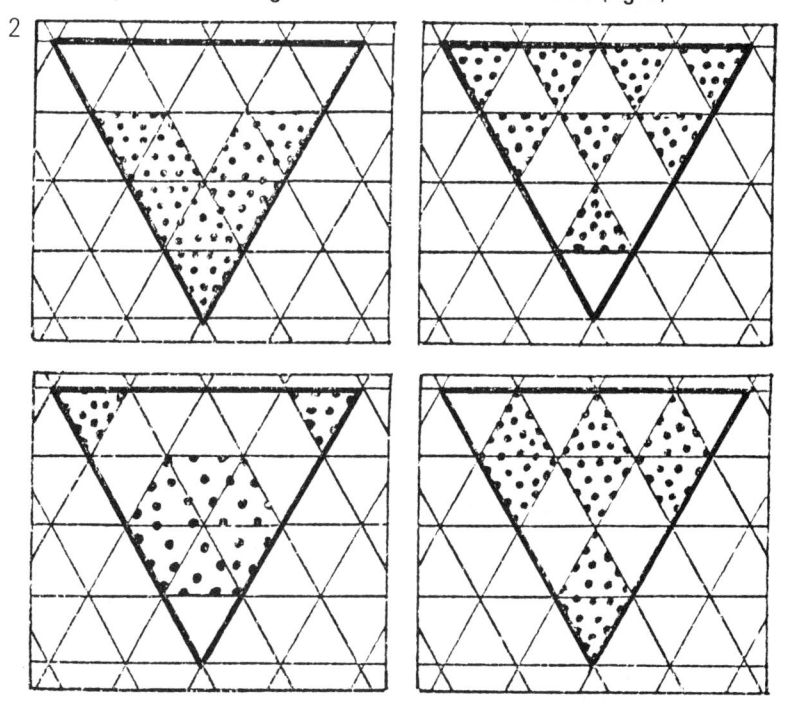

3

TEACHING POINTS
1. Make sure that the children follow the rule 'half in one colour and half in another colour' and appreciate that the two areas are the same although they may be different in shape.
2. Some children may be ready to design flags in four colours, devoting a quarter of the surface to each colour.

EXTENSIONS AND VARIATIONS
1. Another way to emphasise the idea of different shapes with the same area is to encourage the children to investigate *polyiamonds* (fig. 3) which are formed by joining equilateral triangles together. They may have already met *polyominoes* which are formed by joining squares.

Each type of polyiamond is given a name indicating how many triangles are used to make it. Reflections and rotations of the same shape are not allowed.

Children can see how many different polyiamonds of each type they can make, either by drawing on isometric grid paper or by manipulating equilateral triangles made from plastic or card. For example, can they make all twelve hexiamonds? If so, can they sort them into symmetrical and asymmetrical shapes?

Again, it is important to emphasise that all the pentiamonds, for instance, have the same area although they may have different shapes.

See *Sources of Mathematical Discovery* for more information on polyominoes (pages 74–81) and polyiamonds (pages 84–88).

1. Moniamond

1. Diamond

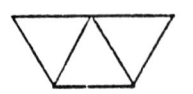

1. Triamond

3. Tetriamonds

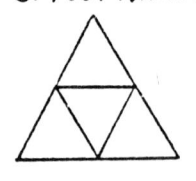

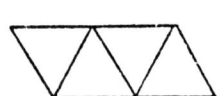

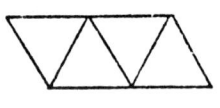

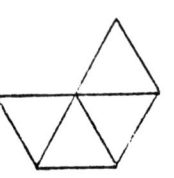

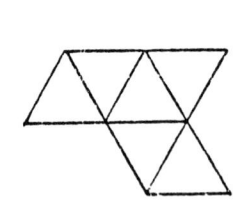

12. Hexiamonds

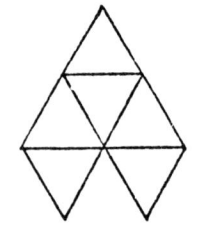

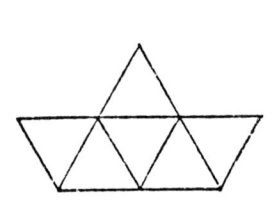

4. Pentiamonds

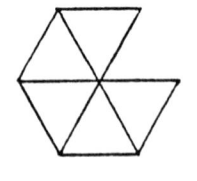

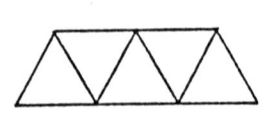

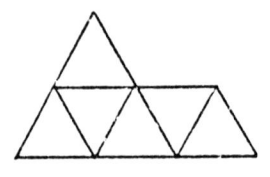

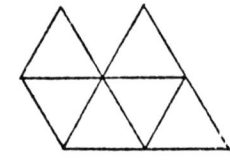

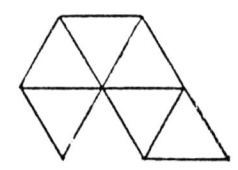

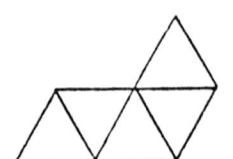

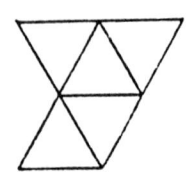

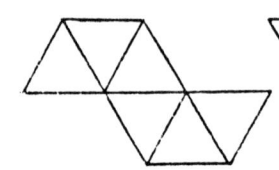

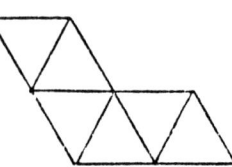

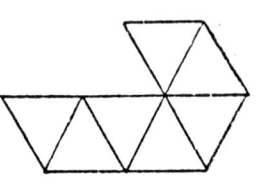

68   AREA 3

2. Encourage children to experiment in making their own grids, using the method outlined in *Teaching points* 4 of *AREA 2*. For example:

"Can you make rhombic or parallelogram grids in different sizes?"

"What happens if the lines are spaced at 2 cm intervals in one direction and at 3 cm intervals in another direction?"

"What are the correct names of the shapes created?"

Get the children to check that the two shaded shapes on each grid have the same area (fig. 4) and then to design other pairs with equal area but different shape.

Some interesting grid patterns can arise and these can be decorated to highlight any symmetries.

(C.f. Islamic designs and *Altair Design Pads*.)

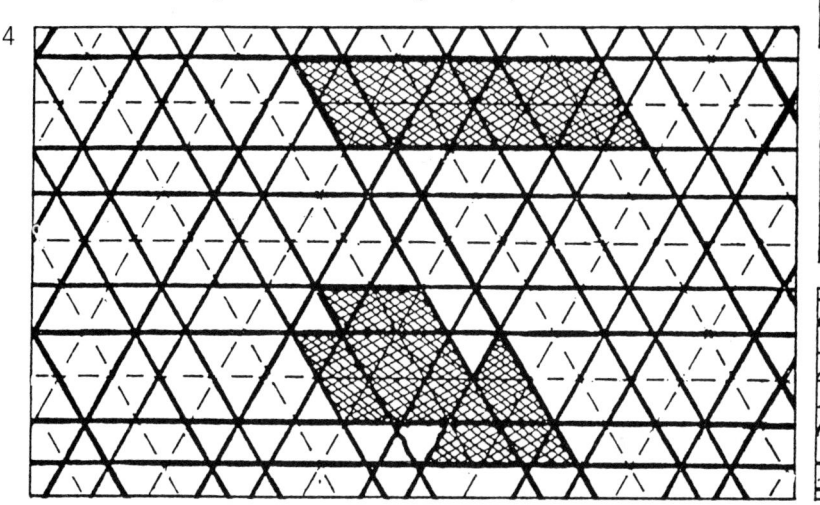

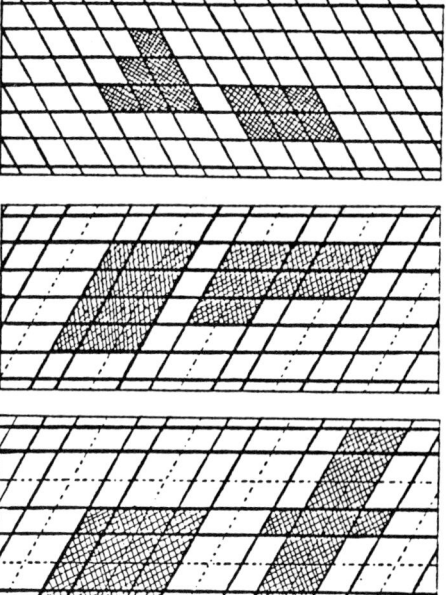

4

3. Show the children a tetrahedron (four triangular faces) or a hexahedron (six triangular faces) made from *Clixi* or *Polydron* (fig. 5).

"Can a net be designed on isometric grid and constructed so that it is the same size as the model?"

"Is there more than one possible net?"

"What other polyhedra can be made using equilateral triangles as faces?"

5

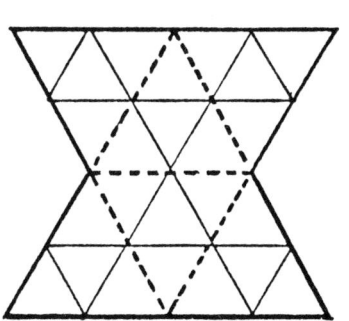

REFERENCES & RESOURCES
Sources of Mathematical Discovery
L Mottershead; Basil Blackwell
Altair Pads Longman
Takehalf A computer program (BBC, RML); SMILE (The first 31); ILEA Learning Resources Branch

AREA 3

SHADOWSHAPES 2 †

MATERIALS
Square of cartridge paper with sides about 20 cm long, crayons, pastels or coloured pencils, card scrap, scissors, circular protractor, self-adhesive stickers (optional), brass paper fastener.

VOCABULARY
Centre, rotate, centre of rotation, template, stencil, perimeter, circumference, rotational symmetry.

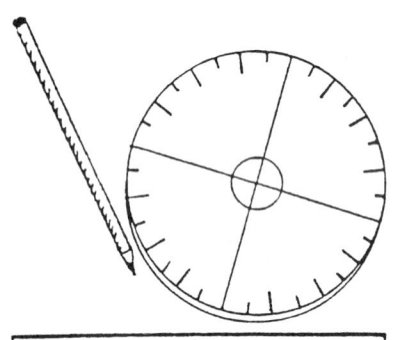

This chapter builds on the earlier simple work in *SHADOWSHAPES 1*, this time using more sophisticated ways of marking out the angles of rotation.

METHOD
1. Mark the centre of the cartridge paper square.
2. Using a circular protractor, mark off ten equally spaced points (that is, every 36°) around the circumference of the protractor (fig. 1).
3. Cut out a simple template from scrap card and push a brass paper fastener through the point about which you want the shape to rotate (fig. 2).
4. Push the paper fastener through the centre of the square of cartridge paper so that the template is free to rotate.
5. Mark a reference point on the edge of the template (not too near the fastener) and line it up with one of the 36° marks (fig. 3).
6. Trace round the perimeter of the template using a hard or soft 'flicked' edge or a mixture of both.
[Experiment first to decide which sort of edge you prefer (fig. 4).]
7. Rotate the template so that the reference point lines up with the next 36° mark (fig. 5).
8. Retrace the template outline in the new position.
9. Repeat steps 7 and 8 until the template has returned to its starting position. In the example (fig. 6), two different edges have been used alternately.

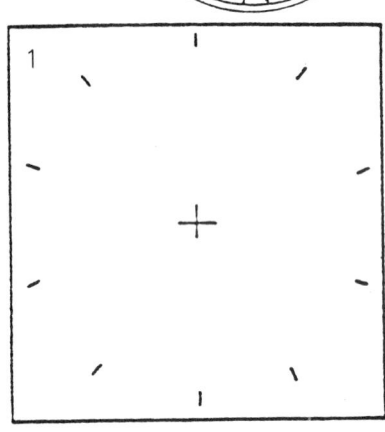

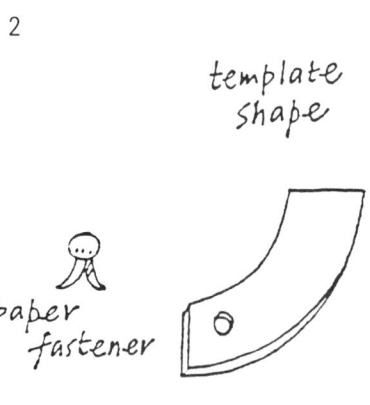

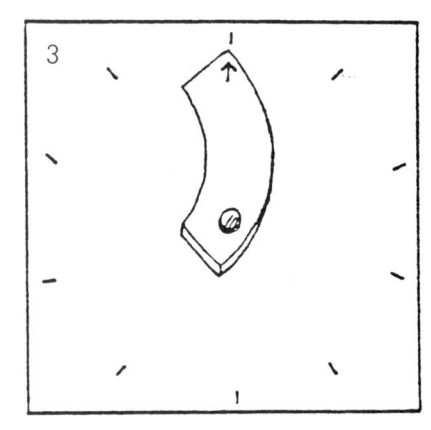

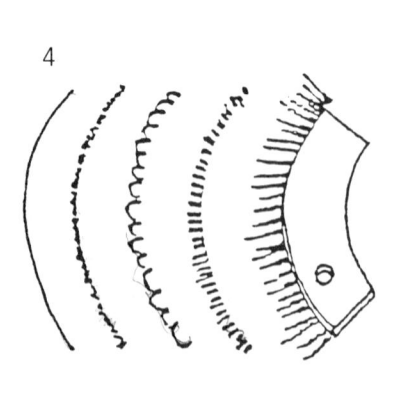

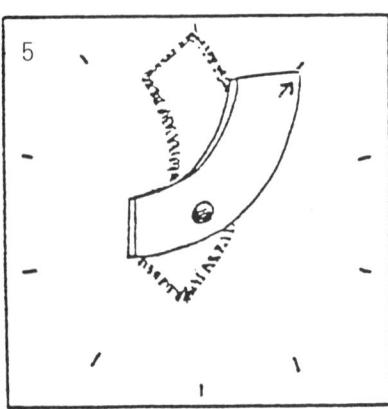

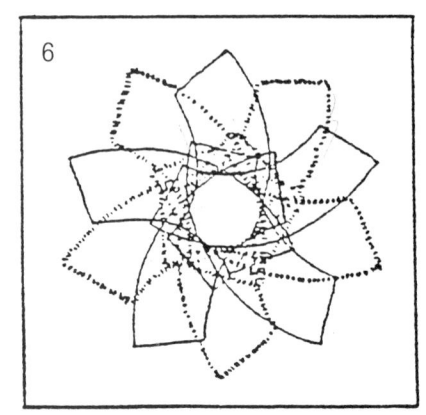

† *Illustrated on page 4 of the second photograph section*

10. Remove the template. The shapes alone make a pattern with rotational symmetry of order 10.
(Taking the different edging into account, the order of rotational symmetry of the pattern is 5.)
11. Add any extra detail or decoration you wish — coloured stickers, etc.

TEACHING POINTS
1. Although the instructions give a fairly 'safe' method, the more adventurous teacher can enhance the potential of this technique by some investigational work carried out either before or during its development. For example:
(a) *"How many ways are there of finding the centre of the square cartridge paper?"* (Step 1 of method)
(b) Experiment with a template in advance to find different ways to 'flick' in order to make hard edges or to 'mix and match' hard and soft edges on the same shape.
(c) *"What colouring sequences are possible to give a cyclic pattern?"*
2. If the final pattern is cut out carefully and secured with a fastener to a larger backing sheet, it can rotate 'windmill' fashion to highlight its rotational symmetry.
3. Devise 'fair tests' to find out:
(a) Which work best for this technique — felt pens, crayons, chalk, etc?
(b) Which types of paper respond best to crayons, felt pens, etc?
4. If children cannot use protractors, the paper folding technique described in *SHADOWSHAPES 1* on page 28 can be used. Alternatively, a selection of simplified circular templates could be made in advance (Fig. 7a).
Also, commercially produced regular polygon templates could be used to mark off the evenly spaced points (Fig. 7b).
5. *"Which angles of rotation will give an exact number of evenly spaced points?"*
In the example, rotations of 36° gave 10 evenly spaced points (36° × 10 = 360°). Had we used angles of 60°, there would be 6 points (60° × 6 = 360°), and so on. This could lead to work on the factors of 360 and discussion about how convenient 360 is for the number of degrees in a complete revolution (fig. 8).

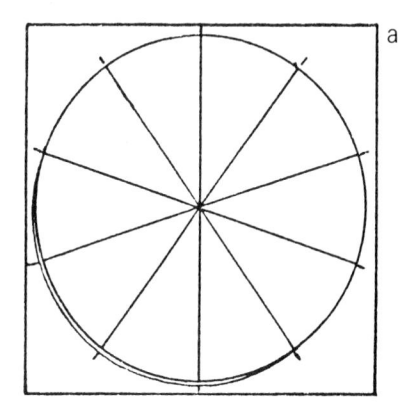

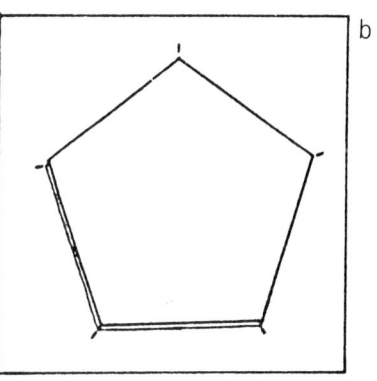

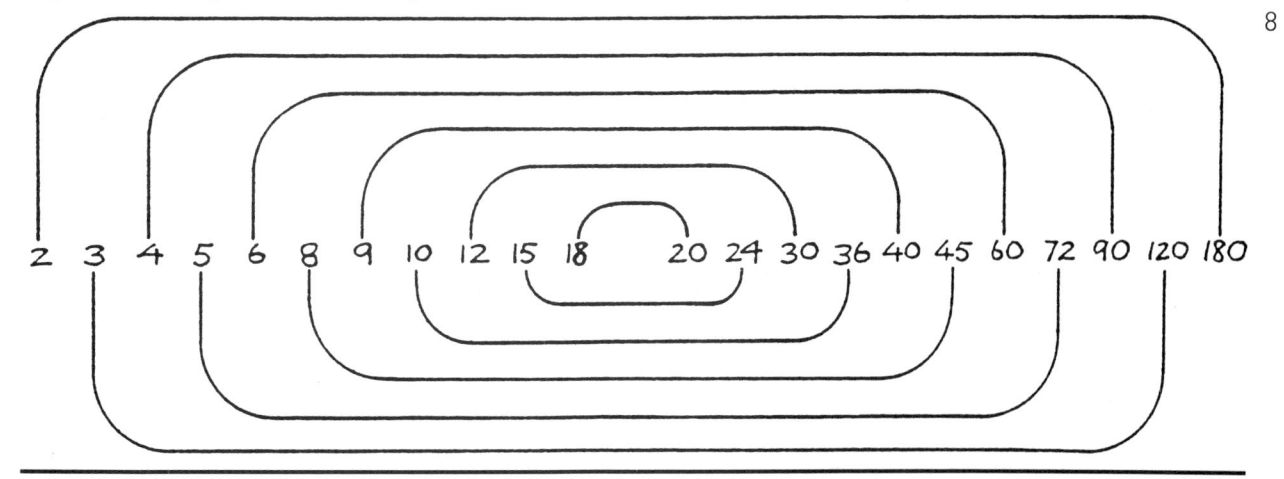

6. Using a calculator if necessary, the child could work out the sequence of degree readings for each of the possible number of evenly spaced points (step 2).

A chart could be made to show the possible sequences (fig. 9).

9

Angle Size	Sequence	order of rotational symmetry
180°	0, 180	2
120°	0, 120, 240	3
90°	0, 90, 180, 270	4
72°	0, 72, 144, 216, 288	5
60°	0, 60, 120, 180, 240, 300	6
45°	0, 45, 90, 135, 180, 225	
40°	0, 40, 80, 120	
36°		

EXTENSIONS AND VARIATIONS

1. Find as many examples as you can of natural forms such as snowflakes or flowerheads or manmade designs, logos or wheel-trims that demonstrate rotational symmetry (fig. 10).

10

11

2. Provide an example of a pattern with rotational symmetry (perhaps one of those shown in figure 10) and see if children can reproduce it by applying the knowledge and skill they have acquired.

3. So far the patterns have been two-dimensional. To give a three-dimensional effect, seeds, pasta, packaging materials, etc. can be fixed with adhesive.

4. Some interesting effects can be obtained with part rotations used freely. In figure 11, for example, the same template has been used for the petals and leaves of the flower.

REFERENCES & RESOURCES
Nature Takes Shape Ladybird
Patterns in Nature Posters Pictorial
Charts Educational Trust

SLINKY CURVES †

The basic activity involves arranging strips of paper in such a way that 'curves' are made from straight lines, but various related activities are suggested in the final part of the chapter.

METHOD
1. Glue two or three horizontal bands of paper on to the front of the gummed square. The bands can be of different widths. (Fig. 1.)
2. On the reverse side of the square, the gummed side, mark out vertically (that is, at right angles to the coloured bands on the front) parallel lines about 1 cm apart (fig. 2).
3. Cut along the pencil lines to form a series of strips.
4. Without glueing, arrange the strips on a backing sheet so that adjacent strips touch each other at one end only. To make each strip touch its next-door neighbour at one corner only without overlapping, it will have to be rotated slightly to form a fan shape (fig. 3).
5. If you wish, reverse the 'touching' and 'nontouching' ends to make a double, or even triple fan shape (fig. 4).
6. Glue down the strips to form a curved pattern made from straight lines.

MATERIALS
Bands of gummed paper 2 or 3 centimetres wide in assorted colours, 15 cm gummed squares, backing sheet, scissors, ruler, pencil.

VOCABULARY
Horizontal, vertical, adjacent, right angles, parallel, rotation, symmetry, distortion, oblong, ellipse.

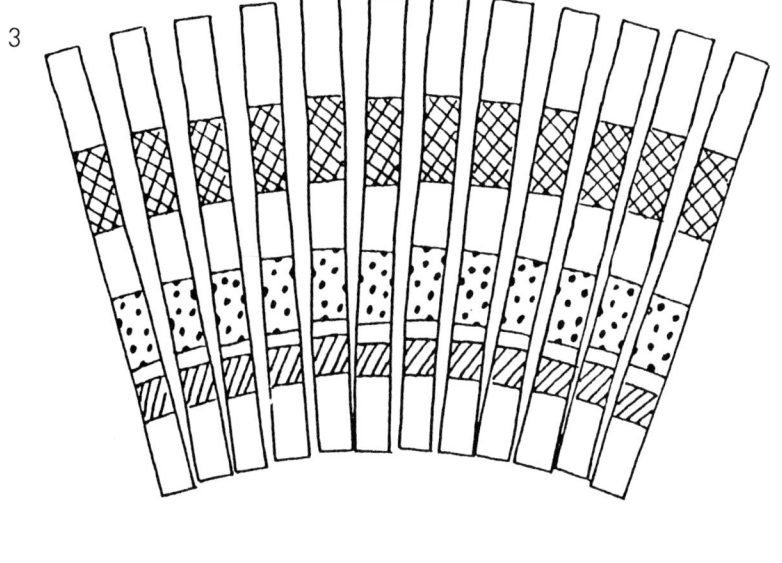

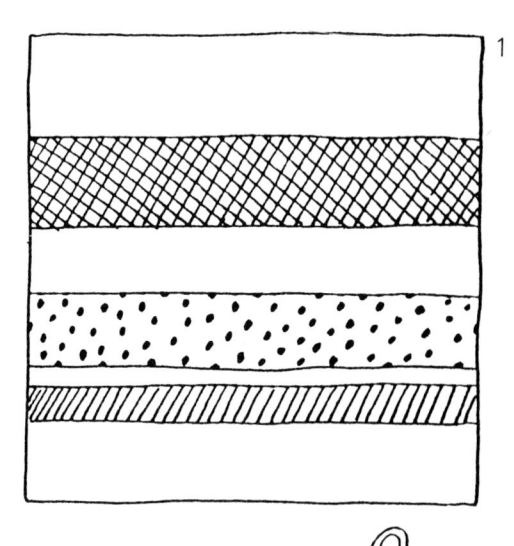

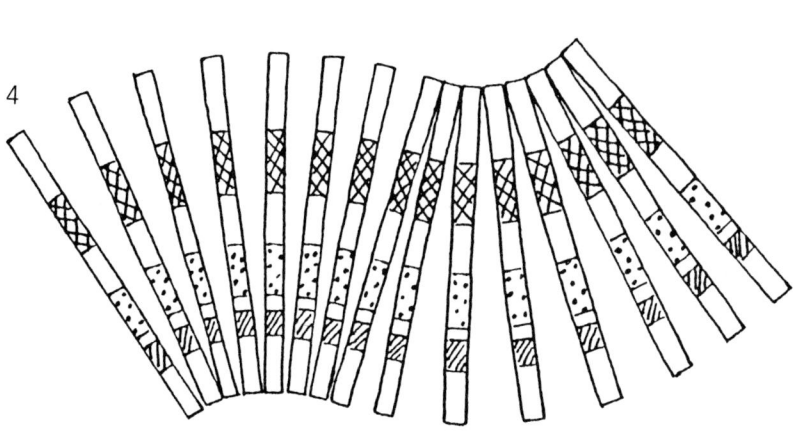

† Illustrated on page 4 of the second photograph section

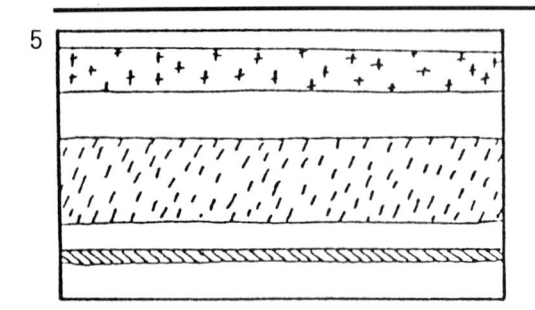

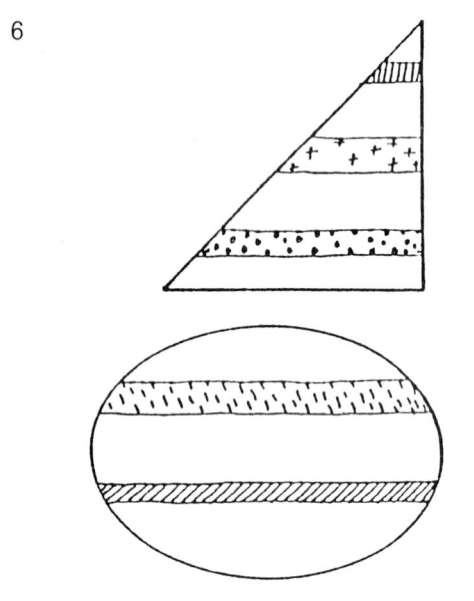

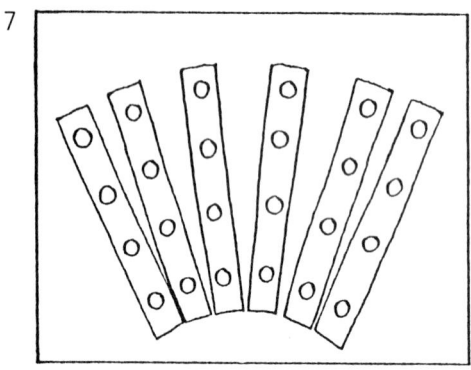

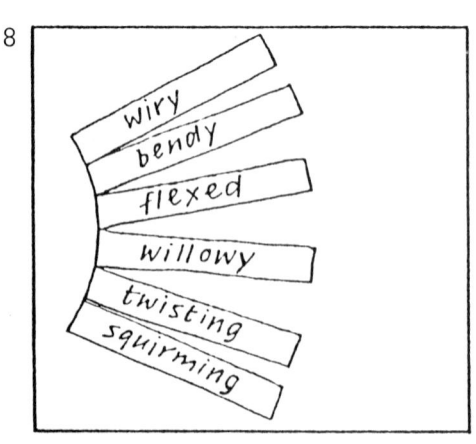

TEACHING POINTS

1. For a more 'open-ended' task, after step 3 ask the children if they can arrange the strips so that the horizontal bands form a curve.
2. It is best not to glue the strips down until all have been arranged on the backing sheet. Children will need to experiment before deciding how much to rotate each strip in order to obtain the best illusion of a curve. Placing the central strip first often helps.
3. In discussion bring out words such as rotation, symmetry and distortion, and highlight the conservation of area of the gummed square in the same way as this was dealt with in *TANGRAM 1*. Ask questions such as:
"What is a curve?"
"Where do these curves come from?"
"Are they really curves?"
4. A group of children could co-operate and experiment to see the effect of varying the amount of rotation of each strip in order to make the best curve.

EXTENSIONS AND VARIATIONS

1. *"What are the possibilities if strips of unequal length or width are used?"* (Fig. 5.)
"Does it matter if the strips are not spaced out evenly?"
"Is a square the best shape to use?"
"What would happen if we used an oblong or a triangle or an ellipse instead?" (Fig. 6.)
2. Investigate other techniques and materials, some three-dimensional, to make similar patterns; for example: ruler and pencil, drinking straws, matchsticks, Cuisenaire rods, perforated edging from computer print-out paper (fig. 7), card-edge prints, lengths of party streamers or even raw spaghetti.
3. Provide a large display sheet and get a small group of children to organise an extended slinking pattern, made from several squares or oblongs, which might just end up looking like a snake! Think of a good title or words that 'spring' to mind to describe the movement suggested by the strips:
wriggling, wiry, twisting, coiling, springy, willowy, bendy, flexible, flexed, sweeping, wavy, undulating, arching, curvilinear, kinky, curly, crinkled, winding, writhing, meandering, squirming, worm-like, serpentine, crimped, distorted, etc.
4. Select some of the words and order them according to the number of letters to produce another interesting slinky curve (fig. 8).
5. *"Is it possible to make an oblong slinky pattern with the same area as the square?"*
6. Experiment with different rules for dissecting or connecting the strips and see what happens. For example, try joining the corner of each strip to the lower coloured band of the previous strip.

74   SLINKY CURVES

7. Position two or three slanting but parallel bands on the blank square or starting shape (fig. 9). Can the children predict what will happen to these slanting bands if they proceed with the basic method.

"What is the best position for the slanting bands to get the best 'curves'?"

(This requires a systematic approach as the strips must be kept in order. If they do become muddled, it is a very good problem-solving activity trying to put them back in order!)

8. Select interesting pictures and advertisements from newspapers and magazines — faces, cars, etc. — and distort them in the same way (fig. 10).

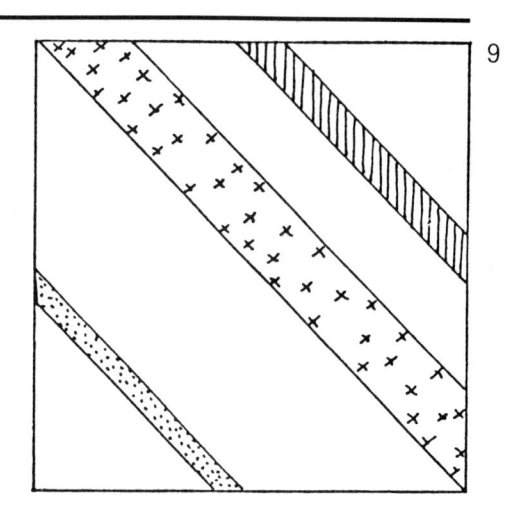

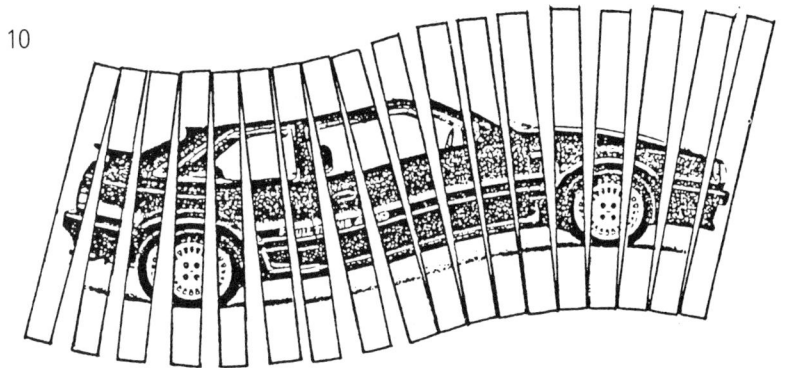

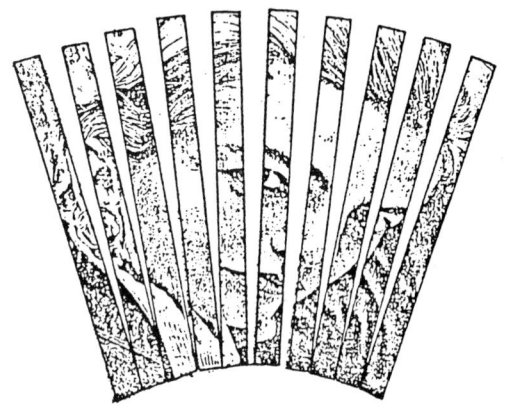

9. Another related activity would be to draw a circle using only a ruler and pencil (fig. 11). Mark the centre of the circle. Place a ruler (or rectangular piece of stiff card) so that one of its parallel sides just touches the centre mark. Draw a short line along the other parallel edge of the ruler. Move the ruler to a new position but with one edge still touching the centre mark, and draw another short line. Repeat this until a circle, with a radius equal to the width of the ruler, is completed.

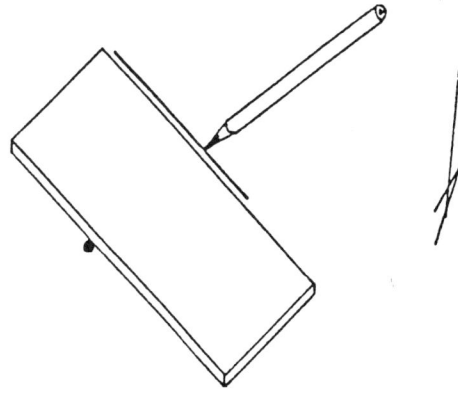

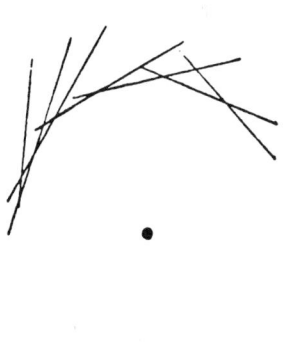

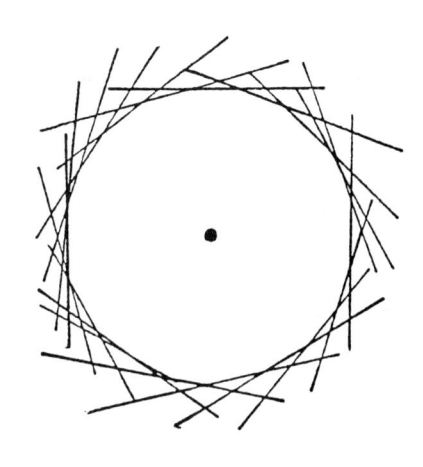

SLINKY CURVES 75

TESSELLATION 3 †

MATERIALS
Card, Sellotape, backing sheets, pencil, ruler, black pen, colouring pencils or felt pens, scissors, gummed coloured paper, tracing paper, pin, 2 sheets of 1 cm isometric triangular grid paper.

VOCABULARY
Edge, midpoint, half-turn, rotate, tessellate, tile, isometric, grid, symmetry, axis, equilateral, hexagon.

The previous two chapters on tessellation used a technique of cutting and sliding or translating from one side of a shape to the opposite side. This chapter looks at another method for creating more intricate tessellating shapes by cutting and rotating.

METHOD
Half side rotation

1. Start with a shape that tessellates (any triangle or quadrilateral, for example), draw it on card and mark the midpoint of each side (fig. 1).
2. Cut out the shape and draw an extra piece (shaded in figure 2) to be cut away from *half* of one side.
3. Carefully cut out the piece, rotate it about the midpoint of the side and add it to the other half of the same side using Sellotape (fig. 3). This new shape will tessellate as it is or you can go on to step 4.
4. Repeat steps 2 and 3 for each side of the original shape in turn, using different shaped rotating pieces if you wish (fig. 4).

[By using tracing paper to copy the piece to be rotated and a pin as a pivot at the midpoint, it is possible to draw the new shape and cut it out in one piece; but it is probably better to try this after some experience of the 'cut out, rotate and stick' method described in steps 1 to 4.]

5. Use the new shape as a template, drawing round it to create a tessellating pattern. It is easier to mark out the first outline of the shape near the centre of a piece of paper and to work outwards.

A few strokes will change this example into 'tessellating squirrels', some the right way up and others upside down (fig. 5).

76 TESSELLATION 3 † *Illustrated on page 3 of the second photograph section*

The example in figure 6 will lead to tessellating seagulls.
Some more ideas created by children are given in figure 7.

TEACHING POINTS
1. When drawing round the template it is advisable to keep the pencil vertical.
2. If thick black pens are used for the perimeters of the tiles, some of the inaccuracies in drawing and cutting are hidden.
3. Alternatively, the template can be used as a pattern to cut out pieces of gummed paper of different colours, either singly or by placing several one on top of the other — but this must be done accurately. These are then placed on a backing sheet and stuck down.

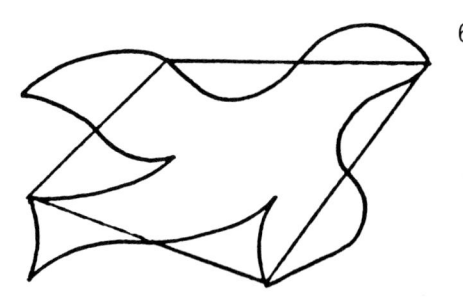

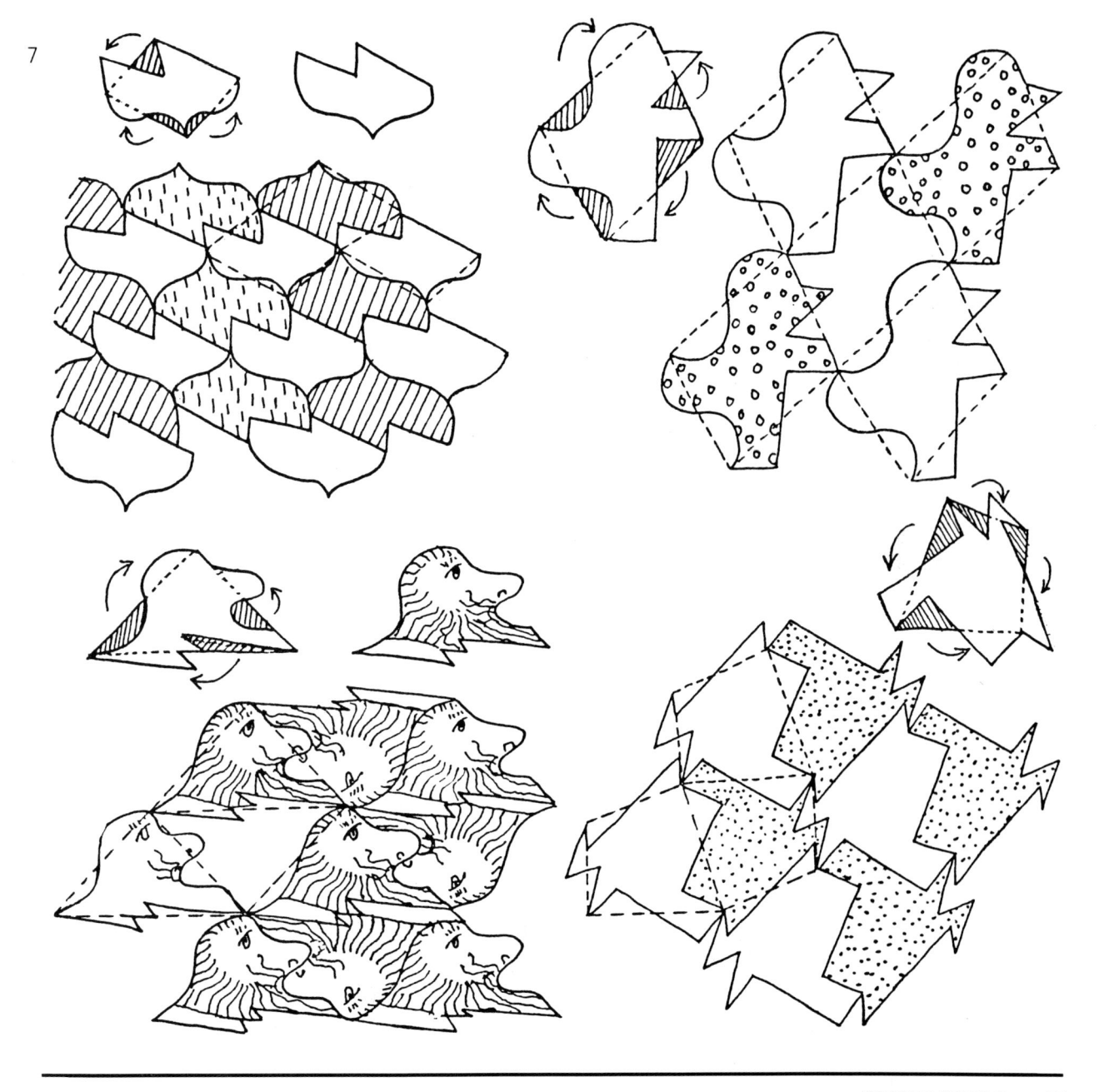

TESSELLATION 3

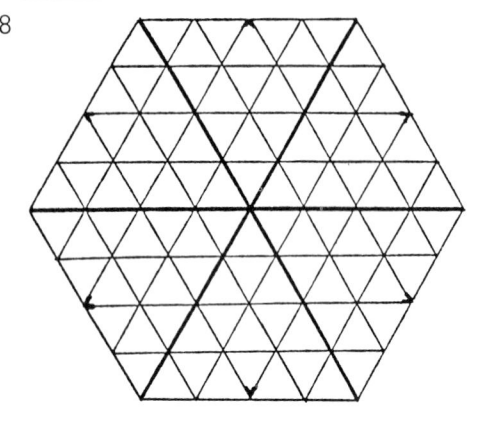

8

METHOD
Half side rotation on isometric grid — 'hexapods'
1. On one sheet of isometric grid paper mark out a regular hexagon with sides 4 cm long and cut it out.
2. Mark the midpoint of each side of the hexagon.
3. Draw the three diagonal axes of symmetry so that the hexagon is divided into six equilateral triangles (fig. 8).
4. On one of the equilateral triangles pencil along the grid lines to mark the section you are going to cut out, starting at the vertex (corner) of the hexagon and ending at the midpoint of its side (fig. 9).
5. Mark the same outline *in the same position* on each of the other five equilateral triangles (fig. 9).
6. Cut out one outlined section, rotate it through half a turn (180°) about the midpoint so that it lines up with the uncut edge of the hexagon (fig. 10).

9

10

7. Sellotape it into its new position.
8. Repeat steps 6 and 7 for each of the other five triangles.
This shape will tessellate. You can use it as a template to create a tessellating design.
9. On the blank side of your second sheet of isometric grid paper you should be able to see the triangular grid lines showing through faintly, especially if you rest it on white paper. Line up your template so that it lies within the grid lines and trace around the template lightly in pencil.
10. Remove the template and go over the pencil lines accurately using a ruler and black pen.

78   TESSELLATION 3

11. Replace the template and move it around your black outline until the 'arms' interlock without leaving a gap. Mark out the new outline lightly in pencil.

12. Repeat steps 10 and 11 until you have covered the sheet. There will be some incomplete tiles around the edges.

13. You may wish to colour your tessellation pattern. If so, think very carefully about how you are going to use the colours before you start. A good plan is to mark each shape lightly with the initial letter of the colour you are going to use. (Fig. 11.)

11

TEACHING POINTS

4. All the interlocking tiles start from the same hexagon so conservation of area can be discussed.

5. There are strong links with rotational symmetry, in this case of order 6.

TESSELLATION 3

EXTENSIONS AND VARIATIONS

1. Try using a different starting polygon on an isometric grid; for example, an equilateral triangle or a rhombus (fig. 12).

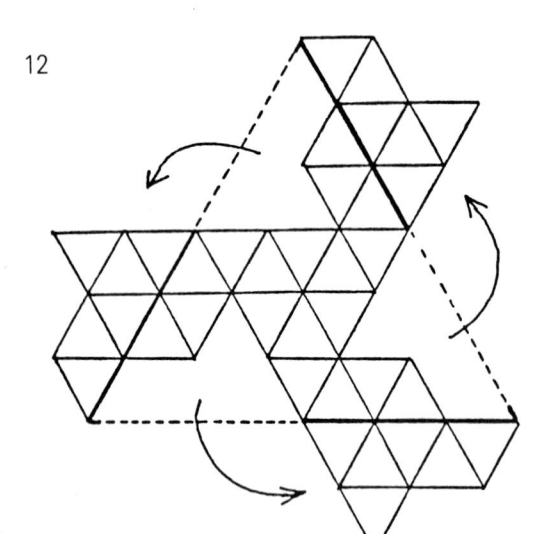

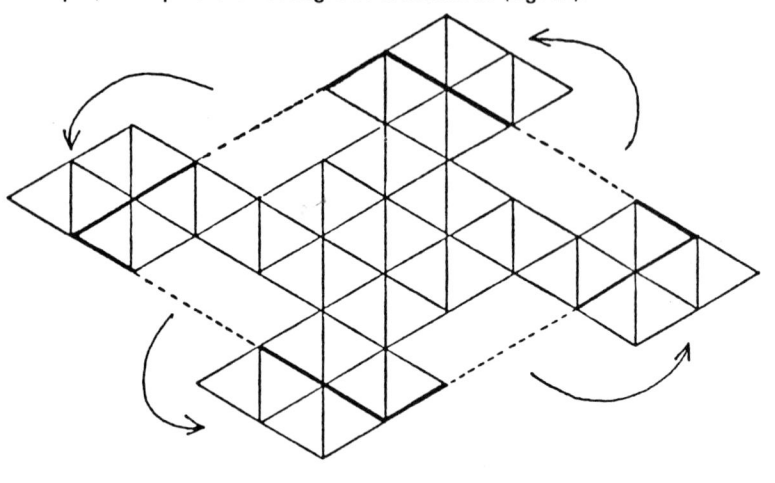

12

2. Try starting with a square on a square grid. This time there is a choice of two ways for drawing the axes of symmetry — either diagonals or medians — and swastika-like patterns can be made (fig. 13). There is an obvious link between patterns on a square grid and cross-stitch work on canvas or binca. (See *CROSS-STITCH PATTERNS* page 61.)

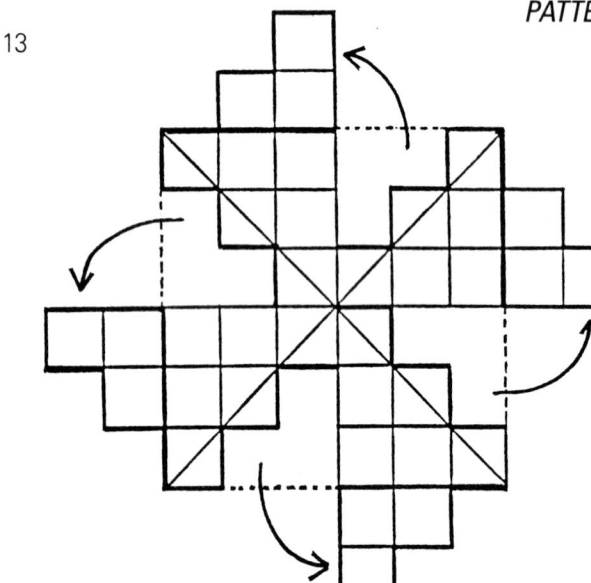

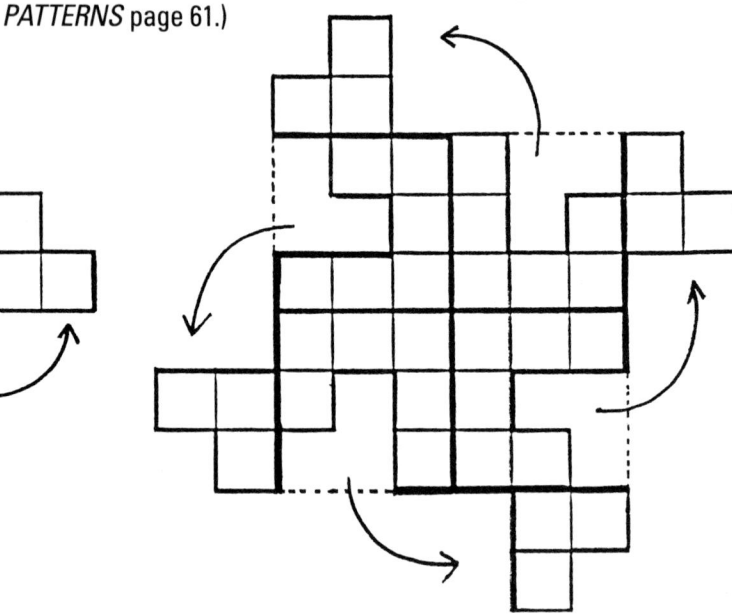

13

REFERENCES & RESOURCES
Nuffield Maths 5–11 Teachers' Handbooks Longman; Book 5, chapter 17 and Book 6, chapter 13
Do-it-yourself Tiles Article in *Mathematics Teaching* number 66; Association of Teachers of Mathematics

3. Investigations can also be carried out on other types of grids, based on the trapezium or hexagon for instance, to see whether it is possible to use this technique to develop a tile that has both rotational and line symmetry.

JACK-IN-THE-BOX †

The basic activity combines the skills of making paper springs and cubes to produce a simple toy, but also suggests experimental and investigative work which can be integrated.

METHOD
1. Glue securely, and over the whole surface, the back of the net of the *larger* cube to the 'wrong' side of the decorated paper.
2. Cut round the perimeter of the net carefully. Do not throw away the scraps you cut off.
3. Rule over the lines of the net of the cube with a ball-point pen so as to crease them. This makes sharper folds so that the cube is easier to assemble.
4. Cut out the net of the *smaller* cube in plain card and crease the edges as before.
5. As a check, fold up the nets into cubes before you glue any tabs. This will show what the finished cubes should look like.
6. (a) On the *smaller* cube, crease the edges and glue all the corresponding tabs together using PVA glue to make a closed cube (fig. 1).
(b) On the *larger* cube, leave one face unglued to act as a lid. On this open cube, glue down the loose tabs around the opening by tucking them flat and glueing them down inside the cube, *except* the one that is at the front of the lid (fig. 2).
7. Line the lid with the scraps left over from the net.

MATERIALS
Marbled paper* or coloured wrapping paper; paper spring*; PVA glue; glue spreader; ball-point pen; ruler; scissors; thread; buttons; scraps of material for collage; nets for cubes* printed on A4 card, one with edges of 6 cm, the other with edges of 3 cm. (*See TECHNIQUES AND MATERIALS at the back of this book.)

VOCABULARY
Cube, net, along, reverse, upwards, downwards, on top of, edge, fold, smaller, larger, closed, open, container, tabs, centre, front, ends, right angle, horizontal, vertical, face, perimeter, circumference.

small cube closed.

1

large cube open top.

2

† *Illustrated on page 1 of the second photograph section*

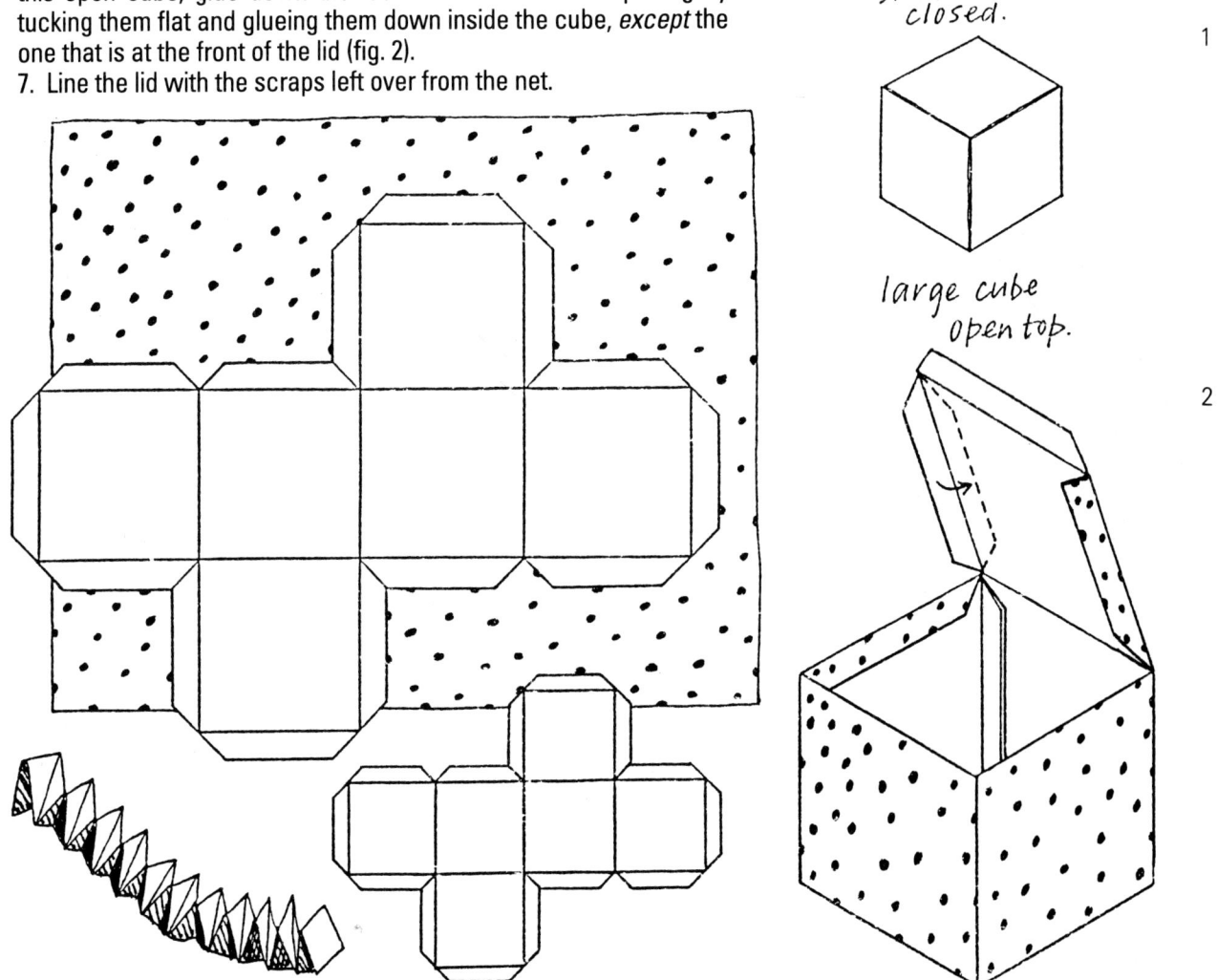

3

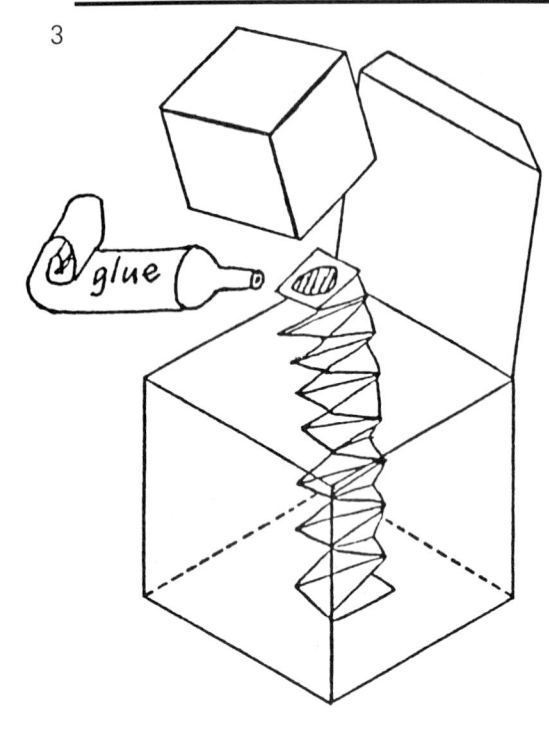

8. Glue one end of the paper spring to the centre of the inside of the base of the large cube (fig. 3).
9. Glue the small cube to the other, free end of the paper spring.
10. Decorate the small cube to look like a head facing away from the hinge of the box, using beads, buttons, felt fabric, feathers, wools, crayons, etc. (You may prefer to do this *before* attaching it to the spring.)
11. Make a thread loop, of about 4 cm circumference (or use a small rubber band), and glue it to the inside of the lid so that it hangs down over the unglued edge when 'Jack' is inside the box with spring compressed.
12. Glue a bead on the front of the box so that the loop on the lid fastens over it (fig. 4). (Small cube-shaped beads are particularly effective.)

4

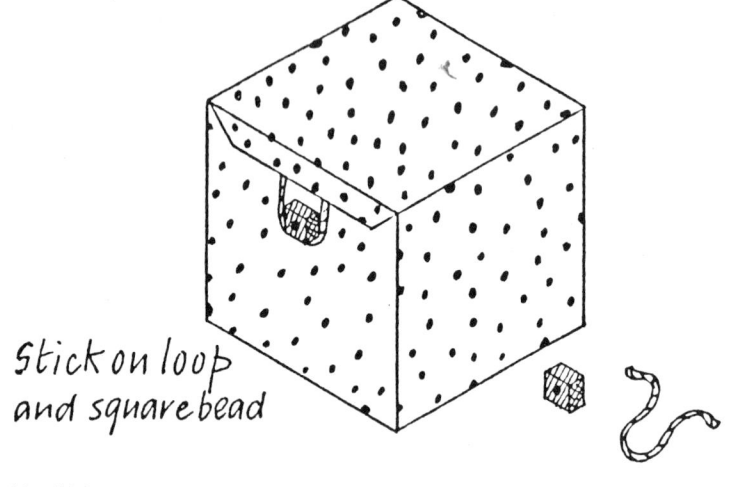

Stick on loop and square bead

'Jack' is now ready to spring from the box as soon as the lid is unfastened! (Fig. 5)

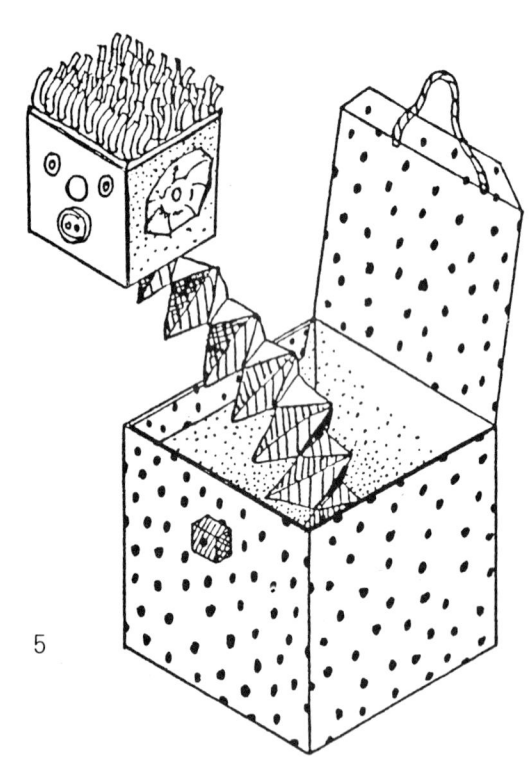

TEACHING POINTS
1. Marbling is best done with a small group of children at a time — they are usually tempted to use far too much paint. Full details for the preparation of marbled paper are given in the *TECHNIQUES AND MATERIALS* section at the back of this book. Alternatively, use 'bubble-print' paper. (See *BUBBLES AND CIRCLES*, page 1.)
2. Apart from the obvious language relating to the properties of cubes and the mathematical techniques used in their construction, the spring is also a piece of applied mathematics. Making the paper spring involves discussion and experience of *horizontal, vertical, right angle, left, right, up, down,* etc.
"*If we have right angles, why don't we have left angles?*"
"*Does the word right in right angle mean the same as it does in the phrase turn right?*"
Mathematics is all about the study of patterns and the four-movement technique used to construct the spring is a repeating pattern. Children will not realise this unless you bring it to their attention.
3. The maximum number of tabs and the double 'skin' both help to give the cubes extra rigidity; the marbled paper also provides aesthetic appeal.

5

4. The cube head is a good base on which to attach features but you could use a ping-pong ball, a cotton wool ball, a pom-pom or even a cardboard disc as alternatives.

5. As Jack-in-the-box mania takes over in the classroom, encourage children to think of features to make their Jack (or Jill) into a real personality by adding such features as spectacles, jewellery, hats, ties, plaits, moustaches, beards, etc. You could also link the character to a theme — circus people, families, animals, etc.

EXTENSIONS AND VARIATIONS

1. Children who are particularly dextrous may enjoy the challenge of designing 'twins in the box' or a 'mum and dad in the box'. The dimensions of the inner cubes and their springs will have to be scaled down to accommodate the extra tenant.

2. Although younger children will need to be provided with ready-made nets for their cubes, older children should be encouraged to design their own nets. This idea could be extended to investigate how many different ways there are of drawing the net of a cube (fig. 6). Shapes made from six squares like this are called *hexominoes*. They belong to the family of *polyominoes*. There are 35 different hexominoes and, of these, 11 can be folded up to form a closed cube. Results could be recorded in a chart (fig. 7).

If the hexominoes are cut from squared paper and only one face of each hexomino is glued down on to a backing sheet, children can fold the nets to verify the results.

Designing your own nets. 6
This shape will fold to form a closed cube:...

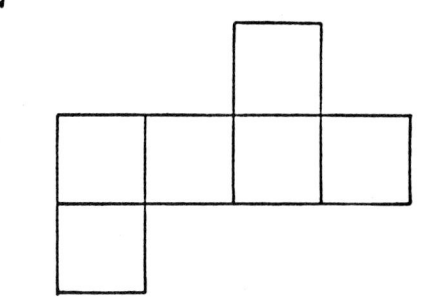

but this shape will not —

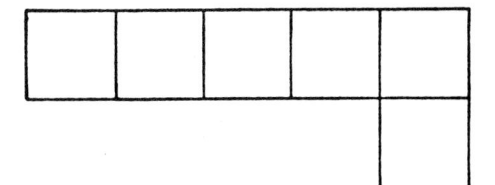

7

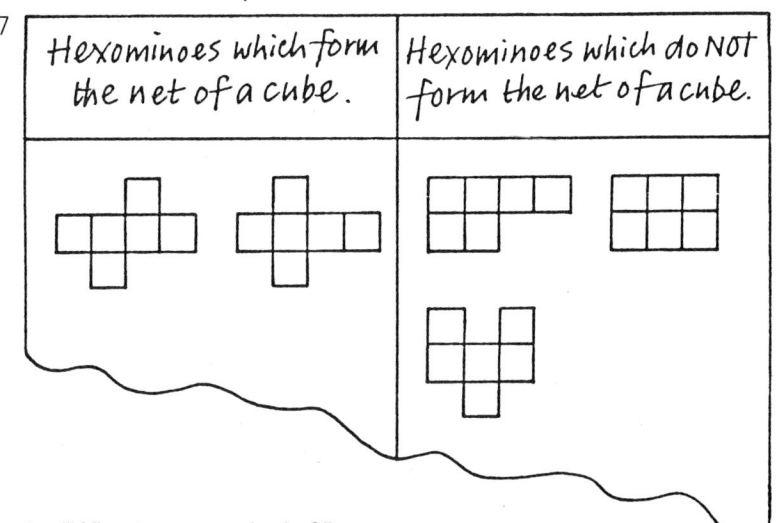

Hexominoes which form the net of a cube.	Hexominoes which do NOT form the net of a cube.

3. *"Why do we need tabs?"*
We have made the nets of the cubes with 14 tabs. This is to make them as strong as possible. A cube can be glued together from a net with only 7 tabs on the edges.

"Is there a rule about where to put the 7 tabs?"
[Tabs are usually placed on alternate edges forming the perimeter of the net (fig. 8).]

4. Comparing the sizes of the two cubes leads to interesting and valuable discussion.

"If the length of the edge of the larger cube is twice that of the smaller cube, what about the areas of their faces?"

"How many times will the smaller cube fit into the larger cube?"

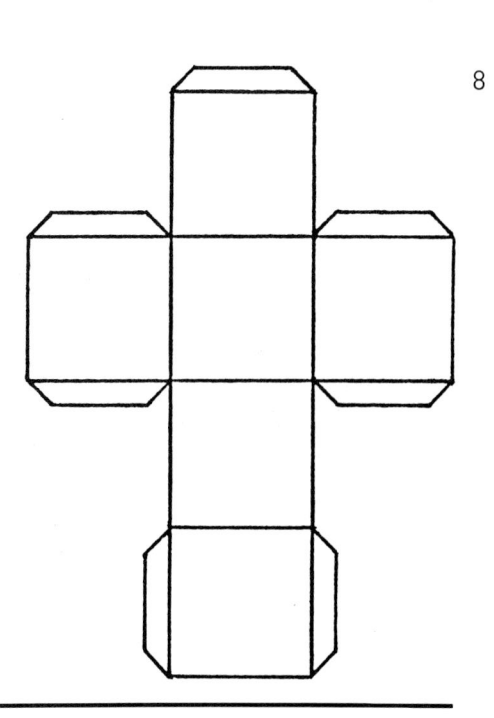

BORDER PATTERNS †

MATERIALS
Centimetre squared paper, pencil, ruler, colouring materials.

VOCABULARY
Repeating, motif, translation, diagonal, 'L'-shaped, evenly spaced, isometric grid, all-over pattern.

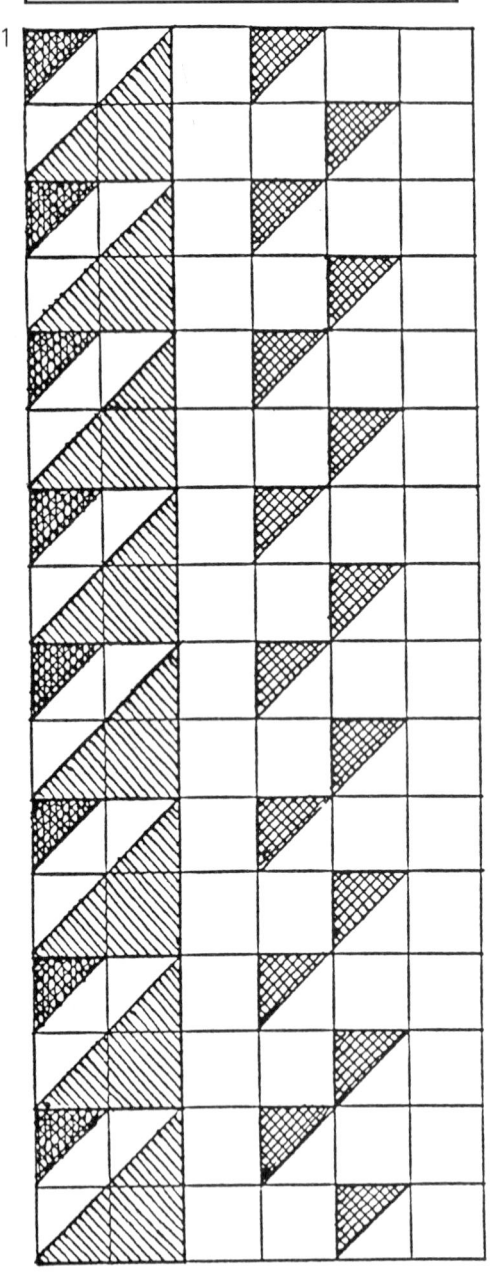

Border patterns are created by translating (sliding) a motif in regular steps without rotation. A method is suggested, using a ruler and a grid, leading to an open-ended design activity.

METHOD
1. Figure 1 shows some examples of border patterns that are composed of repeating motifs. Squared paper makes sure that each motif is translated (slid) the same distance each time.
2. Using only the squares and their diagonals on the squared paper, design a motif that you think will repeat well to make a border pattern. You may wish to draw some trial designs before making a final choice.
3. Repeat the chosen motif several times so that each one is identical to the others and is evenly spaced as in the examples.
4. You may wish to add finishing touches to your design by:
(a) going over the final design in black felt pen;
(b) colouring it in a consistent way, that is so that all the repeats are the same;
(c) cutting it out and double-mounting it on suitably coloured backing paper.
5. The border or strip pattern in figure 2 was also designed using a squared grid to help the artist position the motifs accurately, but the grid has been erased so that it plays no part in the finished design.

6. Design a simple border pattern of this type, making use of a simple natural motif instead of a geometric one. Try to place the repeats as accurately as you can. If you use grid lines, they should not show in the finished design.
7. Write a simple account and prepare a display sheet, explaining in words and diagrams how you tackled this and how you think your design could be used.

TEACHING POINTS
1. Graphic, fashion and textile designers make use of various grids to design accurate, aesthetically pleasing patterns for fabrics, wallpaper, wrapping paper, etc. The teacher should take the opportunity to discuss how mathematical techniques are used to create attractive designs.

---

84   BORDER PATTERNS   † *Illustrated on page 8 of the second photograph section*

2. Examples of translations, which can take the form of a border pattern or of an all-over repeated motif, are abundant in the manmade environment, and examples should be collected and displayed to support the work (fig. 3). Many multicultural, religious and historical examples can be found. Border patterns also exist in three-dimensional form — moulded cornices, picture frames, decorated furniture, etc.

A border pattern extended into an all-over pattern.

Plaited bamboo.

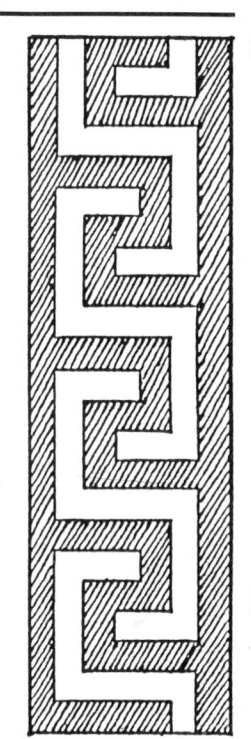

3. Producing border patterns can be time-consuming, so good use should be made of them. Favourite designs can be photocopied to make bookmarks, to decorate work or to enhance displays.

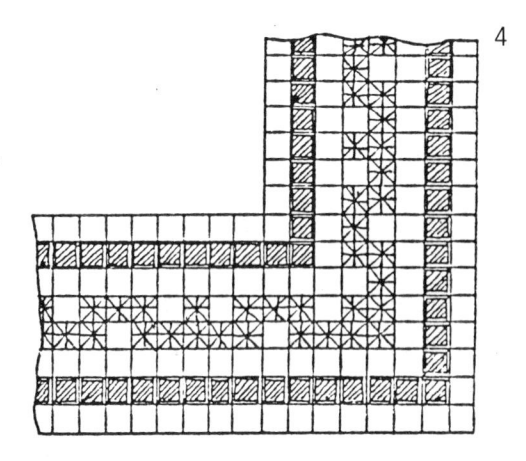

EXTENSIONS AND VARIATIONS

1. *"Design an 'L'-shaped border pattern for the corner of a sheet of writing paper."* This will require the designer to consider how to make the pattern 'turn the corner' without spoiling the design. This may lead to the idea of a mitred corner, often seen on table linen, headsquares, handkerchiefs, photograph frames, etc. (fig. 4).

2. A large variety of grid papers are now available and others can be constructed. (See *AREA 2* and *AREA 3* pages 37 and 67 for examples.) Although squared paper has been suggested, there is no reason why border patterns should not be designed using other grids. Isometric grid, for instance, gives quite different effects (fig. 5). (See page 120 for master copy of isometric grid paper.)

BORDER PATTERNS 85

6

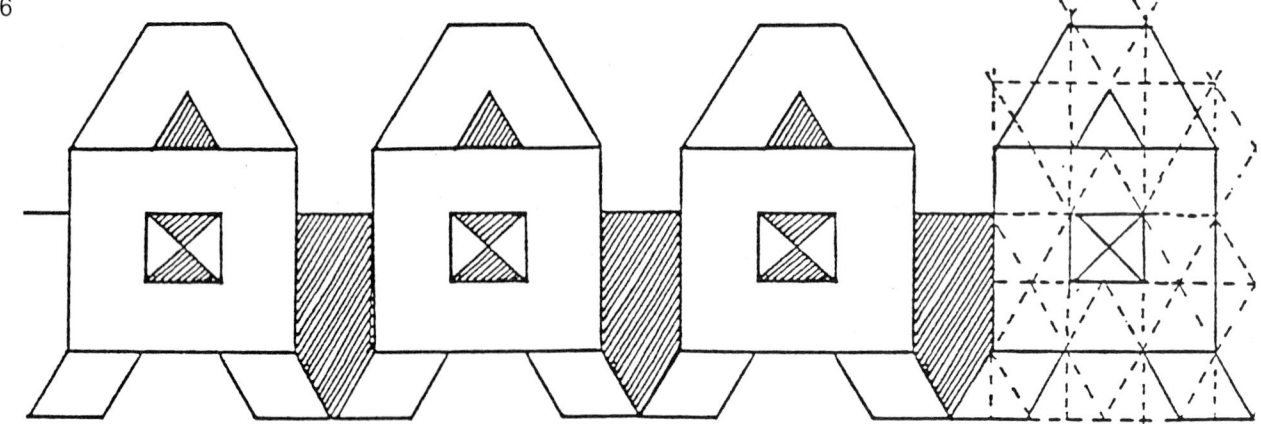

Composite designs, incorporating more than one type of grid, might be considered. In figure 6, for example, both centimetre squared and isometric grids have been used.

3. Some pupils may enjoy using a computer graphic package such as *Logo*. Alternatively, they may wish to use cross-stitching on binca or embroidery canvas — another form of square grid. (See *CROSS-STITCH PATTERNS* page 61.) Examples of Victorian samplers often feature translating patterns. In the example (fig. 7), the repeating motif makes alternating positive and negative images — *a counterchange pattern*.

Border patterns, worked out on grids and coloured by means of fabric crayons, can also be successfully transferred to fabrics. (See *FABRIC SHAPES* page 35.)

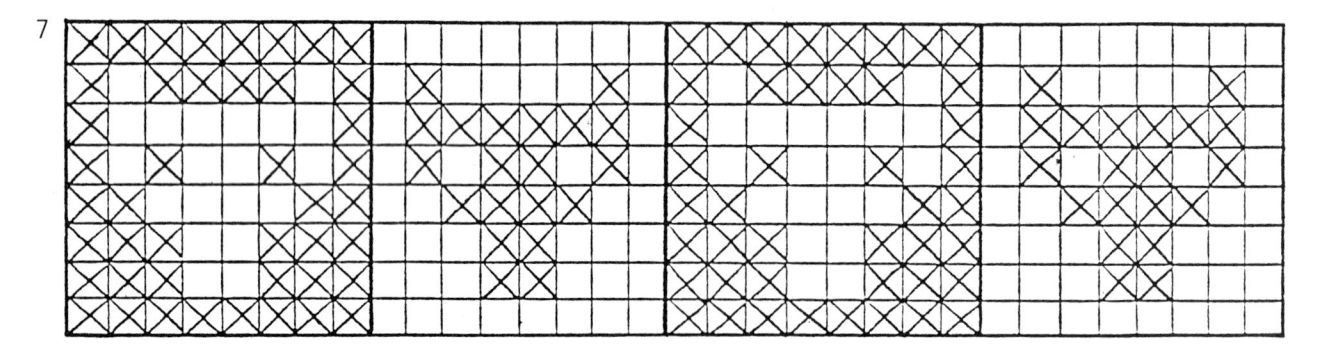

7

REFERENCES & RESOURCES
Draw Patterns Anna Brackett; A & C Black Ltd
The Geometric File Tarquin Publications
How to Make Prints & Patterns Felicia Law & Barry Rowe; Collins
Lettercraft Tony Hart; Heinemann
Newtiles Computer program (BBC, RML); SMILE (The next 17); ILEA Learning Resources Branch
Geometric Motifs Philip & Tacey

4. Extra design restraints can be imposed if appropriate; for example, the repeating motif can either have an axis of symmetry or not; the motifs can either overlap or not.

5. *"Design an all-over pattern for a sheet of wrapping paper suitable for:*
(a) *a birthday present;*
(b) *a Christmas present;*
(c) *your best friend."*

6. A repeating letter or sequence of letters, a monogram for instance, can also be used to form a border or all-over pattern — a theme developed fully in *Lettercraft*.

SHADOWSHAPES 3 †

The earlier work in *SHADOWSHAPES 1* and *2* is extended to deal with centres of rotation both *inside* and *outside* the shape to be rotated, with an emphasis on comparing results for similarities and differences.

METHOD
A. Using the template
1. Mark the centre of a square of cartridge paper.
2. Mark off a number of equally spaced points around the perimeter of the square, either by folding the square or by using a circular protractor as shown in *SHADOWSHAPES 2*. (In figure 1, the square has been folded to make eight equally spaced marks.)
3. From some stiff scrap card, carefully cut out a shape (in figure 2 it is a 5 cm square) so that you have both a template and a stencil. This is best done using a sharp craft knife and a cutting board.
4. Start with the template and mark on it three points *inside* the shape: a is at the centre of the template, b and c are two other points chosen at random, but not too close to an edge (fig. 2).
5. Push a brass paper fastener through the point a on the template and the centre of the cartridge paper square so that the template is free to rotate (fig. 3).
6. Choose a reference point on the template and line it up with one of the equally spaced marks on the cartridge paper.
7. Trace round the perimeter of the template using one of the 'flicked' edges shown in *SHADOWSHAPES 2*.
8. Rotate the template so that the reference point lines up with the next mark on the cartridge paper (fig. 4).

MATERIALS
Squares of cartridge paper with sides at least 20 cm long; scraps of card; circular protractor (optional); crayons; pastels; coloured pens or pencils; brass paper fastener; scissors or craft knife and cutting board.

VOCABULARY
Centre of rotation, inside, outside, template, stencil, rotational symmetry, perimeter.

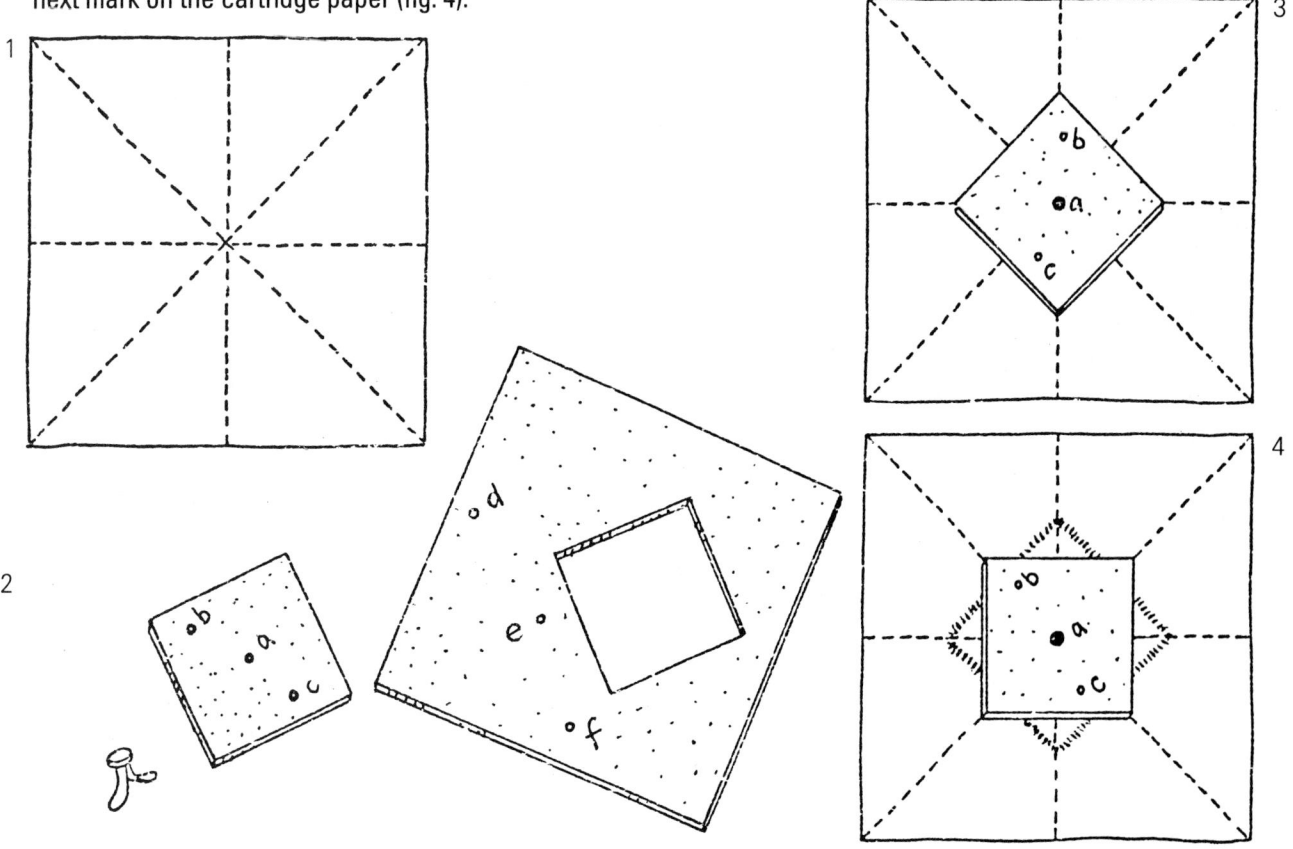

---

† *Illustrated on page 5 of the second photograph section*

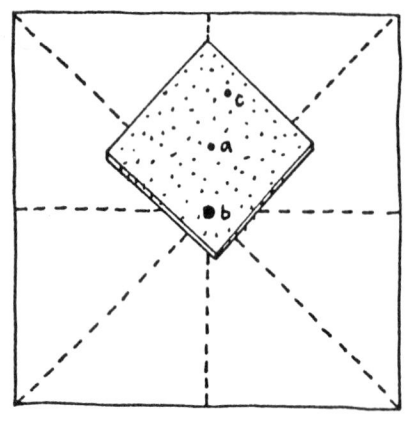

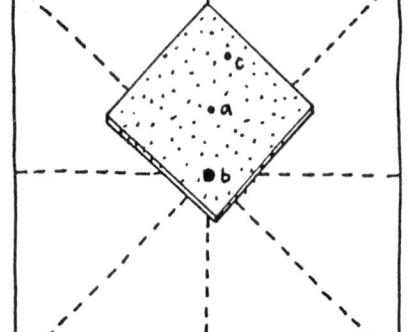

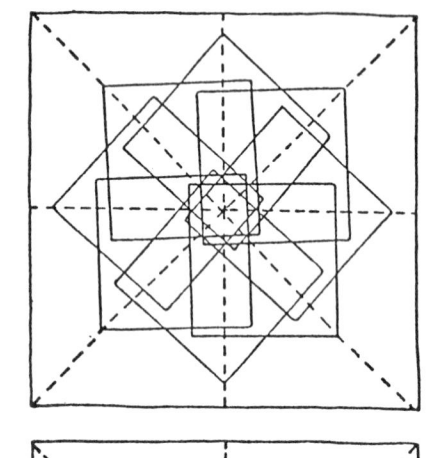

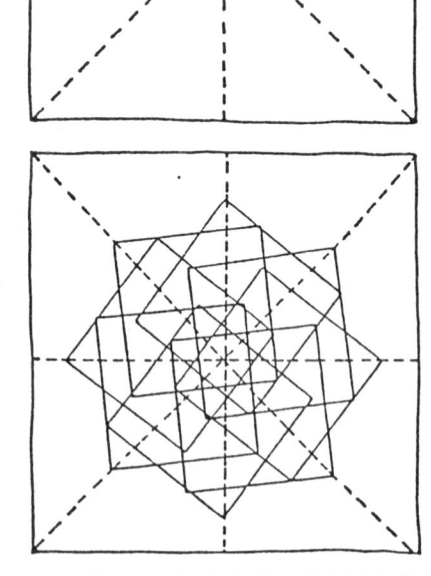

9. Retrace the template outline in the new position.
10. Repeat steps 8 and 9 to complete the pattern. (In the example, because of the symmetry of the square about point a, only one move is required.)
11. Remove the template. The pattern created has an order of rotational symmetry 8.
12. Start with a new square of cartridge paper and repeat the process but this time push the brass paper fastener through point b (fig. 5).
13. Start again, this time with the fastener through point c (fig. 6).
14. Experiment with other points on the template, but notice that each time the central motif of each pattern is a regular octagon because the order of rotational symmetry is 8.

B. Using the stencil

Repeat steps 5 to 14 of method A but this time use the *stencil* and points like d, e and f, which are *outside* the shape. This will lead to patterns similar to those in figure 7.

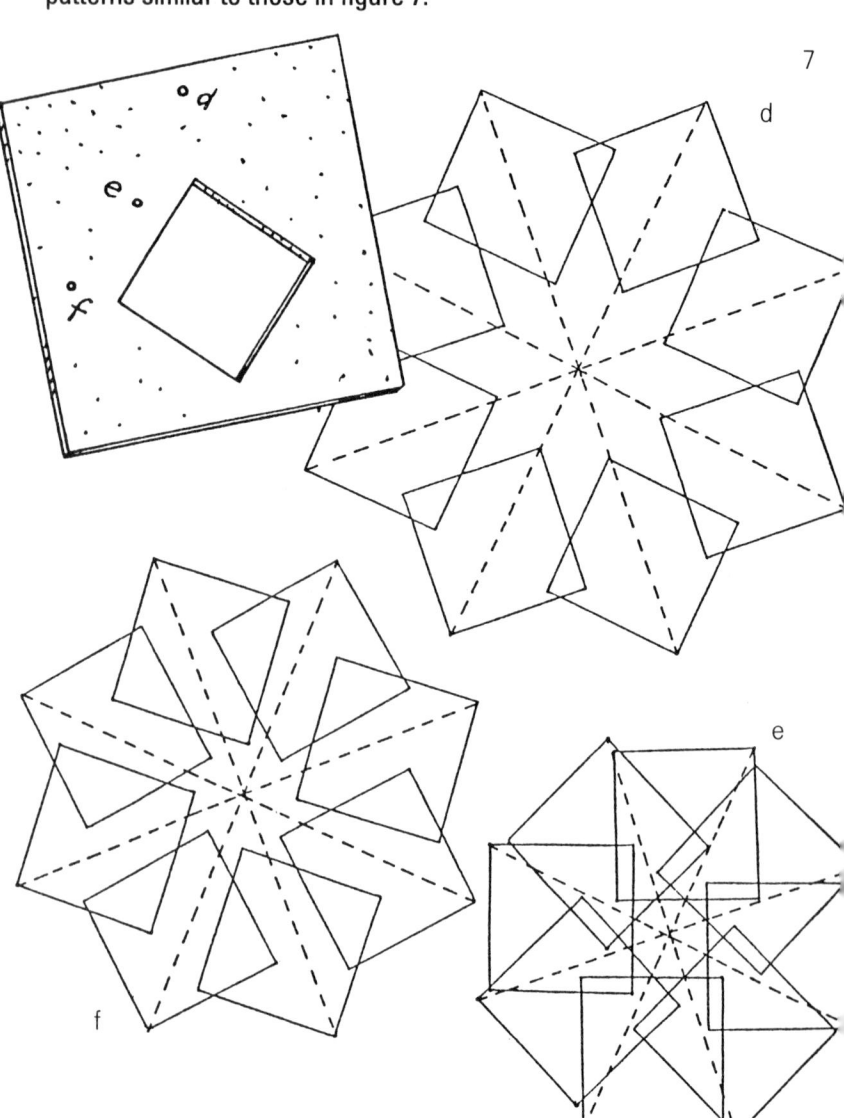

88 SHADOWSHAPES 3

TEACHING POINTS
1. As in *SHADOWSHAPES 2*, different types of edging and colouring sequences can be used to enhance the pattern.
2. Encourage the children to predict what shape the central motif will be when different numbers of equally shaped marks are used.
3. Compare the patterns made by templates and stencils of the same shape.

EXTENSIONS AND VARIATIONS
1. Each child uses a template or stencil of a letter or familiar polygon to make a shadowshape pattern. The patterns and the shapes used to create them are displayed separately.
"Which letter or shape formed which pattern?"
This is not always as easy as you might think!
2. Figure 8 is an example of free pattern (using eye judgement only) created from a square stencil with the centre of rotation outside the square.

8

REFERENCES & RESOURCES
Nature Takes Shape Ladybird
Dial-a-Design Corgi Toys
Patterns in Nature Posters; Pictorial Charts Educational Trust
Newtiles Computer program (BBC, RML); SMILE (The next 17); ILEA Learning Resources Branch

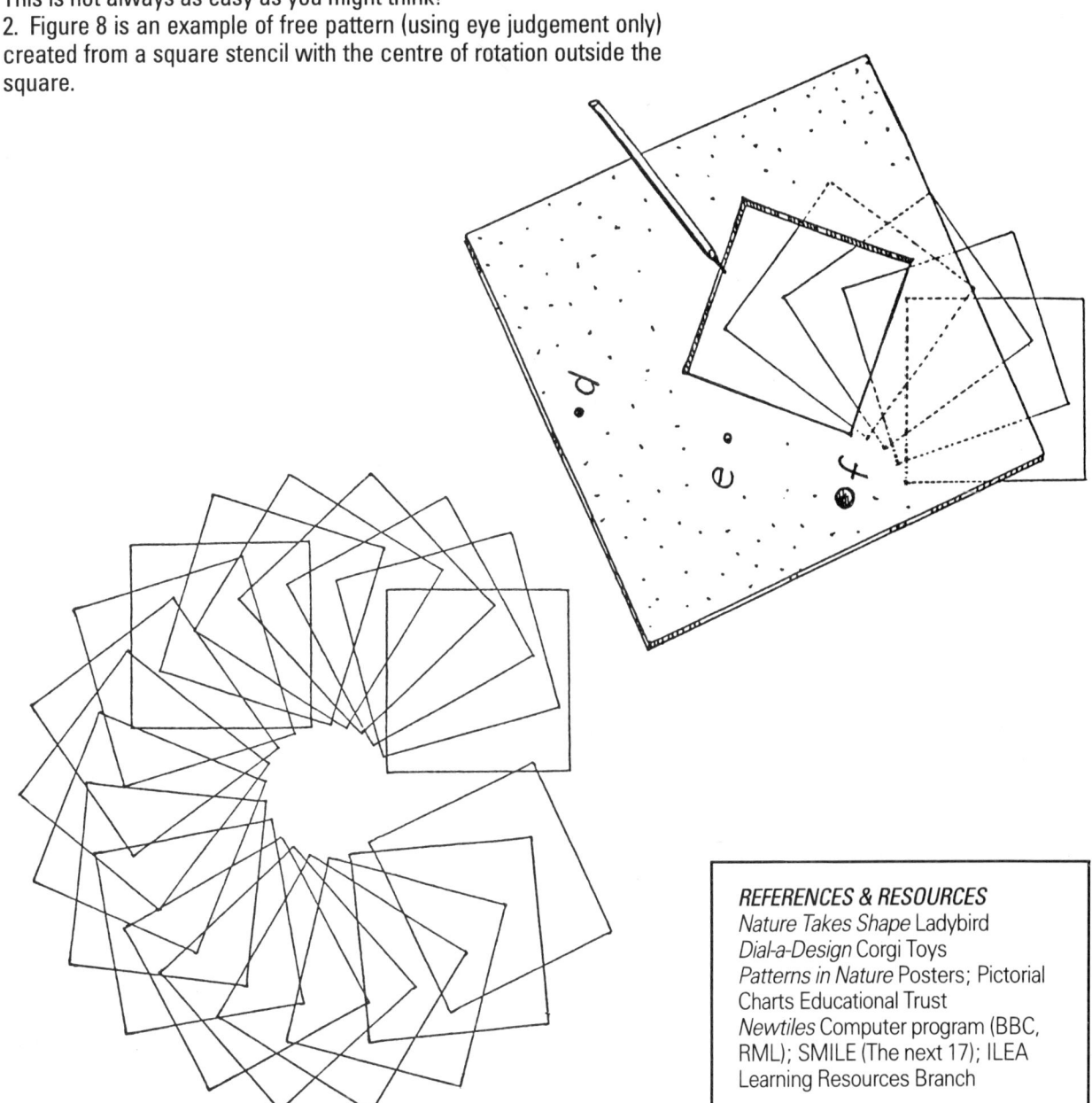

TANGRAM 2 †

MATERIALS
Two gummed squares of different size and colour; backing sheet; pencil; scissors; ruler. (*Optional:* wallpaper paste and small brush.)

VOCABULARY
Square, triangle, parallelogram, quadrilateral, polygon, template, isosceles, right-angled, small, medium, large, area, surface, match, dissect, reflected.

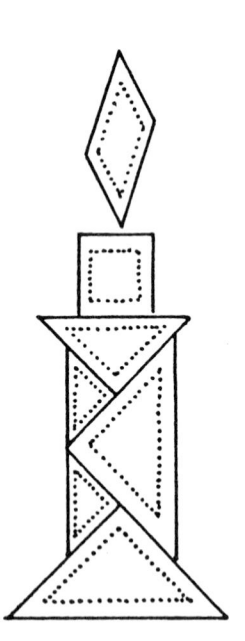

This chapter extends the work done in *TANGRAM 1* using the same basic design but more sophisticated techniques.

METHOD
The Layered Tangram

1. On the back of a large gummed square, mark out the construction lines of the tangram as shown in figure 1.
2. Cut out the seven pieces and assemble them in an arrangement you like so that no pieces overlap.

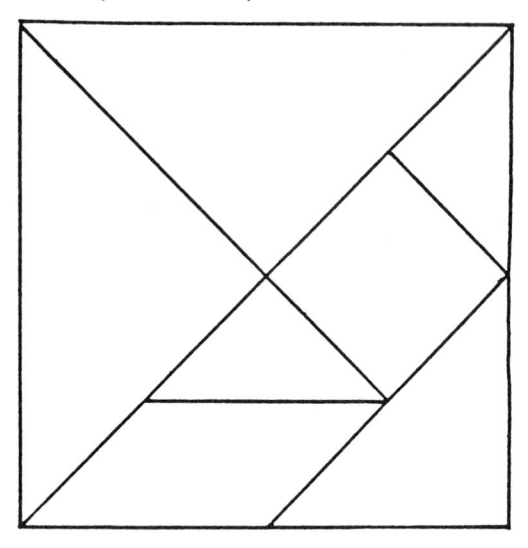

3. Glue the pieces down on to a backing sheet.
4. Cut out the smaller tangram and position each similar piece centrally on top of its 'partner' (fig. 2).
5. Glue the pieces down, making sure that each piece is placed centrally on its larger counterpart.

In the example, a tangram candle has been created in this way. A yellow flame could be added for effect.

TEACHING POINTS
1. See *TANGRAM 1* on page 64 for more information and activities.
2. As well as revising the names of the different polygons, the layered tangram provides a good opportunity to introduce the word *similar* in an informal way to describe figures that have the same shape but are of different size. In a more precise mathematical sense, the word *similar* is used to describe an object that retains its angular measurements but whose sides and/or faces are reduced or enlarged proportionately. Before glueing down the smaller tangram pieces, children should be asked to check that corresponding angles match.
Encourage children to give examples or make a collection of *similar* objects such as photographs and their enlargements, scale models, Russian dolls, etc. There are also shapes within the tangram itself that are similar.
3. Although the squares are gummed, it is better to use paste to secure them as they have a tendency to peel off after a time.
4. If felt squares or thick coloured cards are available, the layered tangram could be made up to give a more pronounced 3-D effect.

† *Illustrated on page 6 of the second photograph section*

CROSS-STITCH PATTERNS (page 61)

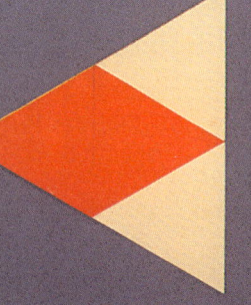

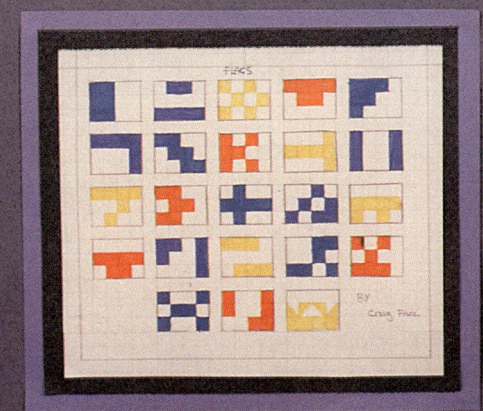

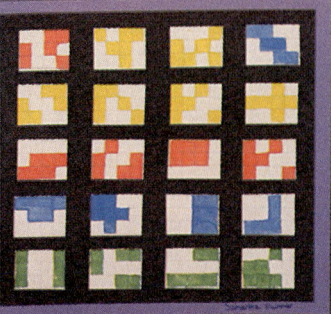

JACK-IN-THE-BOX (page 81)

AREA 3 (page 67)

NAME GAMES (page 58)

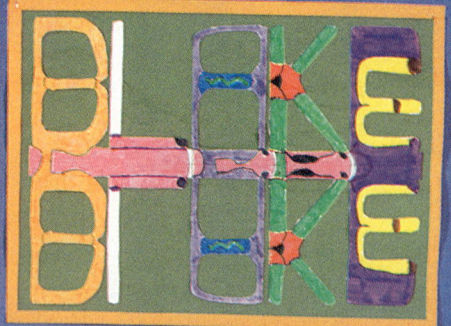

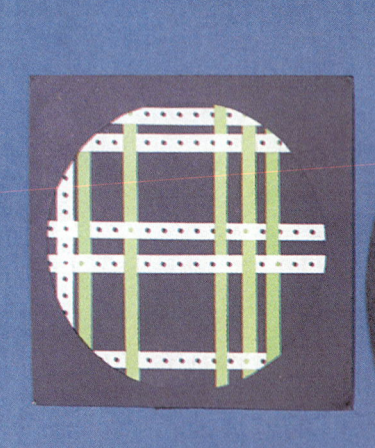

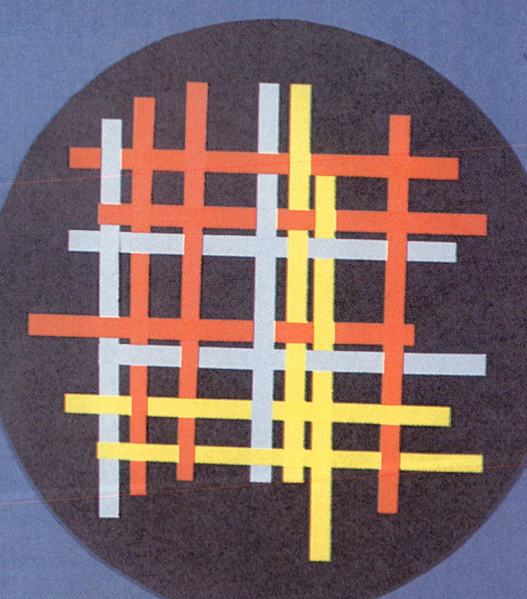

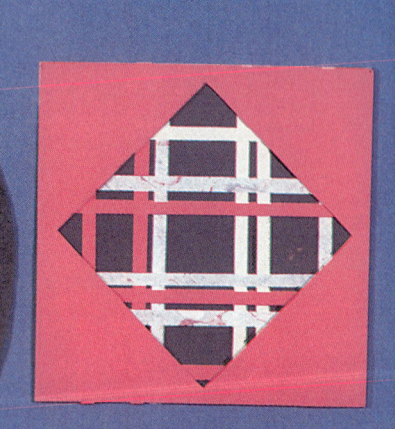

HORIZONTAL AND VERTICAL (page 55)

TESSELLATION 3 (page 76)

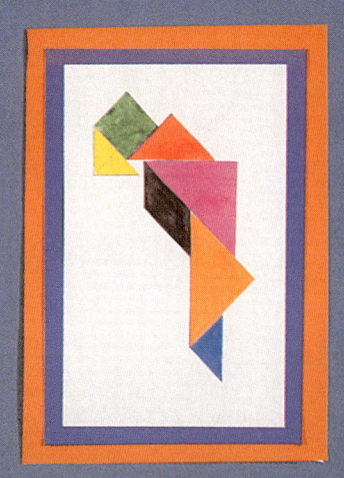

TANGRAM 1 (page 64)

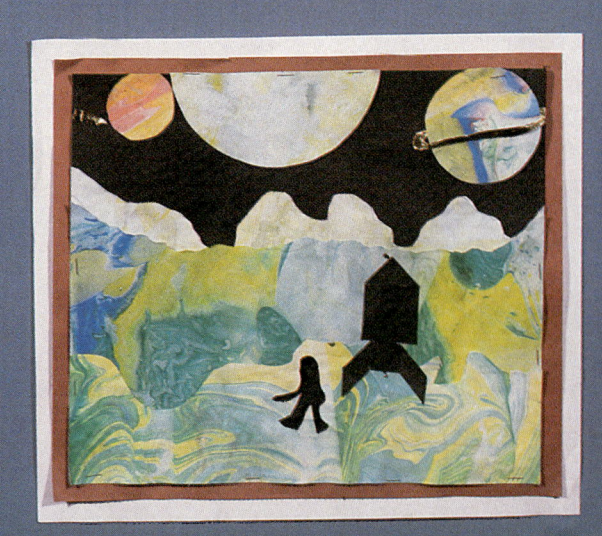

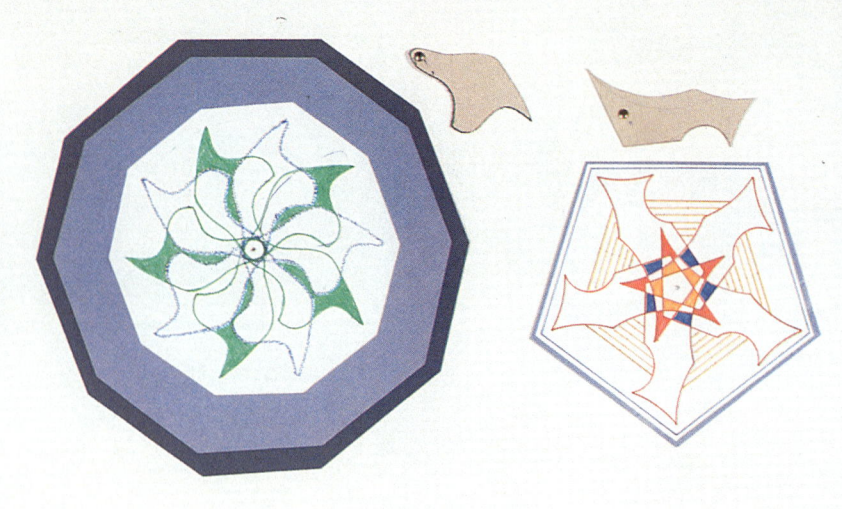

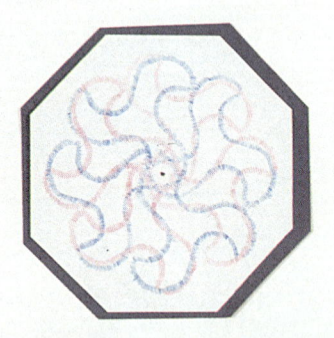

SHADOWSHAPES 2   (page 70)

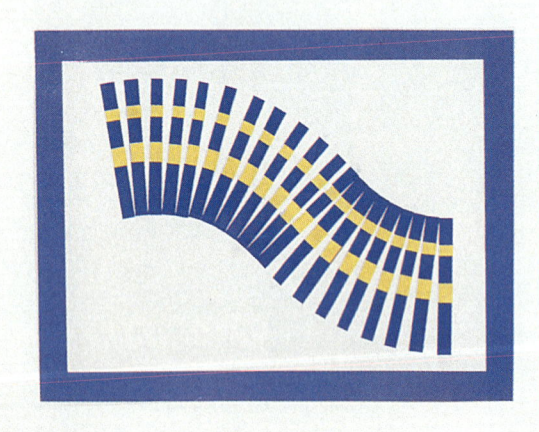

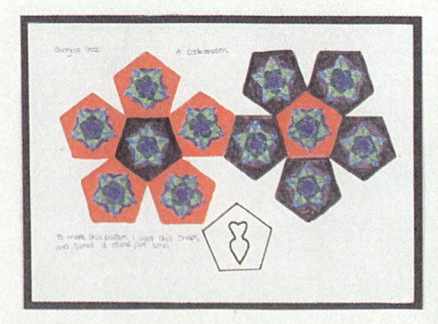

SLINKY CURVES   (page 73)

ROUNDABOUTS 2   (page 52)

TESSELLATION 4 (page 110)

SHADOWSHAPES 3 (page 87)

CIRCLEWEBS (page 100)

TANGRAM 2 (page 90)

ROUNDABOUTS 3 (page 93)

SWOPAROUNDS (page 102)

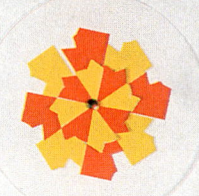

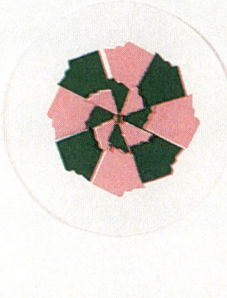

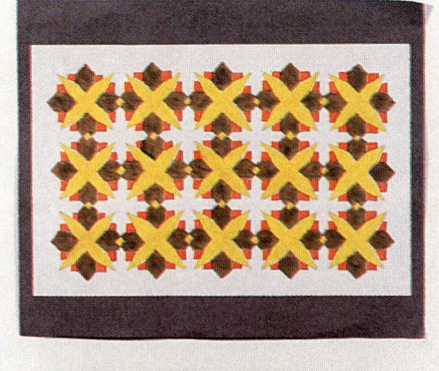

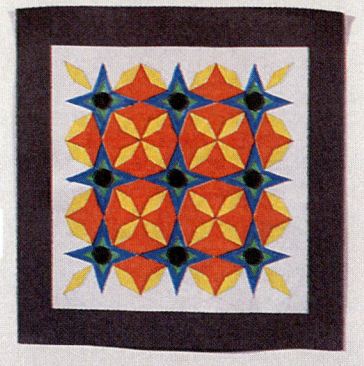

ISLAMIC PATTERNS (page 107)

STARWEAVING 3 (page 97)

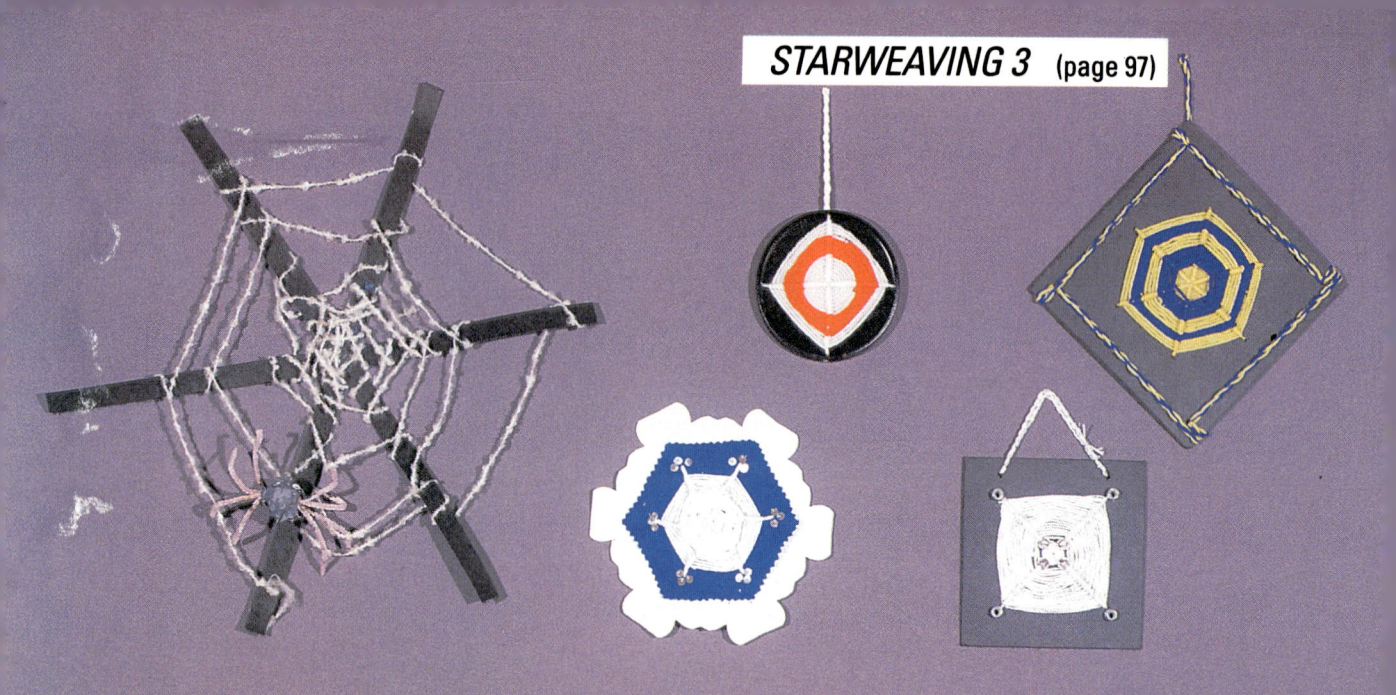

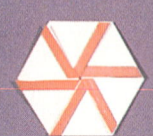

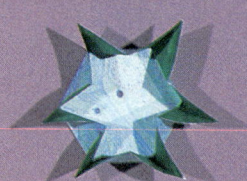

FOLDING STAR CONTAINERS (page 104)

BORDER PATTERNS (page 84)

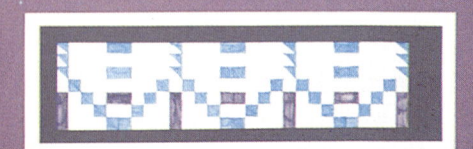

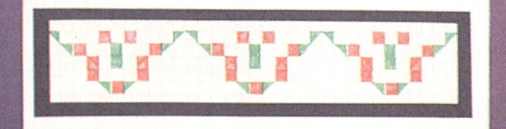

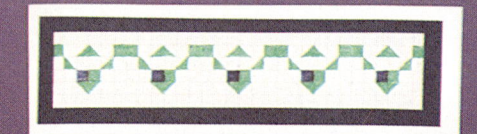

3

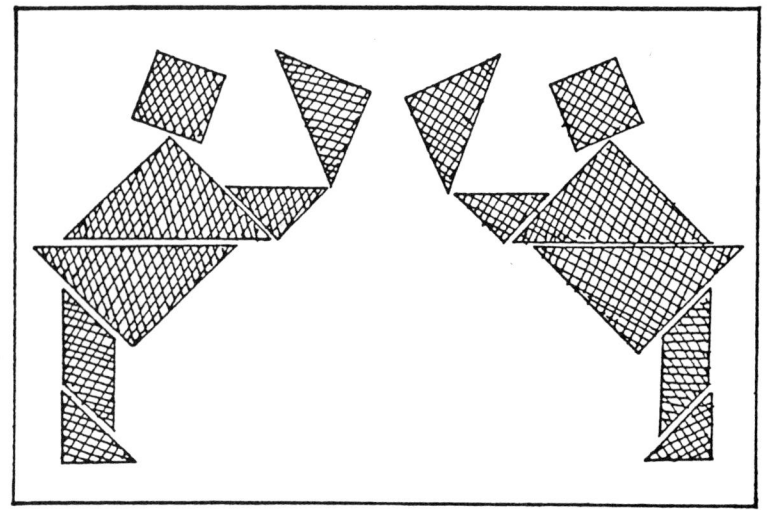

EXTENSIONS AND VARIATIONS

1. 'Twin tangrams' can be designed. Two congruent tangrams are cut out and glued down in such a way that one is the reflected image of the other (fig. 3). This can be offered as a problem to solve — how can it be done?

2. One form of writing that seems to complement the stylised form of the tangram is the *Haiku* — a three line Japanese verse form of 17 syllables divided into three lines of 5, 7 and 5 syllables. After some experience of classifying words according to their syllable count, a *Haiku* could be composed to accompany a tangram picture (fig. 4).

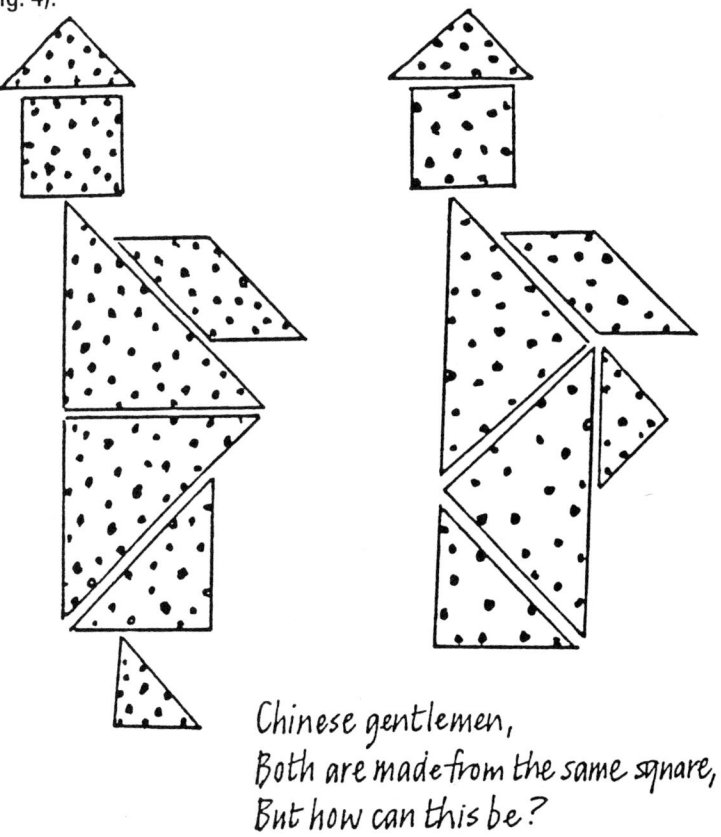

4

Chinese gentlemen,
Both are made from the same square,
But how can this be?

Rocket exploring,
Surrounded by the unknown,
In infinite space.

TANGRAM 2   91

5

Hunger on his mind,
The solitary vulture
Sits aloft a branch,
Awaiting death on the ground,
Scavenger of the desert.

Solitary brave,
Motionless and in silence,
Of what does he dream?
How lost herds of buffalo
Roam the happy hunting ground.

REFERENCES & RESOURCES
Tangrams — 330 puzzles Ronald C Read; Dover Publications
Tangram Joost Elffers; Penguin Books
The Tangram Tree Poster The Mathematical Association
Tangram Puzzles 2 plastic tangrams and 20 graded workcards; Hestair Hope Ltd
Children's materials
Tangrams ABC Kit Susan Johnson; Dover Publications
The Fun with Tangrams Kit Susan Johnson; Dover Publications
Tangram Boxed Game plastic tangram and 70 playcards; Creative Toys

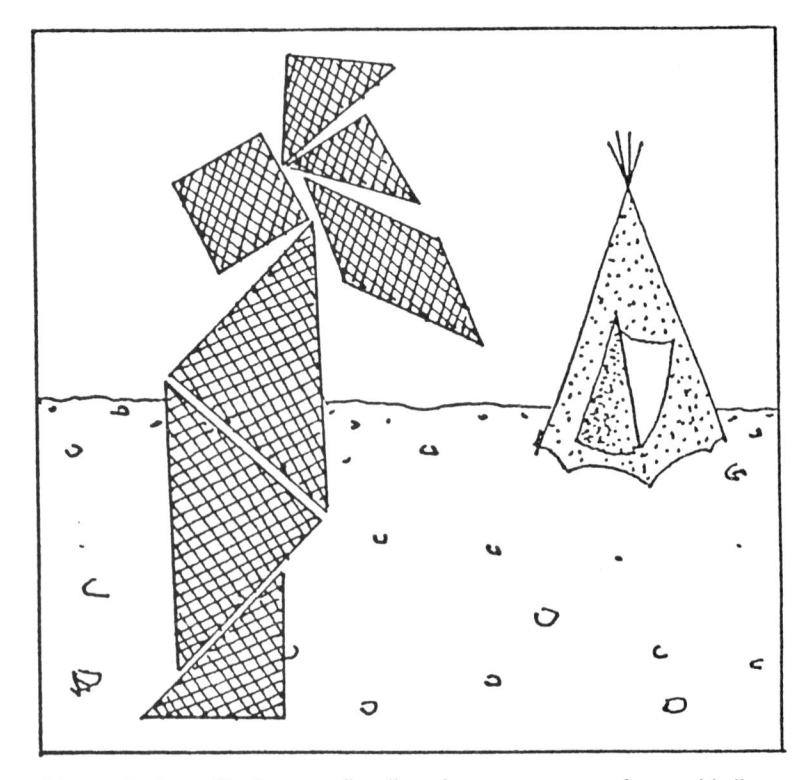

Alternatively, a *Tanka* — a five line Japanese verse form with lines of 5, 7, 5, 7, 7 syllables — could be composed (fig. 5).
3. The technique described on page 41 is highly suitable for making a tangram printing block to produce multiple images in a repeating pattern.

92   TANGRAM 2

ROUNDABOUTS 3 †

This chapter builds on the activities in *ROUNDABOUTS 1* and *2* by considering how the method can be adapted to design a symmetrical pattern to decorate the faces of regular solids.

MATERIALS
Net of a cube on card*; squares of card of same dimension as the cube faces; ruler; pencil; colouring materials; PVA glue; ball-point pen. (*See the back of this book for a master copy of a 6 cm cube.)

VOCABULARY
Stencil, rotate, quater of a turn (90°), face, edge.
(*Optional:* tetrahedron, hexahedron, octahedron, dodecahedron, icosahedron.)

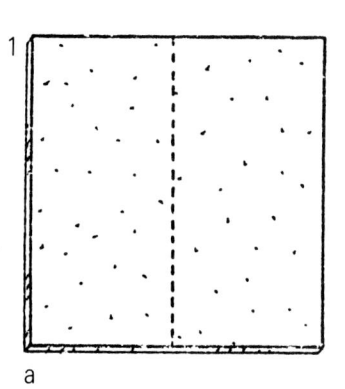

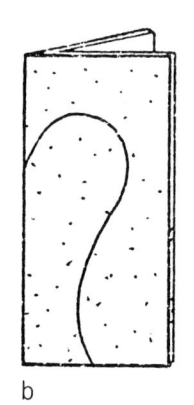

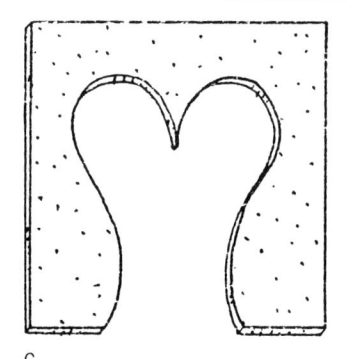

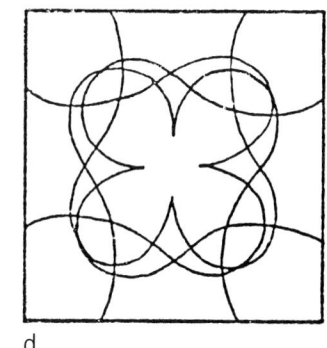

METHOD
1. Take a card square, fold it in half and cut out a section along the fold line, starting at one edge.
2. Flatten out the card which will now be used as a stencil.
3. Overlay the stencil on to another square so that the edges line up exactly and trace round the edge of the cutout carefully.
4. Rotate the stencil a quarter of a turn (90°) and retrace the cutout section.
5. Repeat step 4 twice more (fig. 1).

You may like to try this more than once, experimenting with different cuts until you get a design you like.

6. Transfer your chosen design to each face of the net of the cube. You should find that at each of the edges the pattern matches up exactly (fig. 2).

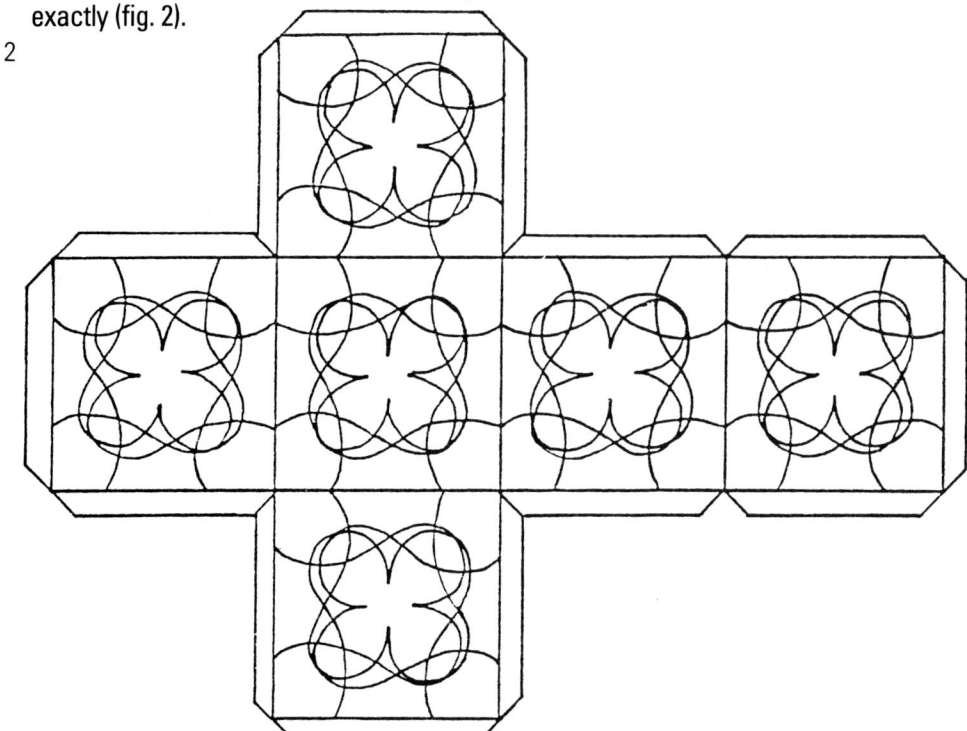

† *Illustrated on page 6 of the second photograph section*

3

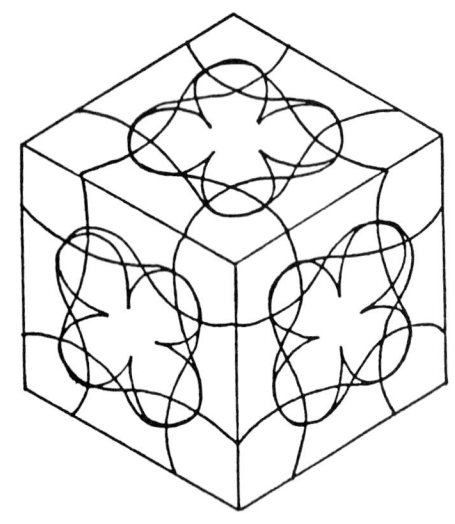

4

7. Decide how to decorate the cube to highlight the matching patterns on each face.
8. Score the edges of the cube carefully on the wrong side, using a ruler and a ball-point pen. Glue the tabs with neat PVA glue, fold and assemble the cube (fig. 3). If you want a cube with a lid, leave one of the faces unglued. The cube could then be used for the *JACK-IN-THE-BOX* (page 81).

TEACHING POINTS

1. This method for creating a decorated cube can be presented in a different way to pose a more open-ended design problem. For example,
"Design a pattern on each face of a cube so that, when assembled, the patterns match and line up along the edges of the cube."
If ATM *Activity Mats* or Galt *Pattern Blocks* are available, they provide a useful lead-in to this activity, particularly if the open-ended approach is used, because the pattern units match along the edges.
2. A coating of diluted PVA glue applied after step 7, and allowed to dry thoroughly, will seal the colours and add an attractive sheen to the finished cube.
3. The master sheets at the back of this book give nets for 6 cm and 3 cm cubes but the technique works equally well for any size. Children who have made a model from the master sheet may enjoy designing a net of their own, of a different size and preferably not of the standard cruciform layout. (See page 83 for investigative activities linked with cube nets.)
Several decorated cubes of different sizes look very attractive suspended as mobiles.
4. At step 1, there are two options for folding the card in half (fig. 4), although figure 1 suggests the nondiagonal fold. Working in pairs, each child could choose one of the options and compare results in order to decide if the use of different axes of symmetry has any effect on the finished pattern.

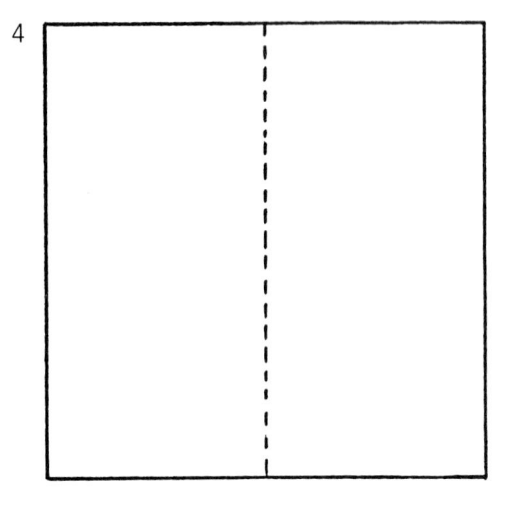

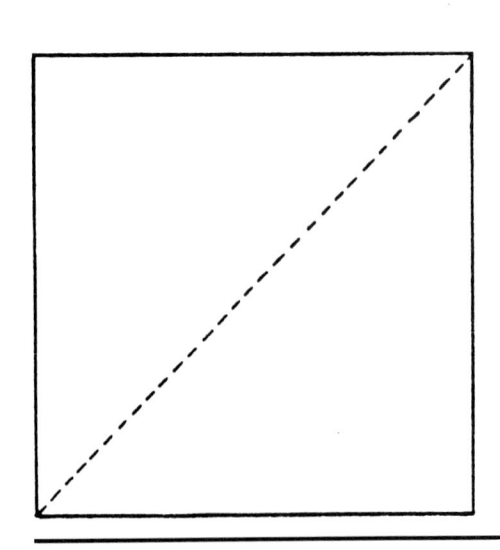

EXTENSIONS AND VARIATIONS

1. *"Is it possible to apply a different symmetrical pattern to each face so that the lines of the pattern still connect at the edges of the cube?"*
2. Some patterns lend themselves to a counter-change technique on adjacent faces.
"Is it possible to use two colours so that a counterchange pattern can be designed on adjacent faces?"
This needs careful planning and a systematic approach at the colouring stage.
3. As an alternative way of decorating, the pattern can be etched into polystyrene sheets such as *Press-Print* and printed off on to each face. (See page 41 for information about *Press-Print* and page 3 for *Printing pad*.)

5

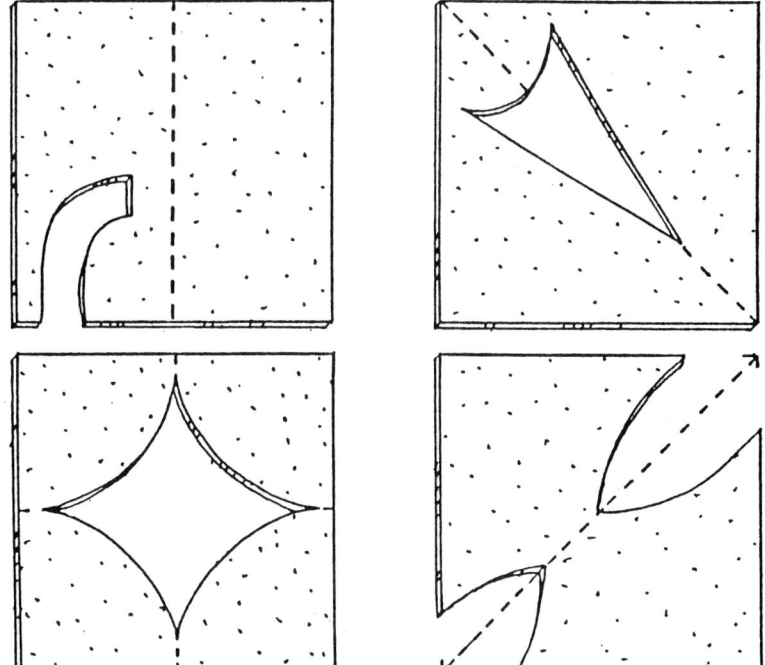

4. Investigate the effects of different types of cutouts and folds.
"Try to predict what will happen if you use stencils like those in figure 5."

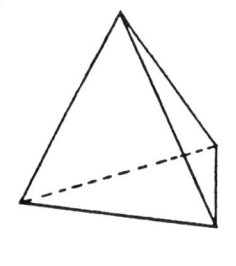

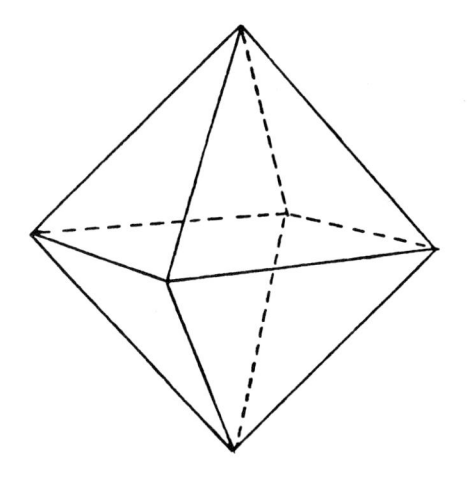

6

5. This technique works just as effectively with other polyhedra whose faces are regular congruent polygons. The tetrahedron, hexahedron and octahedron are constructed with equilateral triangles (fig. 6) and are within the scope of many children. (See page 120 for master of isometric grid sheets.) *Remember to add tabs to outside edges of the net.*
"Are these the only possible nets?" (Fig. 7.)

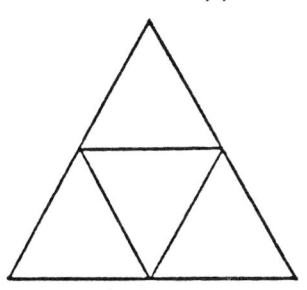

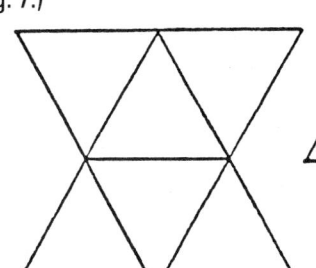

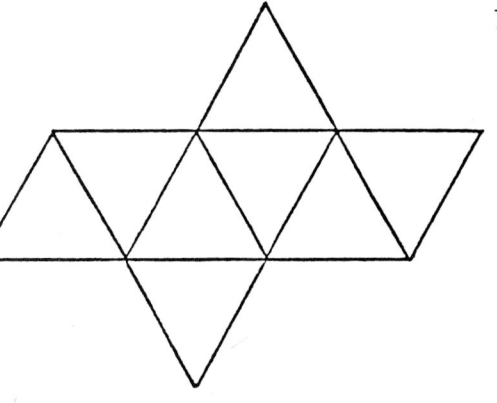

7

ROUNDABOUTS 3   95

8

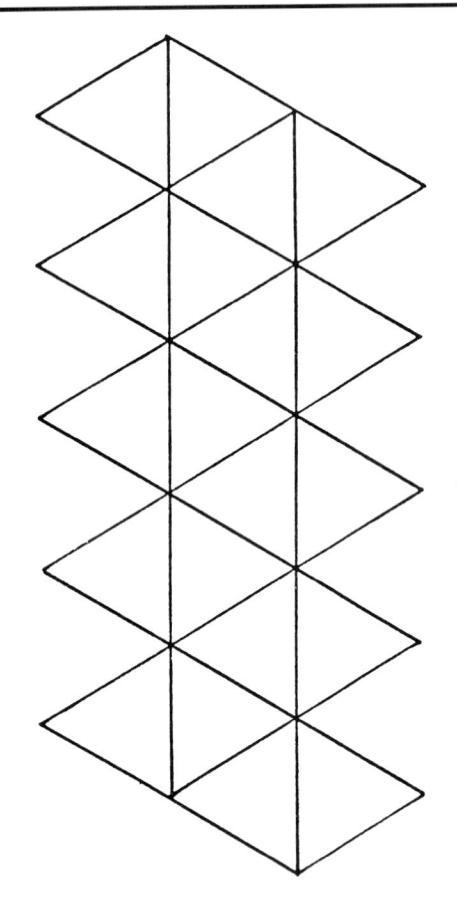

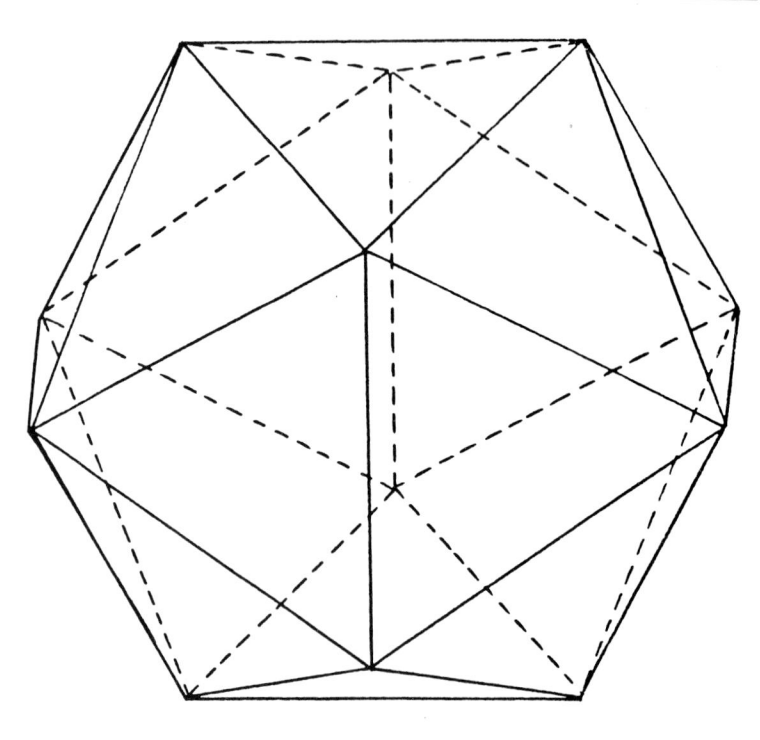

Some may like to attempt the icosahedron, with its twenty faces (fig. 8).

The dodecahedron, with its twelve pentagonal faces, will provide a suitable challenge for some of the more dextrous and patient children (fig. 9).

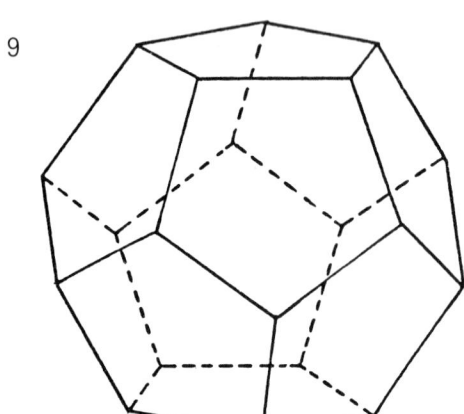

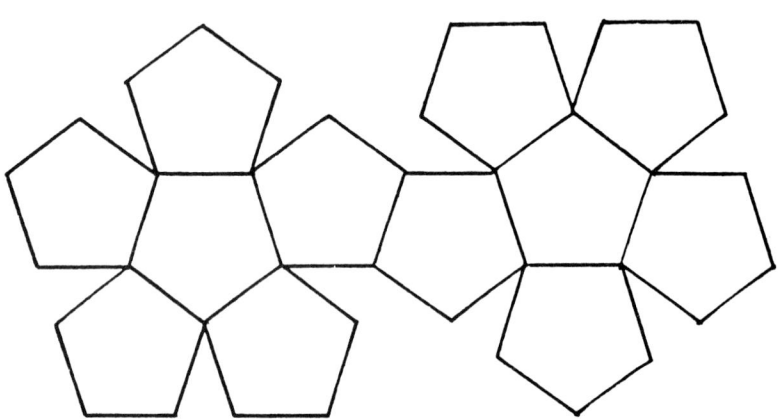

9

REFERENCES & RESOURCES
Pattern Blocks James Galt & Co. Ltd
Activity Mats Association of Teachers of Mathematics
Kaleidocycles Tarquin Publications
Geometric Motifs Philip & Tacey

STARWEAVING 3 †

This chapter moves from the stick-weaving techniques in the previous chapters to the more sophisticated needle-weaving, to create and investigate patterns with symmetrical properties.

MATERIALS
Squares of strong card about 20 cm × 20 cm; squares of coloured activity paper 24 cm × 24 cm; tapestry needle; pair of compasses; circular protractor; PVA glue; smooth wools (four-ply or double knitting); scissors.

VOCABULARY
Square, diagonals, right-angle, centre, tension, anticlockwise, hexagon, hexagonal, circle, circular.

METHOD
1. Find the centre of the square of card by drawing the diagonals.
2. Place the card in the centre of the activity paper and glue down well over the whole surface.
3. Trim the corners of the activity paper diagonally, fold and glue down the 'flaps' (fig. 1).
4. Use the compass point to pierce through the centre of the card and the activity paper.
5. Turn the work over so that the activity paper faces upwards with the centre point showing.

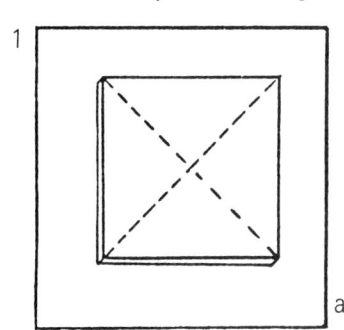

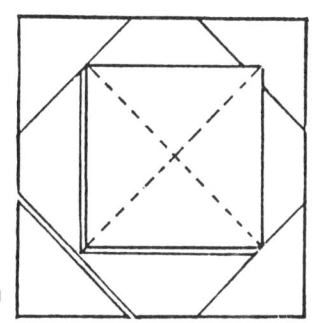

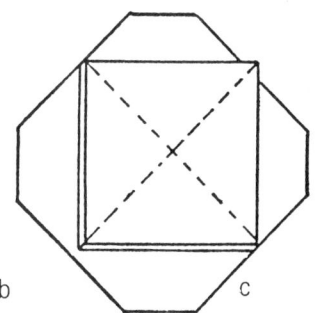

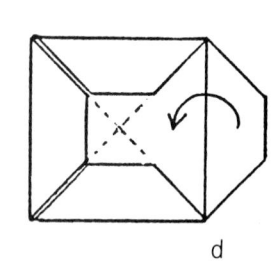

6. Align the centre of the circular protractor on the centre of the paper with the 0° mark in the '12 o'clock' position.
7. Mark off 0°, 90°, 180° and 270° and pierce through these points (fig. 2).
8. Thread up a single length of wool (about 50–60 cm) and tie a large knot in one end.
9. Starting at the centre of the back (the card side), bring the needle up through the centre, down through hole 1, up through the centre, down through hole 2 and repeat for holes 3 and 4.
Keep the tension as taut as possible and finish by coming up through the centre (fig. 3).
You now have a framework on which to needle-weave a square.
10. Working anticlockwise, take the needle back *over* one thread of the framework, then *under* two threads, and then loop the wool back over and under the same thread (fig. 4).

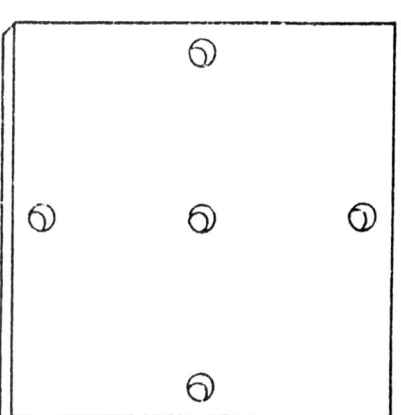

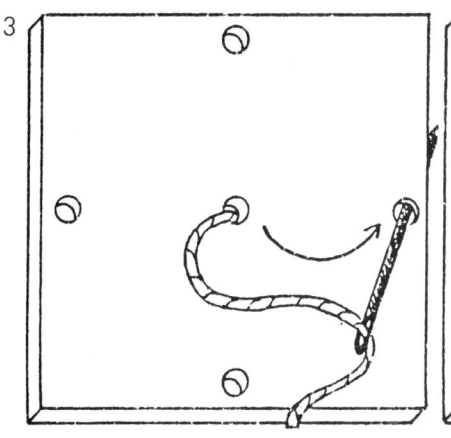

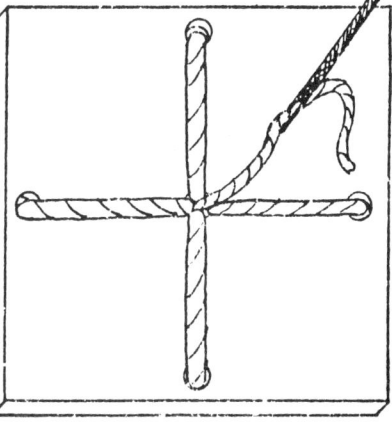

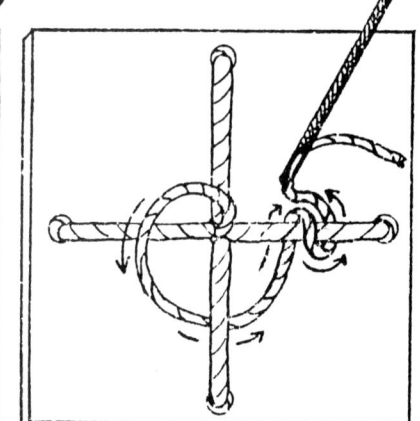

† Illustrated on page 8 of the second photograph section

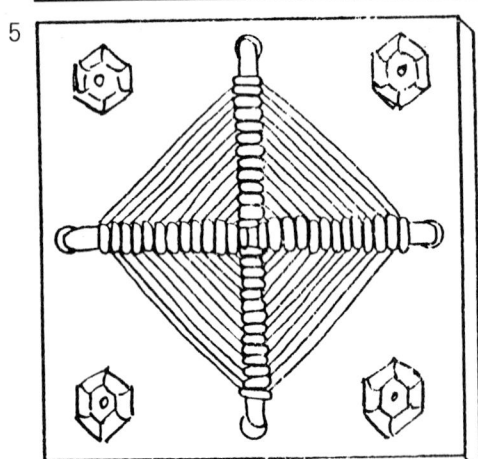

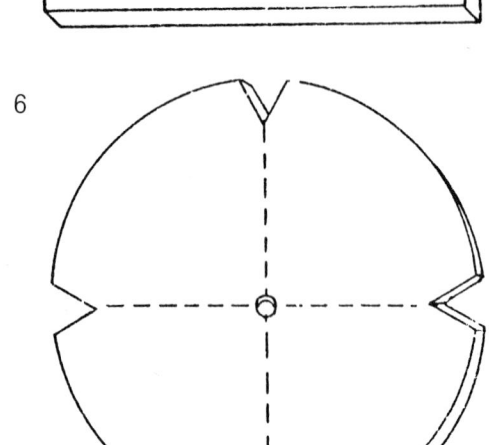

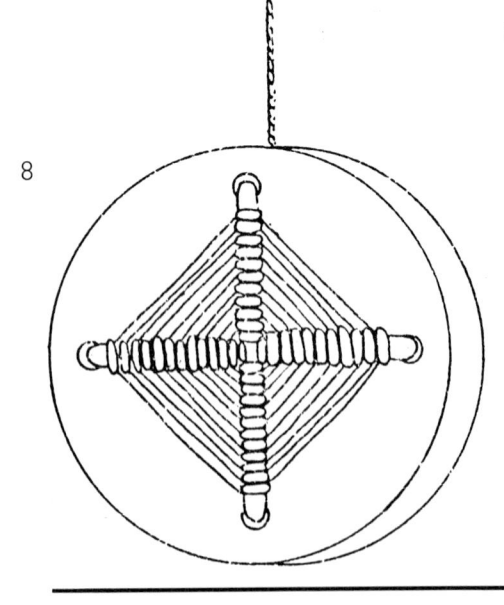

11. Repeat this procedure until there is about 10 cm of wool remaining; then remove the needle, knot on a new length of wool, trim, re-thread the needle and carry on in the same way.

12. When the ends of the spokes are reached, push the needle to the back through one of the pierced holes and fasten securely.

13. Add any surface decoration that you think is suitable — hanging loop, tassels, beads, sequins, buttons, etc (fig. 5).

TEACHING POINTS

1. Use as strong a card as possible and encourage the 'weavers' to thread up the spokes (or, more correctly, *radials*) firmly in order to ensure a good tension in the weaving.

2. Apart from the vocabulary that arises naturally while carrying out this activity, you may also wish to consider discussing the names of polygons (*"What is a regular polygon?"*) and the symmetries that arise — rotational or radial and reflective or line. (*Radial symmetry* is another name for rotational symmetry with the word *radial* meaning *arranged like radii*.)

3. For children who have problems using a protractor, produce a 'cheat' by tracing the circumference of the protractor on to strong card, piercing the centre and snipping out small V-shaped notches to indicate the points to be pierced (fig. 6).

EXTENSIONS AND VARIATIONS

1. Although the basic instructions have been written for a woven square, any regular polygon can be produced by subdividing the 360° in different ways. For example, ⅕ of 360° = 72°, so to construct a regular pentagon, the initial marks will be in 72° steps (0, 72, 144, 216, 288). (See ROUNDABOUTS 2, Teaching point 1 for more information on constructing regular polygons.)

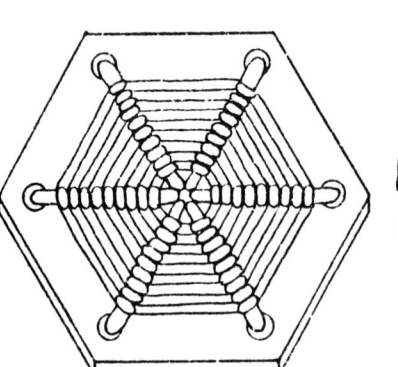

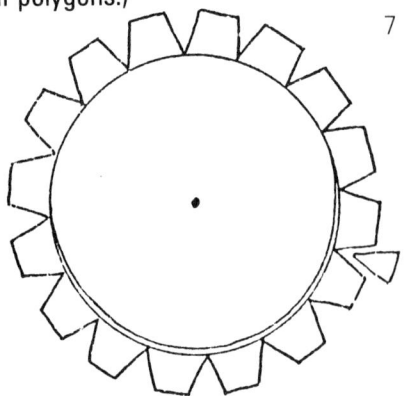

2. Obviously, the shape of the mounting card can be varied to suit the proposed shape of the star.

An hexagonal weaving looks equally effective on an hexagonal or circular mount. This can be modified to simulate a snowflake.

For circular mounts, attaching the activity paper (at step 2) is made easier if small nicks are made all round the edge before glueing down (fig. 7).

3. Mobiles can be made by applying the weaving technique to the back and front of circular cheese boxes that have been prepared by covering the faces with activity paper or PVA paint (fig. 8). The hanging loop is threaded through the top.

Alternatively, if hoops are bound with bias strips of fabric or bandage, spokes can be threaded up at evenly-spaced diameters and the weaving worked inside.

Large macramé rings or old plastic bracelets are particularly useful here. (Fig. 9).

The weaving is equally attractive on both sides, giving a raised pattern on one side and a recessed pattern on the other. (See *STARWEAVING 2* page 48 for more details.)

4. This activity is a form of needle-weaving usually worked on to a fabric background. If you have an embroidery frame there is no reason why you should not try it. The technique is to be found in several forms of embroidery and some children may be interested to find out about and possibly try:

(a) the backstitched wheel stitch (fig. 10),
(b) the Dorset Wheel button (fig. 11),
(c) the 'Spider's Web' stitching used by canal boat people to decorate cushions, etc.

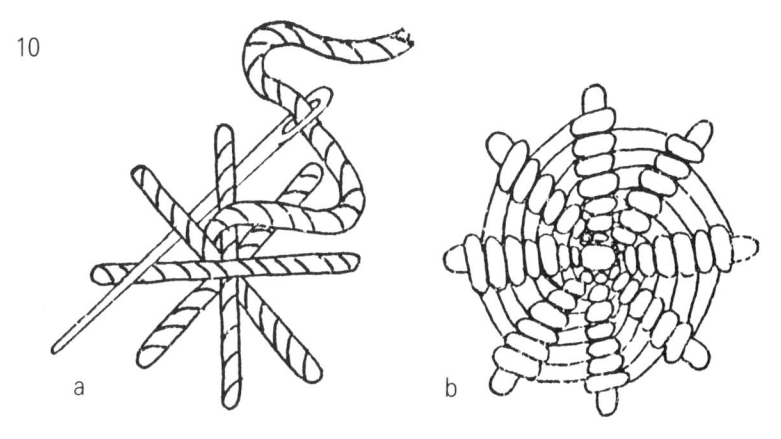

5. Large-eyed beads can be slid on to the radiating spokes at step 9. After bringing up the needle through the centre, slide a bead down on to the wool before taking the wool back to the reverse side. Repeat this for each spoke. The beads are secured by weaving around them and can be positioned to give either a symmetric or an asymmetric effect.

6. More capable weavers can be challenged to investigate how to weave a six-pointed star using the same framework as that for the regular hexagon (fig. 12), or how the pattern in figure 13 might be woven.

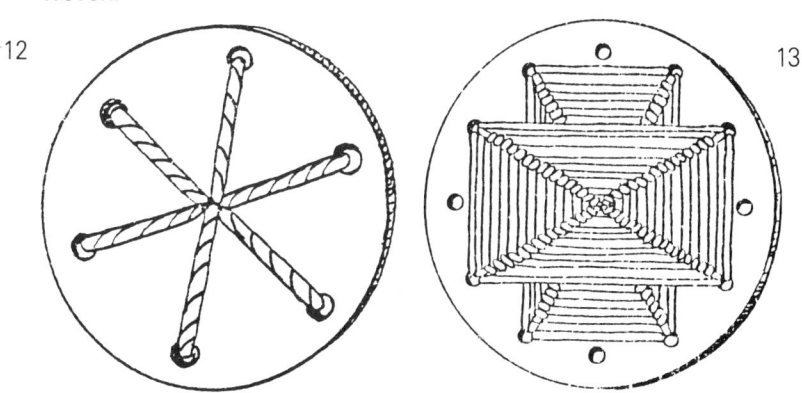

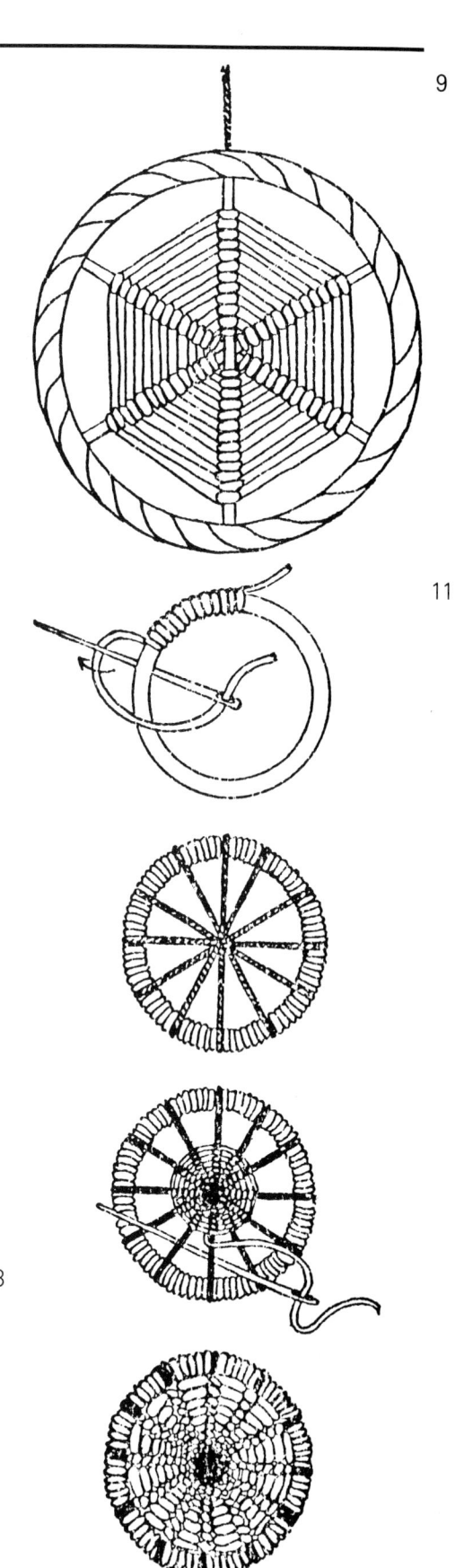

STARWEAVING 3

CIRCLEWEBS †

MATERIALS
Sheet of plain paper, pair of compasses, pencil, eraser, ruler, felt pens or coloured pencils, a pad of newspaper.

VOCABULARY
Centre, circle, circumference, radius, arc, concentric circles, rotational or turning symmetry of order . . . , hexagonal.

The basic activity concentrates on using a ruler and a pair of compasses to develop patterns. It assumes that children have had earlier experience of using pairs of compasses to create 'free-choice' designs.

METHOD
1. Place the sheet of paper on a pad of newspaper and mark the centre of the sheet with a pencil dot.
2. With the dot as centre, use the compasses to draw a feint circle with radius 2 cm.
3. Keeping the same radius, lightly mark off six evenly-spaced small arcs on the circumference of the circle.
4. Use a ruler to join each point where an arc crosses the circumference to the centre (fig. 1).
5. Using the same centre, draw another feint circle, but this time with a radius of 4 cm.
6. Keeping the radius at 4 cm, lightly mark off six arcs on the outside circle, making sure that they are not in line with the arcs on the inner circle (fig. 2).
7. With a ruler, join up each of the marks on the outer circle in turn with a mark on the inner circle (fig. 3).

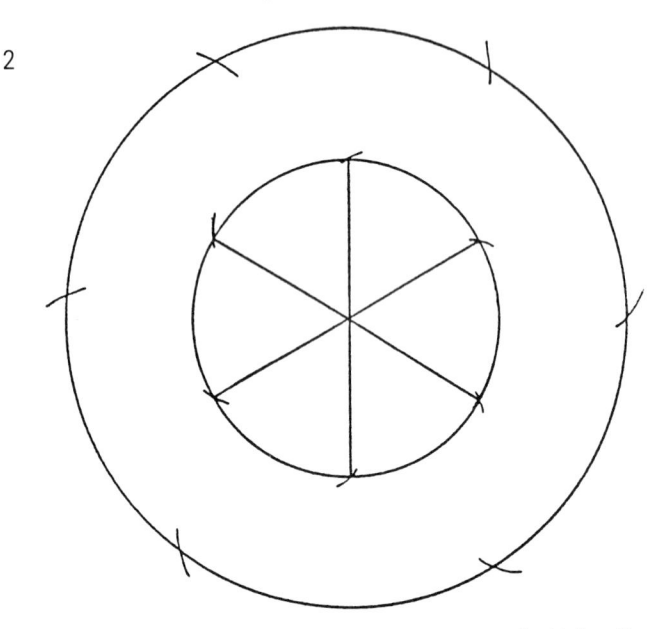

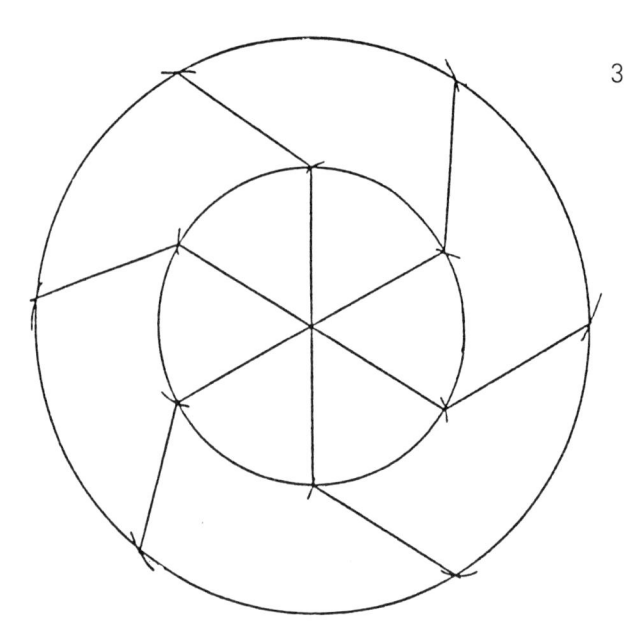

8. Using the same centre, draw a third circle with radius 6 cm and mark off six arcs on its circumference as before.
9. Repeat step 7. Your pattern will now look something like figure 4.
10. (Optional) Draw further concentric circles and more lines using the same method as before.
11. (Optional) Join up the points on the outermost circle to form an hexagonal border.
12. Rub out any parts of the circle you do not want in your final pattern.

† *Illustrated on page 6 of the second photograph section*

13. Turn your pattern round slowly. Can you see why it has 'turning' or *rotational* symmetry?
14. Colour your pattern.

TEACHING POINTS
1. This is an excellent activity for reinforcing vocabulary relating to the circle and measuring skills.
2. If you allow children to stick a pin through the centre of the completed pattern and spin it (preferably before colouring), the rotational symmetry, in this case of order 6, is highlighted.
3. Large versions, using a pair of blackboard compasses or the ancient 'pin and string' method for drawing circles, look very effective when painted or coloured with crayons.

EXTENSIONS AND VARIATIONS
1. Those patterns finished with a hexagonal border, as in step 11, can be cut out and displayed in a tessellating arrangement (fig. 5).
2. Once the basic technique has been mastered, allow children to experiment to find their own variations.

3. Make the pattern in the same way as far as step 10, but then, instead of joining each mark to the previous circle, join some or all back to the centre of the circle (fig. 6).
This pattern has *rotational symmetry of order 6*.
"Can you use the same method of construction to make a pattern that has:
(a) rotational symmetry of order 2 only,
(b) rotational symmetry of order 3 only?"

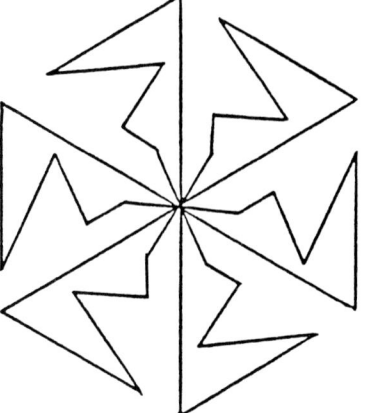

SWOPAROUNDS †

MATERIALS
Pair of compasses, ruler, pencil, scissors, four 10 cm gummed squares (two of each of two colours), backing sheet at least 32 cm square, brass paper fastener (optional).

VOCABULARY
Diagonal, triangle, right-angled, isosceles, congruent, circular, radius, perimeter, rotate, rotational symmetry.

Both guided and open-ended activities, using paper-cutting and counterchange techniques, are suggested to achieve pleasing symmetrical patterns.

METHOD
1. On each of the four gummed squares draw in one diagonal, then cut along the diagonal to form eight identical (*congruent*) right-angled triangles which have two sides equal (*isosceles*). (Fig. 1).
2. Clearly mark the centre of the backing sheet; use it to draw a circle of at least 16 cm radius and cut it out.
3. Arrange the triangles *without glueing* in a rotating pattern so that all the triangles meet at the centre of the circle (fig. 2).
4. When you can do this, remove the triangles and stack them on top of each other with the coloured sides facing upwards.
5. Make sure the triangles fit exactly, then cut from a short side to the long side (fig. 3). Remove the smaller matching sections from the triangles and keep them for future use.
6. Place each of the remaining eight congruent pieces around the centre of the backing sheet so that the colours alternate (fig. 4).

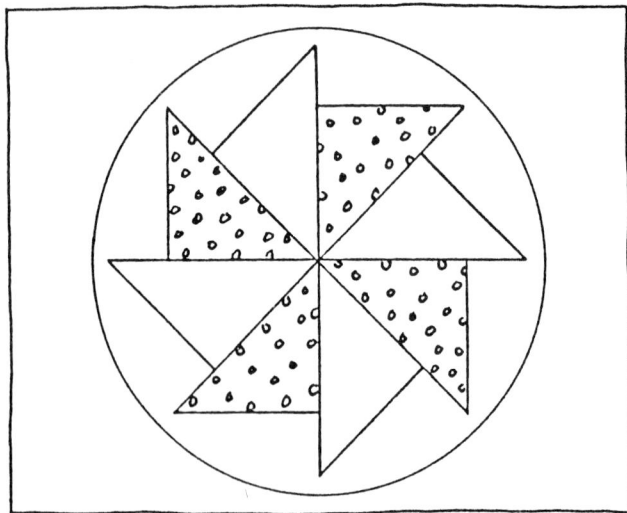

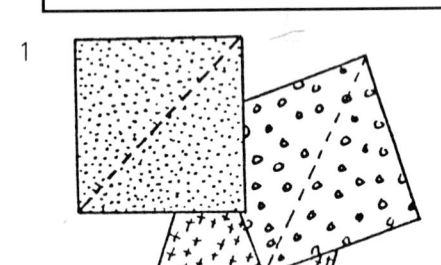

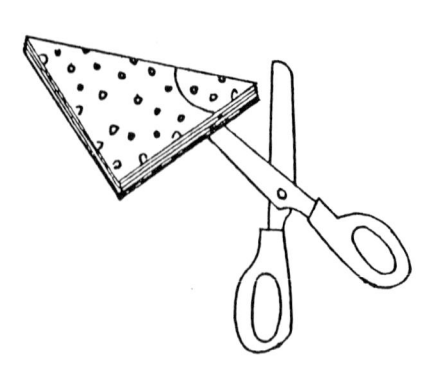

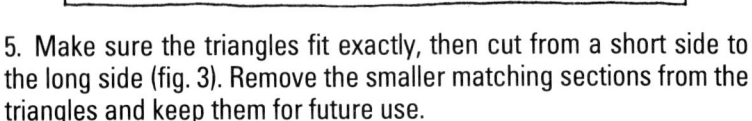

102   SWOPAROUNDS   † *Illustrated on page 7 of the second photograph section*

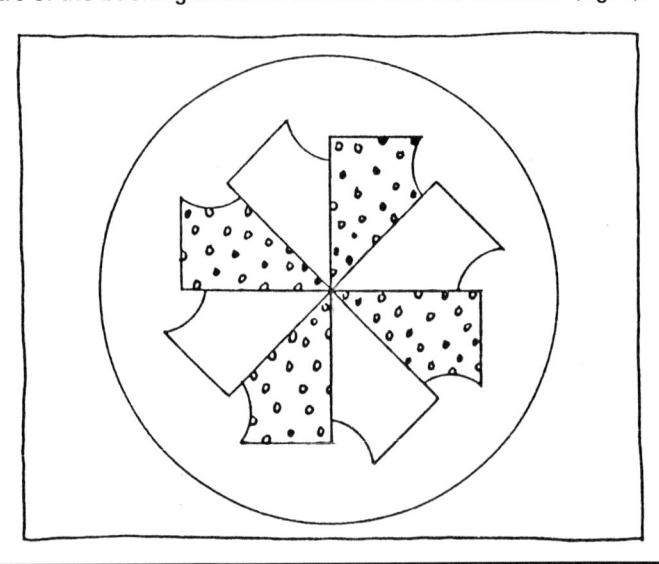

7. Glue the sections down.
8. Place each of the eight sections you cut away in step 5 in a corresponding position around the perimeter of the existing pattern. This can be done in different ways (fig. 5).
9. Glue down the cut out pieces.

You have now constructed a pattern with *rotational symmetry of order 8*.

10. (Optional) Cut out a second circular backing sheet with a radius 2 cm greater than the first one (step 2). Pierce a small hole through the centre of this and the rotating pattern, secure them together with a brass paper fastener so that the pattern can be rotated.

TEACHING POINTS

1. This activity requires a systematic and orderly approach and you may find it interesting to observe and discuss the techniques that children adopt to help them establish the rotating pattern.
2. The order of rotational symmetry raises interesting issues:
"Does the pattern have rotational symmetry of order 4 or 8 and what reasons can be given to justify the choice?"
"Also, why do the eight angles fit together around the centre to form a complete revolution?"
"What size must each of the angles be?"
"How many right angles can be spotted?"
3. The counterchange technique, that is when the cut-away section of one colour is replaced with the corresponding section in the alternate colour, is used extensively in heraldic design (fig. 6). This could provide further interest and research.

EXTENSIONS AND VARIATIONS

1. (a) If only a small section is removed in step 5, these smaller sections can be stuck on top of the larger sections by matching the angles that meet at the centre (fig. 7).
(b) If the larger and smaller sections are made up separately on different backing sheets, they can be cut out around their perimeters and the smaller design fixed on top of the larger with a brass paper fastener. This allows the inner pattern to rotate freely.
2. Other symmetrical arrangements can be investigated. For example,
"Is it possible to modify the design to obtain a pattern that has reflective as well as rotational symmetry?"
"What could happen if sections were removed from both of the smaller angles of the triangles?"

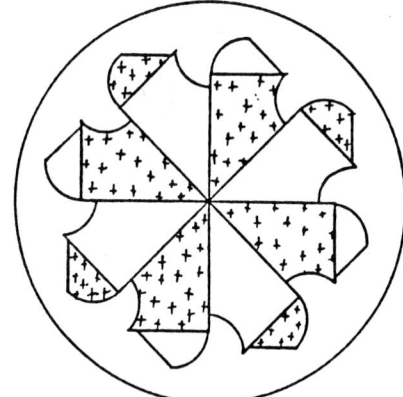

SWOPAROUNDS 103

FOLDING STAR CONTAINERS †

An origami technique is used to convert a piece of hexagonal paper into a star-shaped container without glue or scissors.

MATERIALS
Scissors, pair of compasses, ruler, pencil, 15–20 cm square of gift-wrap paper or marbled paper (see *TECHNIQUES AND MATERIALS* at the back of this book for instructions).

VOCABULARY
Regular hexagon, hexagonal, rotate, axis of symmetry, radius, perimeter, circumference, arc, vertex (corner), edge, base, equilateral, intersect, open, closed.

METHOD
1. With the wrong side of the square of paper facing upwards, find and mark the centre of the square with a pencil.
2. Set the radius of the pair of compasses so that, when a circle is drawn, its circumference lies just inside the perimeter of the square.
3. Using the same radius, step off six evenly-spaced arcs around the circumference.
4. With ruler and pencil, join up the points where the arcs intersect the circumference to construct a regular hexagon (fig. 1).
5. Carefully cut out the hexagon.

In steps 6 to 9, keep the side you wish to form the inside of the container facing upwards.

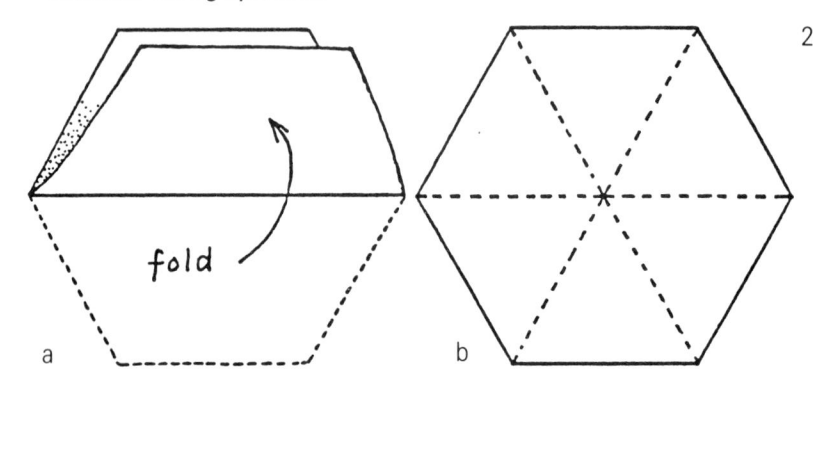

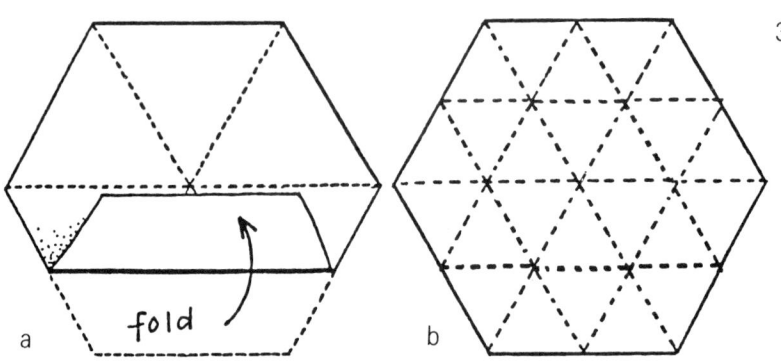

6. Fold the hexagon along one axis of symmetry from corner to corner. Press the fold firmly and then unfold. (Fig. 2a.)
7. Repeat step 6 twice more (for each axis of symmetry) so that you end up with a pattern of six equilateral triangles, created by the three folds (fig. 2b).
8. Take each edge in turn and fold it over so that it lines up with the diagonal passing through the centre of the hexagon. Press the fold firmly then unfold. (Fig. 3a.)
9. Repeat step 8 with each of the other five edges in turn. You should now have made an over-all pattern of 24 equilateral triangles. The small inner hexagon will form the base of the container. (Fig. 3b.)

---

104 FOLDING STAR CONTAINERS   † *Illustrated on page 8 of the second photograph section*

4

5

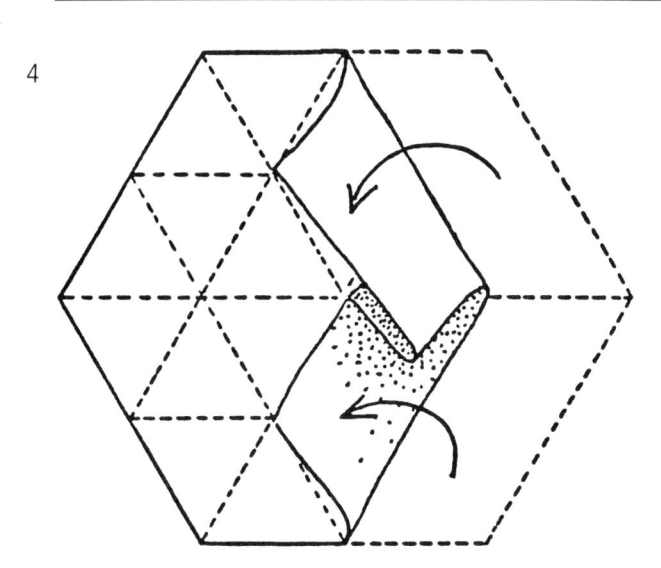

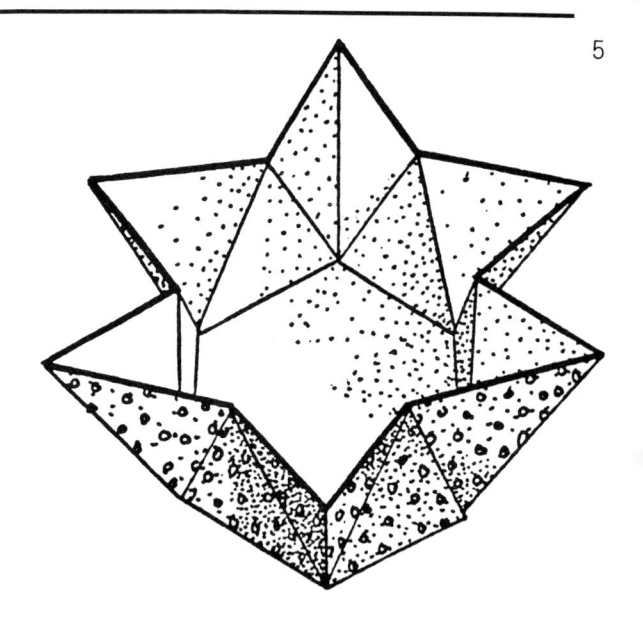

10. To make the 'lid', pinch together, from *underneath*, the two triangles that meet at a corner so that they fit on to each other (fig. 4).
11. Without releasing them, bend them both down in a clockwise direction and flatten them out.
12. Repeat steps 10 and 11 with the five remaining corners.
You should now find that the container has a lid with rotational symmetry of order six. (Fig. 5.)

TEACHING POINTS
1. This idea is best demonstrated to a small group, where the pupils can follow your example before tackling the activity unsupervised. It requires a systematic approach and precise folding.
2. The container is particularly suitable for a small Christmas present, because when it is flicked open it forms a star-shaped open container. In the closed form it could contain a small gift; in its open form it could hold crisps or nuts.

EXTENSIONS AND VARIATIONS
1. An hexagonal card or a snowflake cutout can be designed to fit in the bottom of the container to carry a simple Christmas or birthday greeting. An advent calendar could also be designed by glueing the folding star containers on to a suitable background with a different picture, made from old Christmas cards, inside each one.
2. A stronger container can be made, which is equally attractive inside and out, if two thin layers of paper are made up as one; for example:
(a) tissue paper inside and marbled paper or gift-wrap paper on the outside;
(b) two sheets of gummed paper stuck together.
3. If at step 5 you cut around the circumference of the circle instead of the perimeter of the hexagon, then proceed to fold in the same way as before, you will find that, on completion, a small hexagon will appear at the centre of the lid as if by magic (fig. 6).

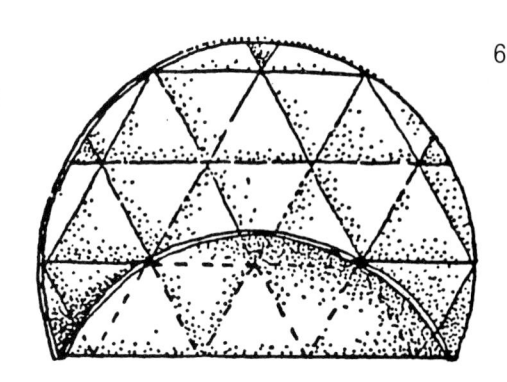

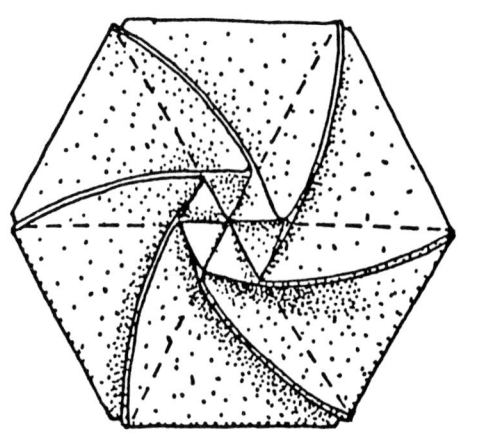

6

FOLDING STAR CONTAINERS

7

Lid → A ... A
glue tabs A and B here.
B ... B

Base →

8

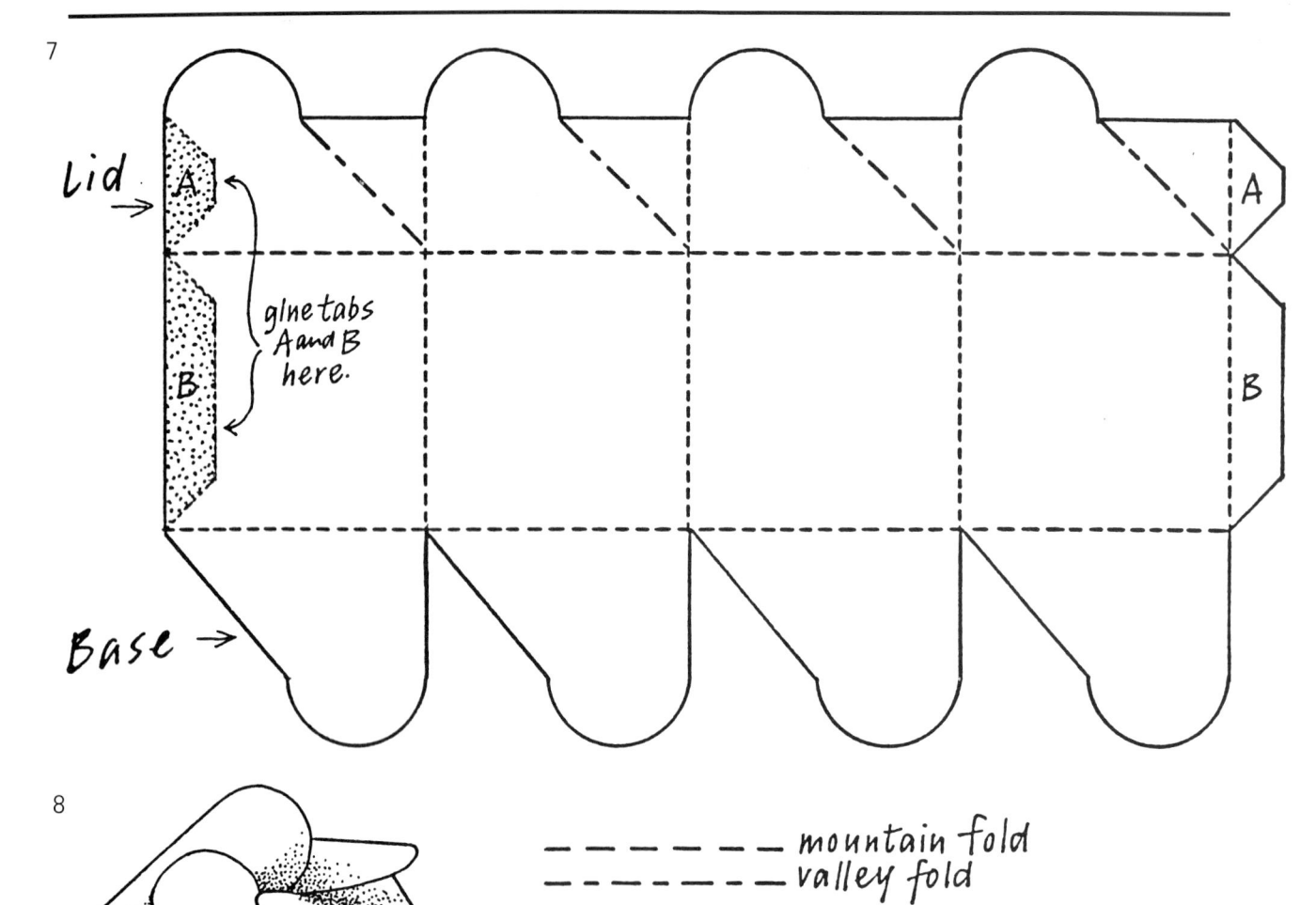

------ mountain fold
- - - - - valley fold

4. Encourage children to consider using other methods of construction of the hexagon, possibly using isometric grid paper or a protractor to measure out the corners of the hexagon.

5. Allow experimentation with different regular polygons. By folding in all the lines of symmetry of a regular pentagon, for instance, or a regular octagon (more difficult!) other containers can be constructed.

6. This container is created by using simple origami techniques. Allow more dextrous pupils to make other containers to be found in books on origami, an excellent source of extension material which uses symmetrical paper folding as its main construction technique.

7. A class collection and examination of a wide range of three-dimensional packaging materials will reveal many types of lid mechanisms, some simple, some more complex. The lid of a *J-Cloth* box, for instance, is quite intricate. Much of the packaging for gifts for special occasions has interesting features, for the most part too complex for young hands to construct, but the net in figure 7 makes up into an attractive cube container with a four-petal lid (fig. 8). It can be made in card, preferably covered in advance with decorated paper to add to its strength and aesthetic appeal.

8. In *The Gift Box Book*, fifteen fascinating gift boxes ready to cut out and make up, should inspire even the most reluctant pupils to have a go, and the more creative to design their own.

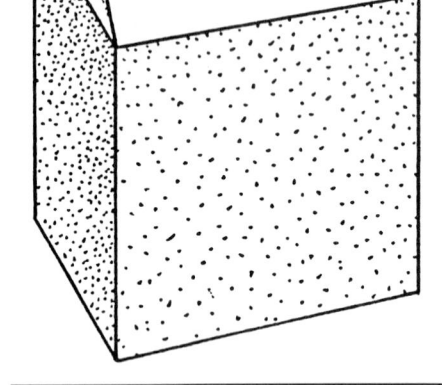

REFERENCES & RESOURCES
Origami in Colour Octopus Books
The Gift Box Book G Jenkins and A Wild; Tarquin Publications
Gift Wrapping — Creative Ideas from Japan A teacher's reference book; K Bkiguchi; Kodansha International Ltd.

FOLDING STAR CONTAINERS

ISLAMIC PATTERNS †

The use of geometric designs in mosques, Arabic architecture and artefacts has great religious significance. It is a form of sacred geometry. To carry out this activity without delving into this aspect is to undervalue it. Local museums, mosques and reference books can provide a wealth of suitable background information.

MATERIALS
Centimetre squared paper, thin paper such as computer print-out paper, pencil, ruler, colouring materials.

VOCABULARY
Axes of symmetry, symmetrical, intersection, construction lines, perimeter, tessellation, reflection, rotation, translation.

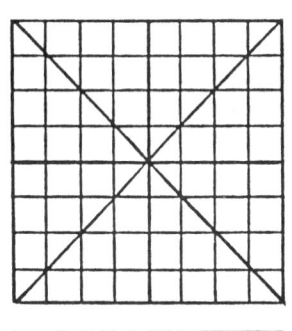

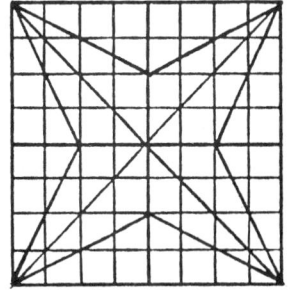

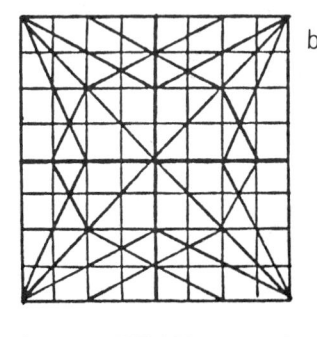

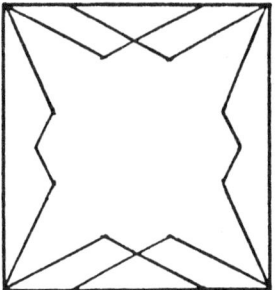

METHOD
1. Secure a blank sheet of thin paper over centimetre squared paper and mark out the perimeter of a square 8 cm × 8 cm using the grid lines as a guide.
2. Draw in the axes of symmetry (fig. 1).
3. Build up a symmetrical pattern, using the intersections of grid lines and axes of symmetry to help (fig. 2).
4. Choose some of these lines or parts of them and go over them boldly, making sure that the final choice of lines is symmetrical about at least two axes. (You may have to experiment until you get a pattern you really like.)
These bold lines will now become the 'master' pattern for the next step. (Fig. 3.)
5. Take a fresh sheet of thin paper and, using the square grid, mark out 8 cm squares *very lightly* in pencil.
6. Place the pattern 'master' under the sheet and line it up in one of the pencilled squares. Trace the pattern and continue in this way until you have covered the whole sheet (fig. 4).
7. Erase any unwanted grid lines and work out a suitable symmetrical colouring arrangement.

† Illustrated on page 7 of the second photograph section

TEACHING POINTS

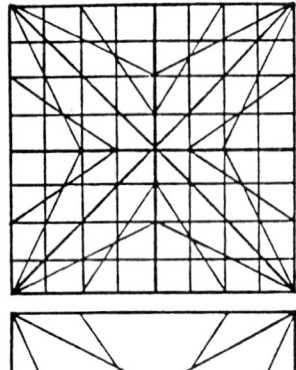

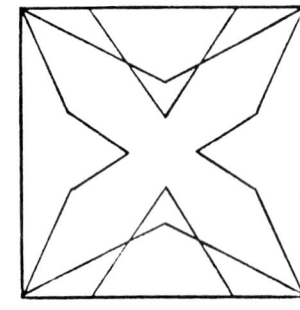

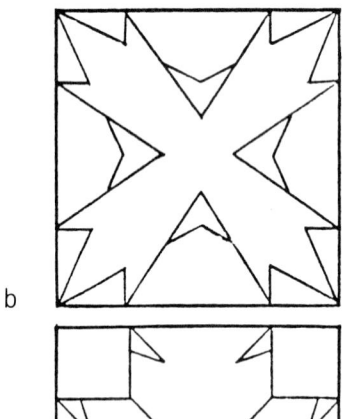

1. This activity highlights how construction lines, which can be removed later, are often an integral part of the design process.
2. Copying the repeated pattern unit many times by hand can become tedious and it is suggested that, once the activity has been carried out with paper and pencil, computer assisted design packages such as *Islam* can take over and extend the work.
3. Polygons that occur within the design can be named and classified.
4. This activity is linked with several areas of mathematics — reflection, rotation, translation and tessellation — which should be brought out in discussion. It is also worthwhile to link the activity with a study of the Muslim religion, Islam.

EXTENSIONS AND VARIATIONS

1. Allow a small group of children to carry out the first three steps of the method in the same way, that is using the same construction lines, then develop their own designs in step 4. In figure 5 there is an example showing three different designs developed from the same construction lines.

Alternatively, a pair of children could start from the same base, then one child develops a design with two axes of symmetry while the other creates a design with four axes of symmetry.

2. Although the square has been used as the module for creating an Islamic pattern, the same technique can be used just as well with either an equilateral triangle or a regular hexagon as the module (fig. 6a,b). For these, isometric grid paper is used in the same way as the square grid. (See master sheet at the back of this book.)

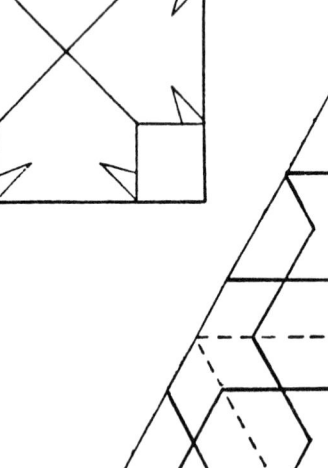

108 ISLAMIC PATTERNS

6 b

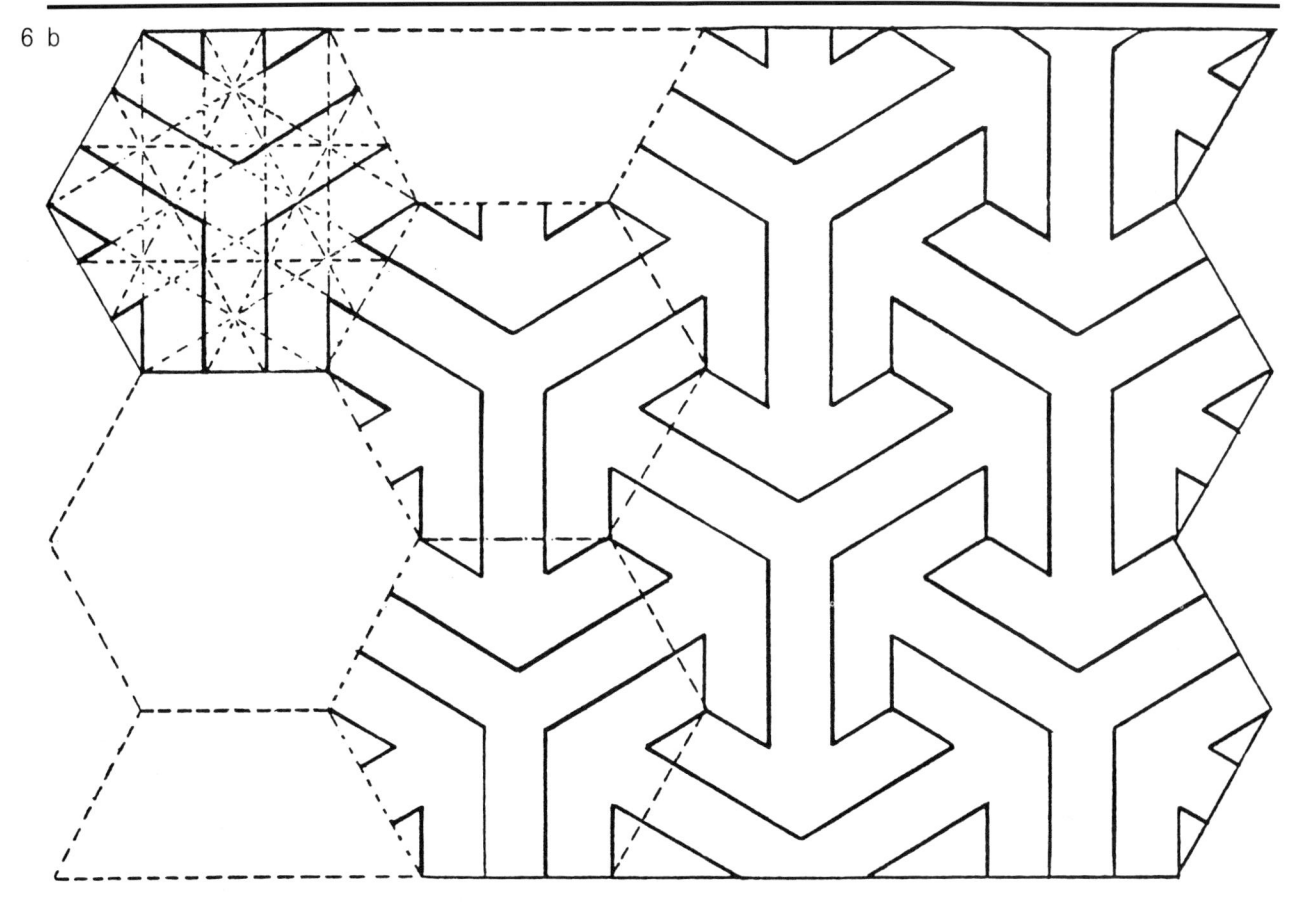

3. More adventurous designers may enjoy adapting the technique for semi-regular tessellations; for example, a grid consisting of regular octagons and squares (fig. 7).
4. Islamic patterns are often 'interlaced'. See if the children can find out what this means and why the technique is used so extensively. Compare with the interlacing used in Celtic patterns.
5. Find out about patterns in other religions; for example, Rangoli patterns, Mandalas, etc.

7

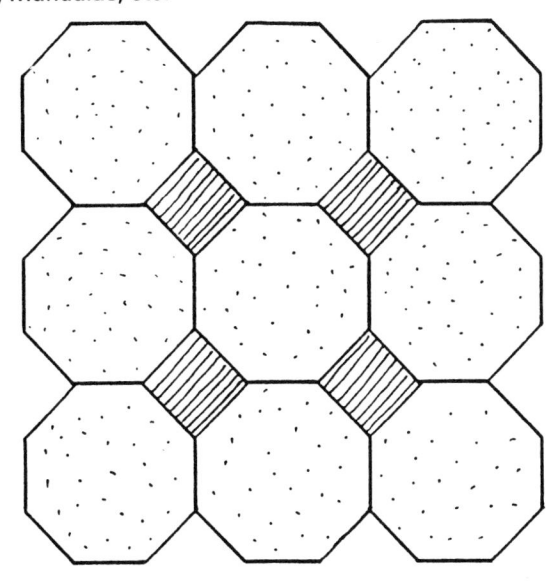

REFERENCES & RESOURCES
Islamic Design Posters Tarquin Publications
Polysymmetrics Tarquin Publications
Overlapping Hexagon Charts Pictorial Charts Educational Trust
Activity Mats Association of Teachers of Mathematics
Arabic Geometrical Pattern & Design Dover Publications
Geometric Concepts in Islamic Art El-said and Parman, World of Islam; Festival Publishing Company Ltd.
Islam Computer program on Junior Maths 2 Disc; EARO
Oriel Paper Stained glass window kit; Philip and Tacey.

ISLAMIC PATTERNS

TESSELLATION 4 †

MATERIALS
Card, Sellotape, backing sheets, pencil, ruler, black pen, colouring pencils or felt pens, scissors, tracing paper, pin.

VOCABULARY
Edge, vertex, rotate, adjacent, grid, pivot.

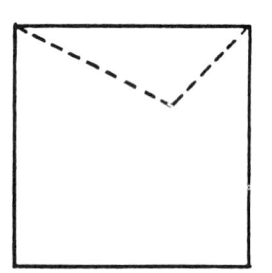

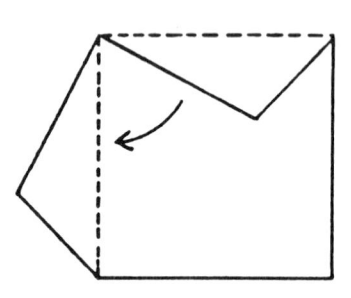

A further method for creating tessellating patterns consists of cutting and rotating a piece about *a vertex* (instead of the midpoint of a side). Shapes that tessellate and have at least two adjacent sides of the same length are ideal for this technique, which was developed by Mauritz Escher to produce his famous and intricate designs.

METHOD
1. Start with a shape that tessellates and has at least two adjacent sides of the same length. (Equilateral triangle, square, rhombus, regular hexagon, for example.)
Draw it on card and cut it out.
2. Draw a piece to be cut away, starting at one vertex and ending at the next (fig. 1).
3. Carefully cut away the piece and rotate it about one vertex until it is aligned with the adjacent edge of the original shape (fig. 2).*
4. Sellotape these two edges together to form the template of a new shape, which will tessellate as it is or you can go on to step 5.
5. Repeat steps 2, 3 and 4 on another pair of equal adjacent sides (fig. 3).

TEACHING POINTS
1. *If the starting shape is drawn in the centre of a piece of card and not cut out, the 'cut away' line can be traced on to tracing paper and, using a pin as a pivot to rotate it about a vertex, copied in its new position on the outside of the original shape.
The tile template can then be cut out in one piece.
2. Notice that in the example the two sides were rotated in a clockwise direction, giving rise to this overall pattern (fig. 4).

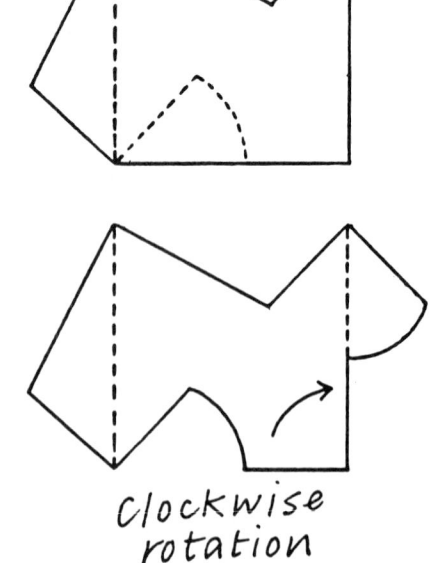

clockwise rotation

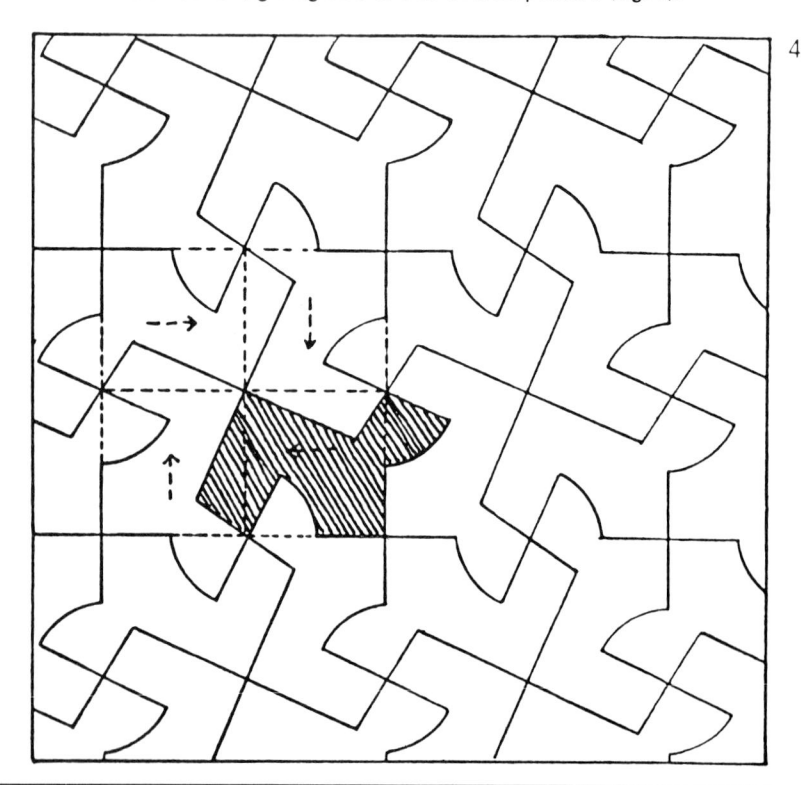

† Illustrated on page 5 of the second photograph section

Had the two sides been rotated in an anti-clockwise direction, the pattern in figure 5 would be formed.

Comparison of the two possible versions and the ways in which groups of four 'dog-like' shapes fit around a point leads to some interesting discussion on rotational symmetry.

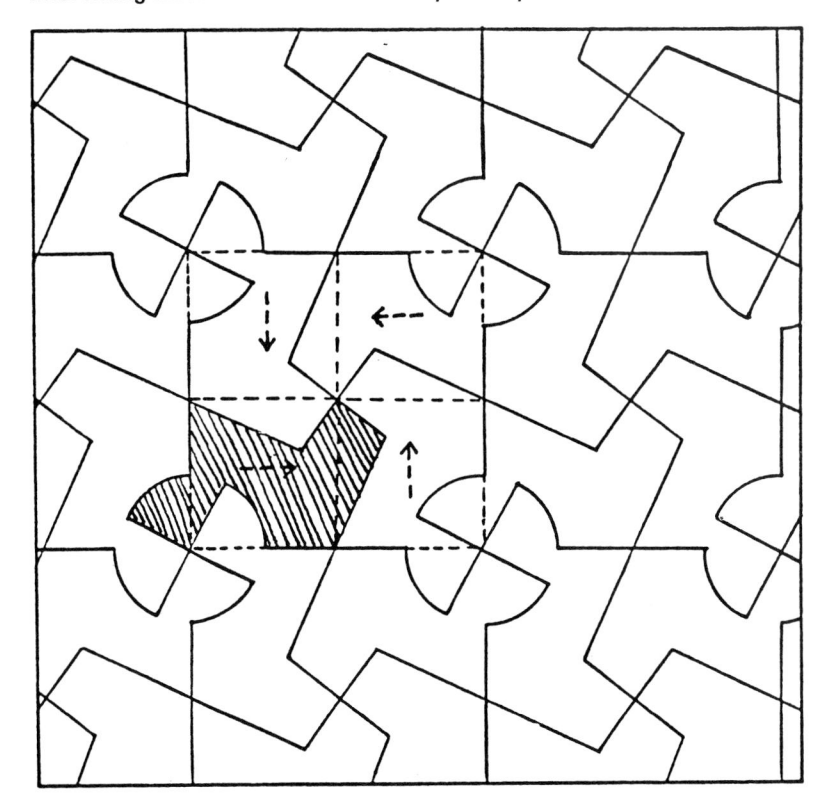

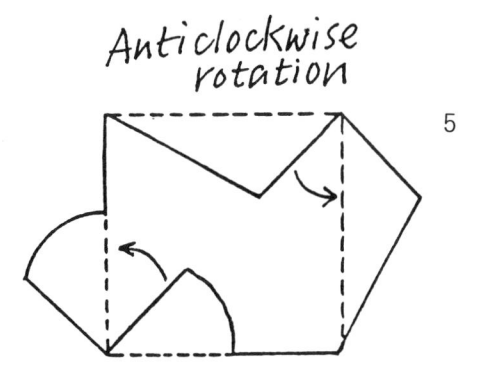

Anticlockwise rotation

5

EXTENSIONS AND VARIATIONS

1. Some children may be keen to investigate what happens if the 'piece' is rotated about each of the vertices in turn of a shape with four, or six, equal sides. This is illustrated by an example starting with a rhombus (fig. 6).

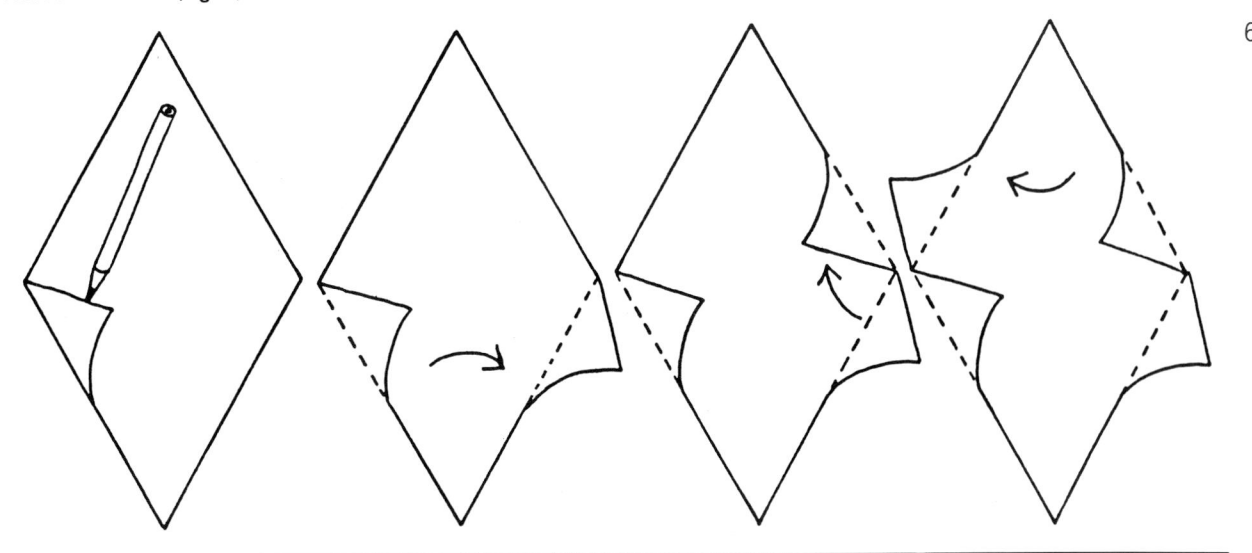

6

TESSELLATION 4   111

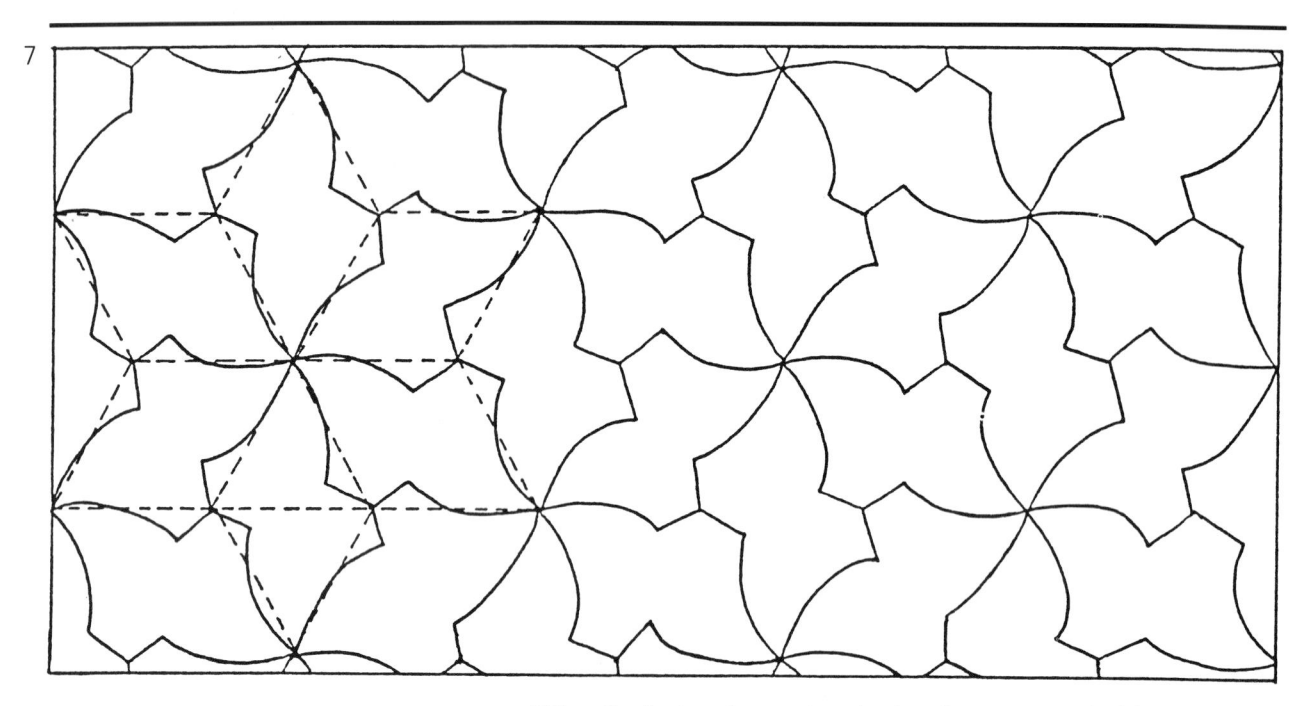

Either the 'cut and rotate' or the 'tracing paper and pin' method can be used for this particular example (fig. 7).

2. The more adventurous might wish to try creating some 'Escher-type' tessellations. On the opposite page is a simplified version, based on a square, of his famous *Study of a Regular Division of the Plane with Reptiles*. The original one is based on a regular hexagon. This example cannot make use of the 'cut and rotate' method because the alteration to each side involves a line that cuts back and forth across the original straight boundary; so the 'tracing paper and pin' technique must be employed (fig. 8).

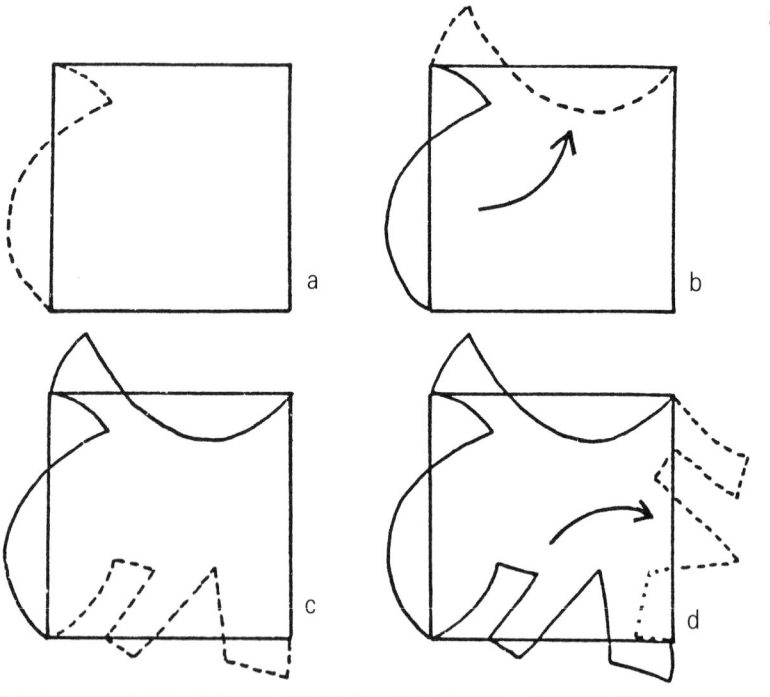

f

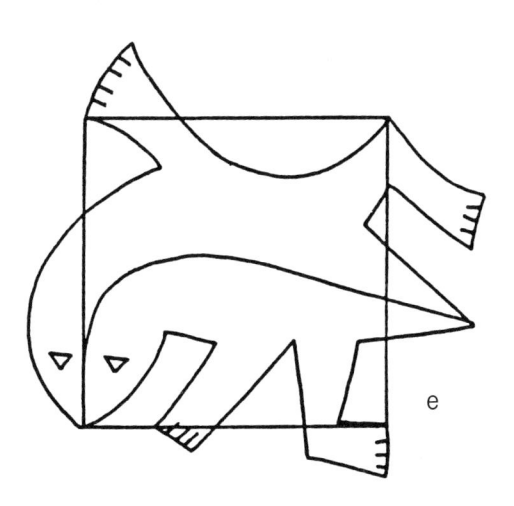

e

REFERENCES & RESOURCES
Sources of Mathematical Discovery
L Mottershead; Basil Blackwell
A Way with Maths Langdon and
Snape; CUP
The Tessellations File de Cordova;
Tarquin Publications
Nuffield Maths 5–11 Teachers' and
Pupils' Book 6; R Wyvill; Longman
Creating Escher-type Drawings
Ranucci and Teeters; Jonathan Press
Teeter's Escher-type Posters
Creative Publications/
Jonathan Press
Escher Posters Selection from
Tarquin Publications
M C Escher Kaleidocycles Tarquin
Publications
Tessellations A computer program
(BBC); CUP

TESSELLATION 4   113

MARBLED PAPER

MATERIALS
Newspaper, flat container (desk tray or roasting tin), model paints (or any oil based paints), turpentine substitute, vinegar, plastic straws, foil, cloth rag, A4 cartridge paper, spring clothes pegs.

METHOD
1. Prepare a table and drying areas in advance by covering them generously with newspaper.
2. Line a flat container with foil and place it centrally on the work table.
3. Pour in cold water to a depth of 3 cm. Add a few drops of vinegar to soften the water. The paints will then blend better.
4. Using a different straw for each colour of model paint, trickle a *few* drops of 2 or 3 colours on top of the water. Stir very gently if the colours do not blend sufficiently.
5. Lay a sheet of cartridge paper gently on top of the water and leave it for a few seconds.
6. Take hold of one narrow edge and pull the sheet *up and along* at the same time so that it is pulled across the surface of the water without being immersed.
7. Remove the sheet and place it aside to dry with the marbled side uppermost. Drying is best left overnight so it is advisable to plan a 'marbling session' in advance.
8. Clean up working area, removing paint from fingers with rag dipped in turpentine substitute.

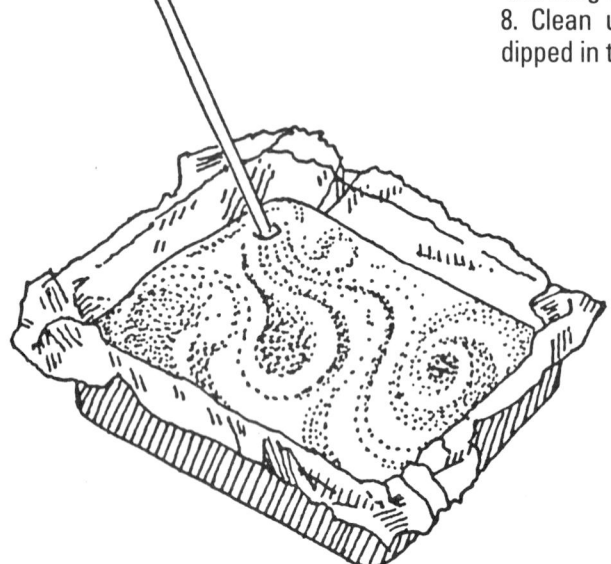

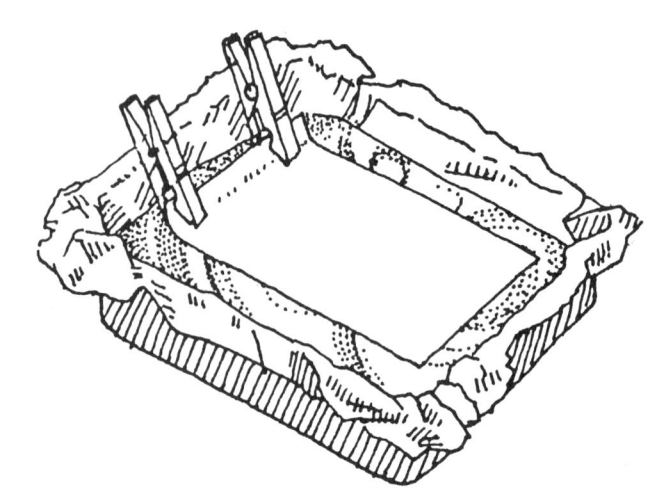

TEACHING POINTS
1. Where possible, work with a small group of children so that careful supervision ensures that children do not use too much paint as this gives inferior results. To get rid of unwanted paint from the surface of the water, float some newspaper on the top to absorb the excess.
2. Children can avoid getting paint on their fingers if they use spring clothes pegs to lift sheets from the flat container.
3. Allow each child to make several sheets of marbled paper at one sitting — it has many decorative uses, several of which are referred to in this book.
4. Model paints are particularly good for marbling but you can also use remnants of household gloss paint, thinned down to a creamy consistency with turpentine substitute, or marbling inks, which are expensive but easy to use. Gold and silver metallic model paints can also be considered for a festive effect.

TECHNIQUES AND MATERIALS

PAPER SPRING

METHOD
1. Take the two contrasting strips of sugar paper and glue the ends at right angles to each other (fig. 1).
2. Fold the horizontal strip to the right (fig. 2).
3. Fold the vertical strip upwards (fig. 3).
4. Fold the horizontal strip to the left (fig. 4).
5. Fold the vertical strip downwards (fig. 5).
6. Continue folding in this four-move pattern until the whole length of each strip is used. Glue the ends to stop the spring unwinding.

MATERIALS
Glue; 2 long narrow strips of sugar paper of contrasting colours, 3 cm wide. (For the Jack-in-the-box spring, the strips need to be about 84 cm long — the length of the A1 size sheet.)

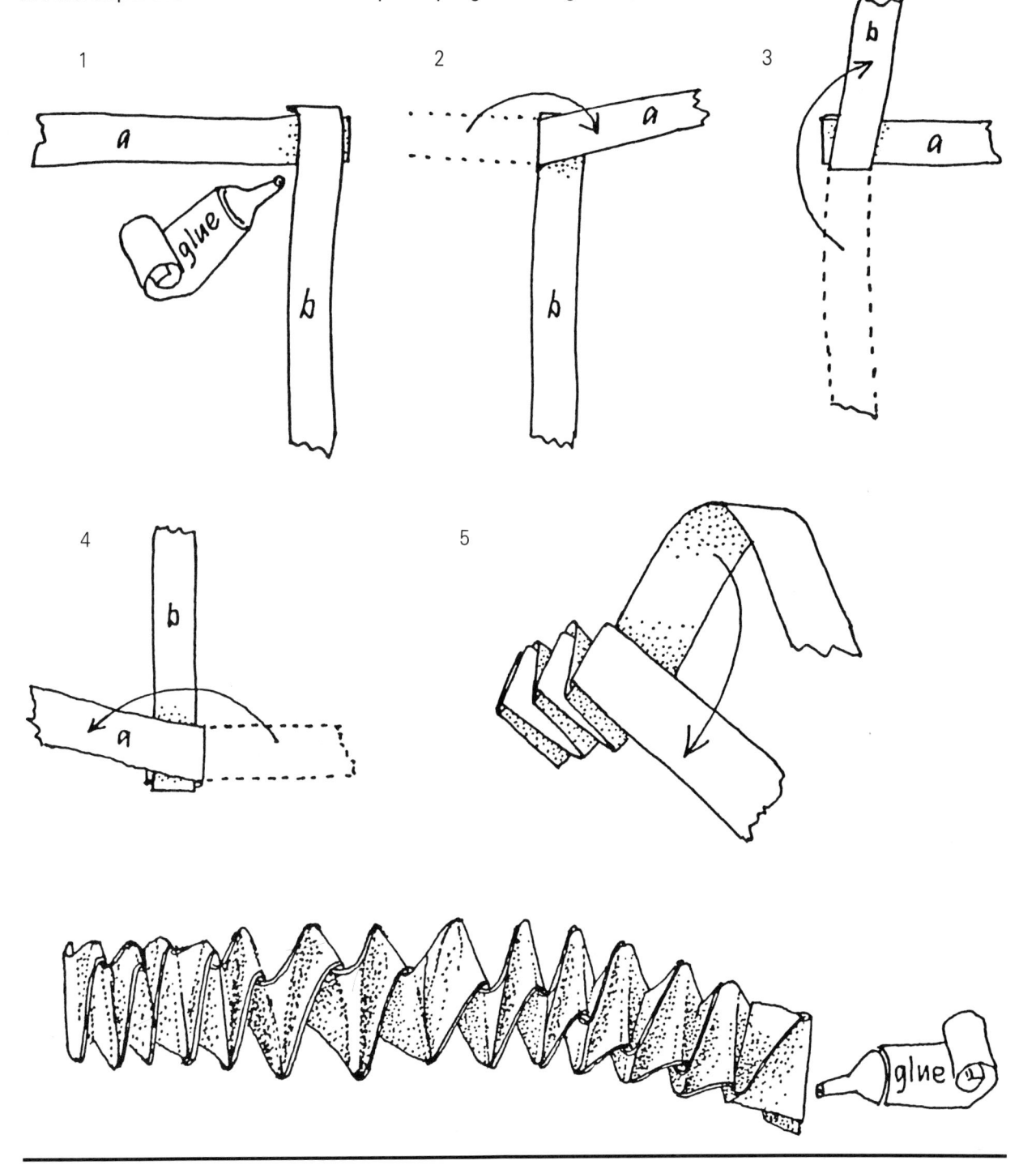

TECHNIQUES AND MATERIALS

A STAR IS BORN

This method shows how to fold a five-pointed star.

MATERIALS
A rectangle 28 cm × 21 cm. (An A4 sheet with 17 mm cut off the length.)
For a larger star make the rectangle 41 cm × 30 cm. (An A3 sheet with 10 mm cut off the length.)
Ruler, pencil, scissors.

METHOD

1. Start with the rectangle in *landscape* position (fig. 1a) and fold it in half to make a 4-page leaflet with the crease on the left-hand side.
2. Find M, the midpoint of the base, by folding (fig. 1b).
3. Fold the left-hand top corner down to M and make a sharp crease (fig. 1c).
4. Fold back the bottom left-hand right-angled triangle until it is hidden behind the rest (fig. 1d).
5. Bring down the top edge to bisect the acute angle (fig. 1e). There are now 10 thicknesses of paper.
6. Turn over from top to bottom. Mark S 5 cm from O. *(8 cm for the larger star.)*
Draw the straight line SA and cut along it (fig. 2).
7. Open out to give a five-pointed star (fig. 3).

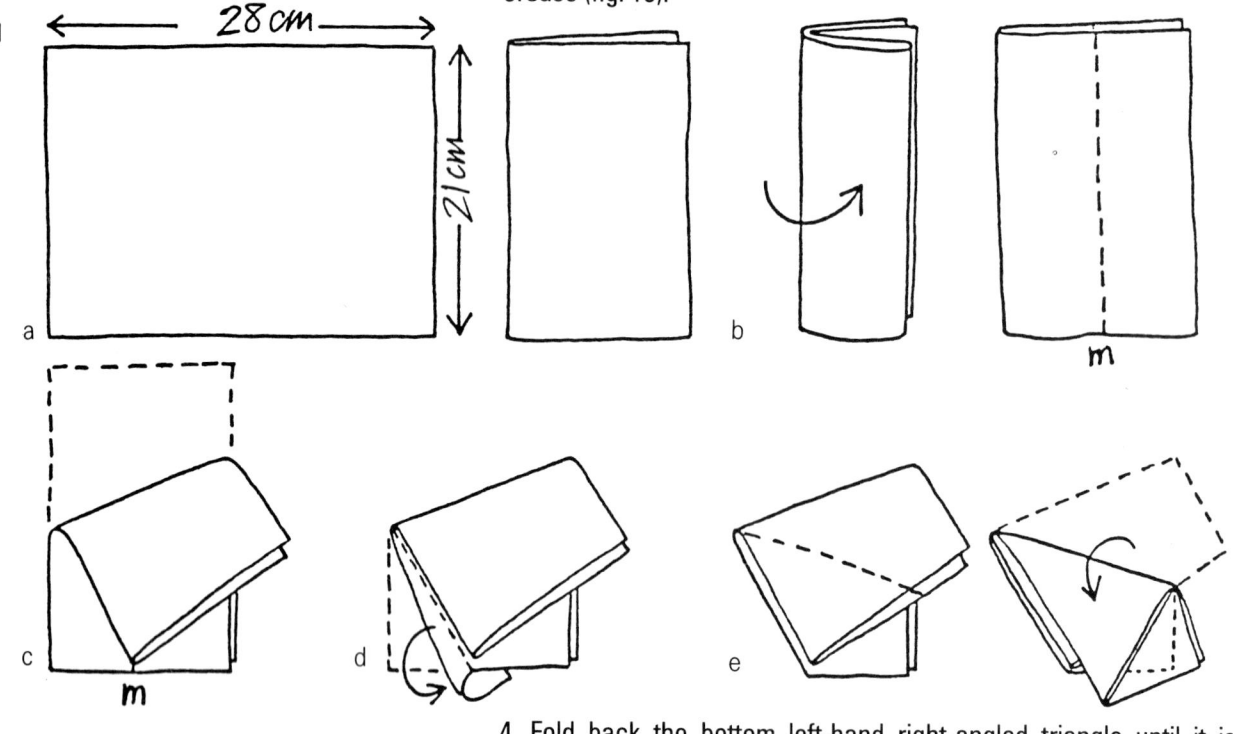

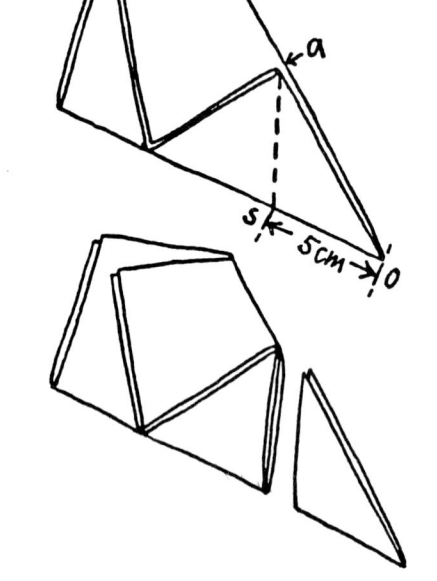

This method of folding is reputed to have been suggested by Betsy Ross, a seamstress, to George Washington when he wanted to make the stars for the flag of the United States of America.

116 TECHNIQUES AND MATERIALS

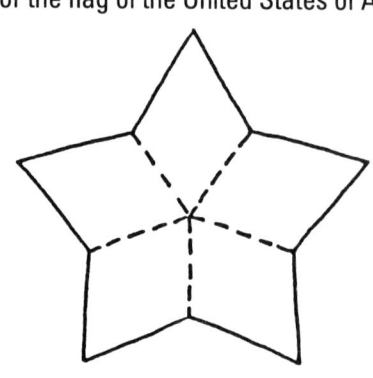

CHINESE TANGRAM

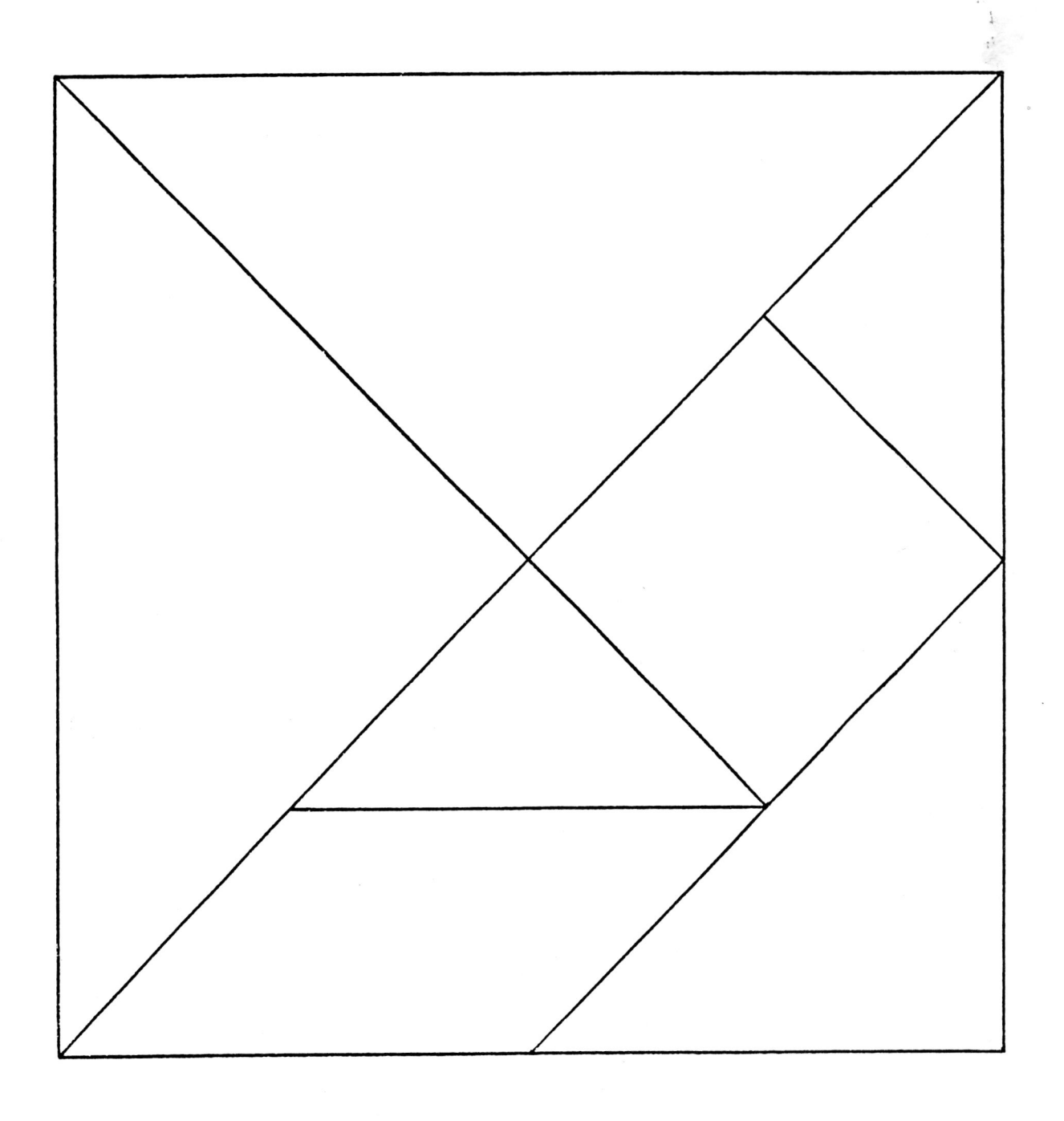

TECHNIQUES AND MATERIALS

NETS FOR CUBES

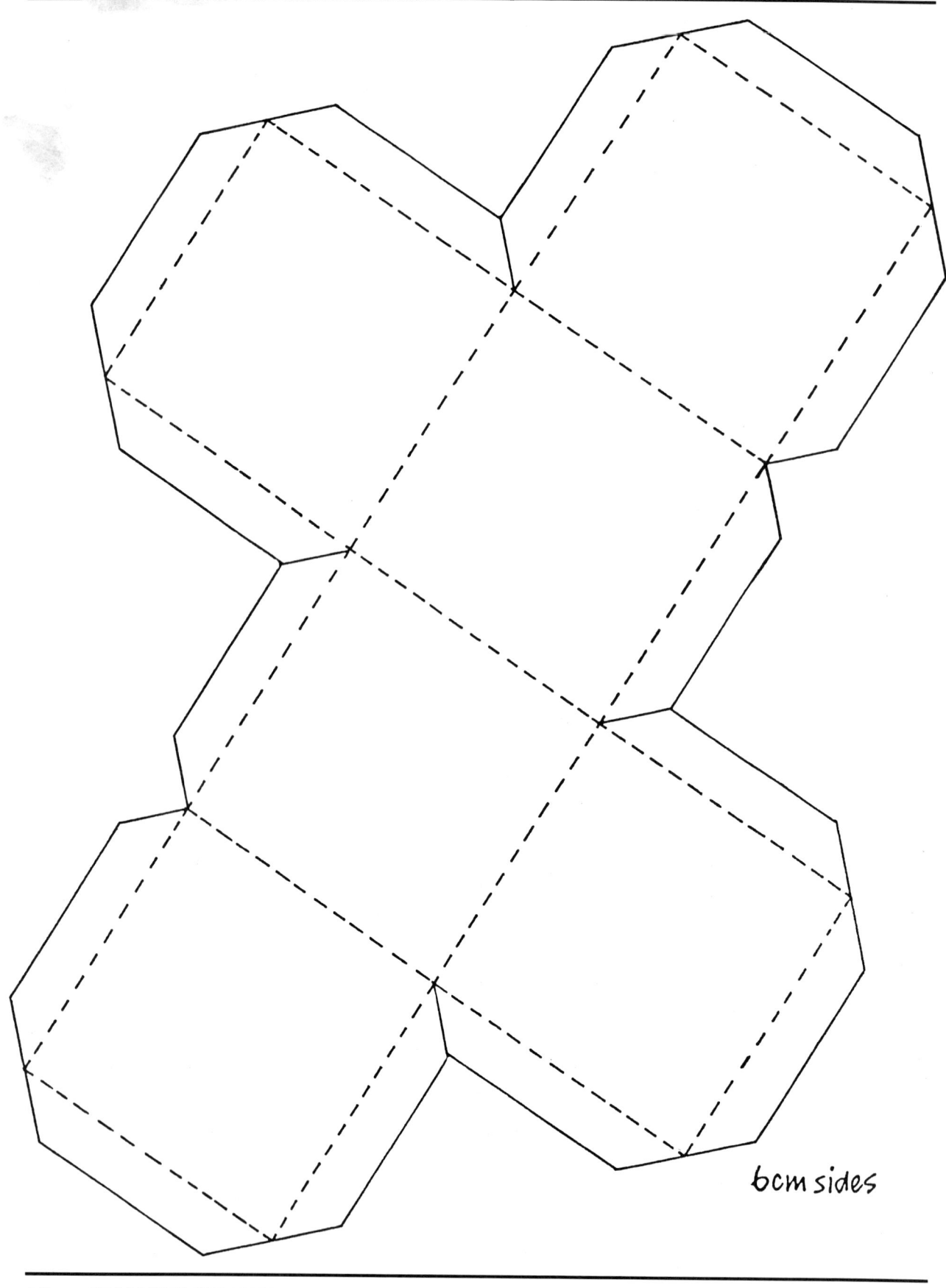

6cm sides

118　TECHNIQUES AND MATERIALS

cut
fold

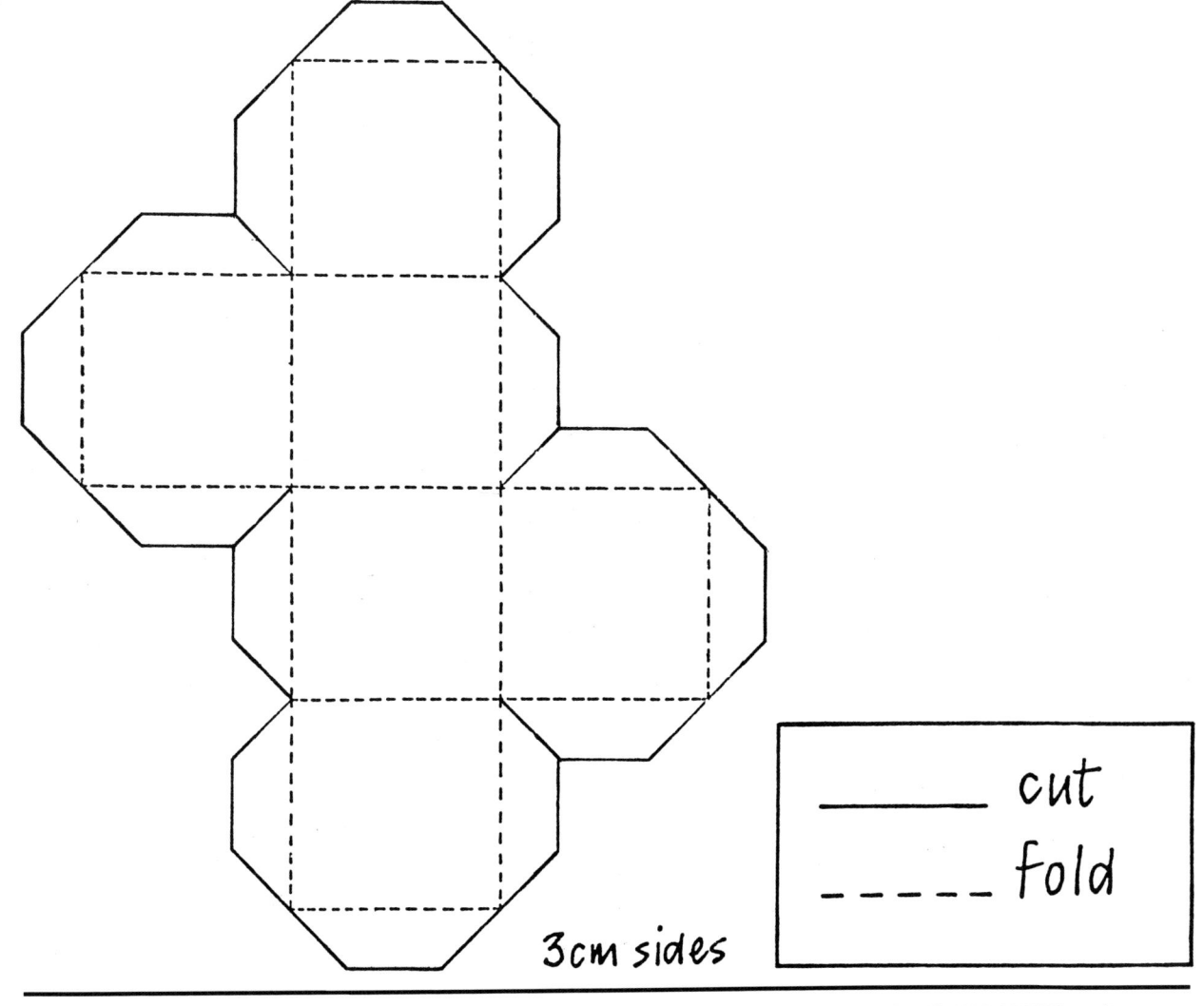

3cm sides

TECHNIQUES AND MATERIALS 119

ISOMETRIC GRID (1 CM)

PAPER SIZES

Paper comes in standard sizes, and the most commonly used international standard is the 'A' series.

This is based on a modular system, each size being half the size of the previous sheet (fig. 1). A4 is the most commonly used sheet size for letters. Both A3 and A4 sheet sizes are often used for drawing pads.

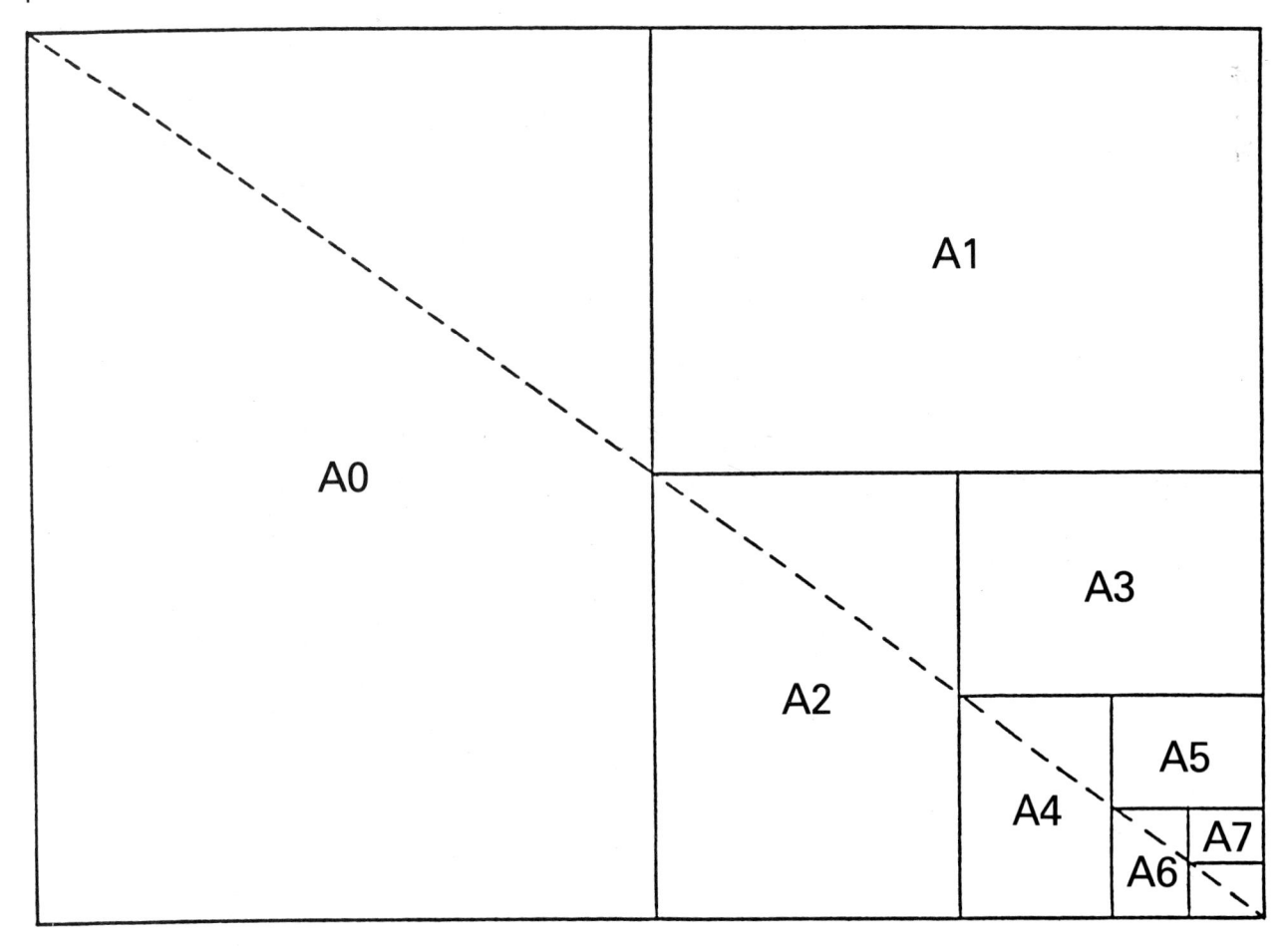

	Size in millimetres	Approx. size in inches
A0	841 × 1189	33½ × 46¾
A1	594 × 841	23⅜ × 33½
A2	420 × 594	16½ × 23⅜
A3	297 × 420	11¾ × 16½
A4	210 × 297	8¼ × 11¾
A5	148 × 210	5⅞ × 8¼
A6	105 × 148	4⅛ × 5⅞
A7	74 × 105	2⅞ × 4⅛

TECHNIQUES AND MATERIALS

SUPPLIERS' ADDRESSES

E J ARNOLD & SON LTD
Parkside Lane
Dewsbury Road
LEEDS
LS11 5TD

ASSOCIATION OF TEACHERS
OF MATHEMATICS
7 Shaftesbury Street
DERBY
DE3 8YB

BEROL LTD
Oldmeadow Road
King's Lynn
NORFOLK
PE30 4JR

BINNEY & SMITH LTD
Ampthill Road
BEDFORD
MK42 9RS

CORGI
The Mettoy Co Ltd
NORTHAMPTON

JAMES GALT & CO LTD
Brookfield Road
Cheadle
CHESHIRE
SK8 2PN

HESTAIR HOPE LTD
St Philip's Drive
Royton
OLDHAM
OL2 6AG

THE MATHEMATICAL
ASSOCIATION
259 London Road
LEICESTER
LE2 3BE

PICTORIAL CHARTS
EDUCATIONAL TRUST
27 Kirchen Road
LONDON
W13 0UD

PLAYAWAY SUPPLIES LTD
Boundary Road
Shawfield Industrial Estate
Rutherglen
GLASGOW
G73 1DB

TARQUIN PUBLICATIONS
Stradbroke
Diss
NORFOLK
IP21 4JP

TASKMASTER LTD
Morris Road
LEICESTER
LE2 6BR

MICRO SOFTWARE

AUCBE
Endymion House
Hatfield
HERTFORDSHIRE
AL10 8AU

CAMBRIDGE MICRO SOFTWARE
The Edinburgh Building
Shaftesbury Road
CAMBRIDGE
CB2 2RU

EARO SOFTWARE
Back Hill
Ely
CAMBRIDGESHIRE

HILL MACGIBBON SOFTWARE
Bartholomew House
92 Fleet Street
LONDON
EC1Y 1DH

SMILE
ILEA Learning
Resources Branch
275 Kennington Lane
LONDON
SE1 5QZ